Books by Jean H. Shepard

SIMPLE FAMILY FAVORITES

HERB AND SPICE COOKING

COOK WITH WINE

THE HARVEST HOME STEAK COOKBOOK

EARTH WATCH: NOTES ON A RESTLESS PLANET

THE FRESH FRUITS AND VEGETABLES COOKBOOK

The Fresh Fruits and Vegetables Cookbook

by Jean H. Shepard

FOREWORD BY
DR. PHILIP L. WHITE
DIRECTOR,
DEPARTMENT OF FOODS AND NUTRITION
AMERICAN MEDICAL ASSOCIATION

Little, Brown and Company
Boston — Toronto

Most of the drawings in this book are from *The Vegetable Garden,* by Vilmorin-Andrieux, published in London by John Murray in 1885.

LIBRARY OF CONGRESS CATALOGING IN PUBLICATION DATA

Shepard, Jean H
  Fresh fruits and vegetables cookbook.

  Includes index.
  1. Cookery (Fruit) 2. Cookery (Vegetables)
I. Title.
TX811.S45   641.6'4   75-4570
ISBN 0-316-78496-6

Design by Barbara Bell Pitnof

Published simultaneously in Canada by Little, Brown & Company (Canada) Limited

To Aunt Jennie

Foreword

Consumers are aware of the importance of fruits and vegetables to nutritional well-being but too often fail to put their knowledge into practice. We fail to make the most of the abundance of the plant kingdom. This is true despite the fact that per capita consumption of fruits and vegetables is greater now than it was fifty years ago.

Consumption of most fruits and vegetables has increased, but important changes in patterns of their use are occurring. During the past four or five decades, the use of *fresh* fruits and vegetables has declined nearly 50 percent, while the consumption of processed forms has increased fourfold. The net result has been a slight increase in total consumption of all fruits and vegetables.

Fruits and vegetables (in all forms) are of immeasurable importance to health since they contribute great amounts of vitamins and minerals. Ninety-five percent of our Vitamin C and 50 percent of our Vitamin A come from fruits and vegetables, with a cost of but 10 percent of total calories and 1 percent of the fat consumed on the whole. Wise selections among the fruits and vegetables can assure much needed improvement in the nutritional value of many diets.

Retention of nutritional value is an important aspect of the management of the products of the vegetable world. There is much we can learn about preferred methods of preparing vegetable foods to retain their inherent values. This book is devoted to just that — how to use fruits and vegetables for maximum pleasure and benefit. You see, great damage to fruits and vegetables can occur in our homes during storage, while preparing and cooking, and while holding after cooking, i.e., in chilling or reheating. We can save money and nutrients while enjoying great dining pleasure by following the methods described in this book.

—Philip L. White, Sc.D.
Director, Department of Foods and Nutrition
American Medical Association

Introduction

Fresh fruits and vegetables are essential to our diet for reasons of health and nutrition; these reasons are discussed in detail in a later chapter (beginning on page 277). However, apart from their nutritive and vitamin properties, their low-fat and low-calorie content, and their fine alkalizer propensities, there are several very important reasons why we should include fresh fruits and vegetables in our diet today.

The present abundant supply and huge variety of fresh fruits and vegetables that are available on the market at all seasons make them a sensible choice to cook and serve regularly in any number of ways. Even in midwinter, a shopper in one of the large supermarkets probably can buy forty-seven different fresh fruits and vegetables plus many varieties. The produce industry itself is moving toward making these products more and more abundant in higher quality throughout the year in all forms. For example, fresh corn and strawberries, which were not available in the winter twenty years ago, are now on the market all year round. Other fresh commodities for which the period of abundance has lengthened include melons, grapes, pears, some varieties of apples, and peaches. More readily available, too, are the less well-known commodities such as artichokes, avocados, pomegranates, and the new hybrids like tangelos, ugli fruit, and the like. No longer need the shopper's horizon be limited to the prosaic green pea when the grand and colorful array of produce offered at the supermarket may include Jerusalem artichokes, four varieties of squash, and a mouth-watering group of salad greens to choose from.

Not only are fruits and vegetables of all kinds and in all forms more available than they used to be, but nutrients are better protected against destruction. Improved cooling methods immediately after harvest and the refrigeration of commodities all the way to the consumer now largely protect produce from the loss of Vitamins C and A and folic acid. This includes precooling before loading, thermostatic control of better insulated cars and trucks during transit, better packaging to maintain proper temperatures, improved loading patterns of rail cars and trucks to maintain desirable circulation of cold air in hot weather and warm air in cold weather, and better control of temperature fluctuation in storage.

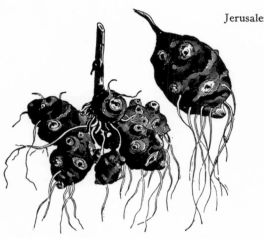

Jerusalem Artichoke (⅛ natural size)

Ongoing genetic research leads to plant breeding of new varieties, improved quality (of taste, color, texture), better disease resistance, and adaptability to mechanized production. Chemical research is providing new compounds to regulate growth, the development and fruiting of plants, and new controls for pests and weeds; and engineering research is producing mechanisms and methods for improved growing and distribution of produce and precision instruments to determine the internal quality of fruits and vegetables without destroying them.

Along with their importance to diet and health, and with all the assurances of supply, distribution, availability, quality, variety, and nutrient protection, there is still another factor to be seriously considered in the purchase of fruits and vegetables. For the busy family, there is nothing like the speed and ease of preparation of these real "convenience" foods.

This is especially true of fruits; most can be eaten as is or with a minimum of preparation. So many vegetables, too, can and should be eaten raw — sliced or chopped into a salad. Other vegetables, with a little boiling or baking, butter or margarine, and your favorite seasoning, are ready to serve in record time.

On the other hand, there is no limit to the degree of embellishment possible in preparing them as gourmet dishes or sauces. Alone as main or side dishes or combined with meats, fish, poultry, or cheese, their versatility lends color, variety, and piquancy to everyday meals. Either way, fresh fruits and vegetables mean good eating for today's busy household.

It is impossible in discussing the value of fruits and vegetables to ignore the economical aspect of cooking and serving them regularly. In a time of soaring food prices, they are relatively inexpensive and the wisdom of utilizing them to the fullest for one or two meatless meals a week is obvious. For suggestions along these lines, see the Menus for Meatless Meals (pages 269–274).

Finally, for all those who are fresh-food oriented but are often totally unfamiliar with its preparation and cooking, and for the more experienced everyday cook whose outlook has been limited to the common carrot and to whom the Jerusalem artichoke remains a mystery, I hope this book will provide the kind of information necessary to eliminate embarrassed questioning and hurried selections of stock items or their canned and frozen versions.

In the following pages are descriptions of all the fresh fruits and vegetables available today; information on what to buy and what to avoid, and how to store, prepare, cook, and serve them. Recipes are given that use them in all categories of cooking, as well as a nutrient highlight chart, an herb and spice guide, and a list of vitamin and nutrient ingredients. All are designed to help inform the shopper of their intrinsic value and variety and to help the cook make the best possible use of these marvelous foods.

Only one thing has been left unsaid in their behalf: fresh fruits and vegetables are probably the most delightfully varied and deliciously flavorful of all the basic food groups.

Contents

Serving: The Recipes

Fresh Fruits and Vegetables for Your Health

Buying and Storing

Mammoth Pumpkin
(1/10 natural size)

Buying Tips

While nothing can replace your own experience in selecting good quality fruits and vegetables, specifically suited to your own uses, keep in mind the following general rules. For detailed information on each fruit and vegetable, consult the Dictionary of Fresh Fruits and Vegetables.

When buying fruits and vegetables demand freshness. Check for clean, crisp produce of bright, lively characteristic color and normal shape. Grossly misshapen fruits and vegetables are usually inferior in taste and texture, difficult to prepare, and wasteful. Check as carefully for signs of deterioration. Fruits and vegetables should be comparatively dry, as excessive moisture will hasten decay.

It is important to remember in selecting fresh fruit that size and appearance are not everything. Large-sized fruits are not necessarily of the best quality nor are they always economical for your purposes. In general, medium sizes are preferred for most uses. Very large fruits may be coarse and overmature, while extremely small ones may be immature with a relatively small edible portion.

Although quality and appearance are often closely associated, attractive appearance does not always mean fine quality. A fruit may have a lovely unblemished color but a relatively poor eating quality because of a varietal characteristic or some internal condition such as overmaturity. Similarly, a superficially blemished fruit of less attractive color may have superb eating quality. In short, fruit should be purchased for best eating quality rather than outer appearance.

Root vegetables should be bought without the tops unless the tops are to be eaten, as they draw nutrients and moisture from the roots. If the tops are to be eaten, select those whose tops are young, tender and green.

Remember that degree of maturity (the state at which the fruit or vegetable is harvested) is different from ripeness and that both vary with the individual commodity. For example, all leafy vegetables should be immature at the consumer level, while ripeness in many cases is undesirable; i.e., a ripe cucumber would have hard seeds, poor flavor, and be inedible. Where pertinent, this information is carefully given on individual commodities in the Dictionary of Fresh Fruits and Vegetables.

Buy only what you need and can use without waste or can properly store for a reasonably short time in your refrigerator, even if the commodity is cheaper in quantity. Long storage of fresh fruits and vegetables at home is not practical. Always sort fruits and vegetables before storing them. Discard or use at once any bruised or soft produce, and never store them with sound, firm fruits and vegetables.

Where home storage is indicated as "cold and humid," a temperature as near 32° F. as possible is desired, with high humidity achieved by keeping the commodity in a film bag or in a hydrator compartment in the refrigerator or both. Where "cool" temperatures are suggested, 50° to 60° F. is meant or at least room temperature away from the sun or any other source of heat. To keep a fruit or vegetable "dry" simply means exposing it to the air of an ordinary room or open to the movement of air currents in the refrigerator so that surface moisture will evaporate. Do not keep produce so damp or wet as to show droplets of moisture.

It is a mistake to buy off-quality commodities at a reduced price since the waste in preparation will very likely offset the price reduction. Even if the decayed areas are trimmed off, rapid deterioration will probably spread to the salvaged areas and storage for any length of time will be impossible. Lower-priced commodities are rarely a bargain unless the reduced prices are a result of an overabundant supply.

Try always to buy in season. Quality is higher and prices more reasonable at this time. Out-of-season produce is almost always more expensive. Your best guide to "in-season" shopping is the monthly announcements made by the U.S. Department of Agriculture, through the newspapers, radio, and television, of the commodities in greatest supply.

Finally, handle fruits and vegetables with care when it is necessary to judge quality. In the end, the loss to a grocer in terms of waste and spoilage is passed on to the consumer in higher prices. *So don't pinch!*

A Consumer's Glossary of
Fresh Fruit and Vegetable Terms

BLACKHEART: a brown or black discoloration of the small center branches, as in celery.

BLOSSOM END: the end opposite the stem end; the blossom end is often more rounded than the stem end.

BREAKDOWN OF TISSUE: decomposition or breaking down of cells due to pressure (bruise) or age (internal breakdown).

BUD CLUSTER: a group of small flowerets that compose the head of broccoli.

CORM: a short bulblike underground upright stem invested with a few thin membranes or scale leaves, as in the crocus.

CURD: the white, edible portion of the cauliflower.

DECAY: decomposition due to bacteria or fungus infection.

FLOWERET: one of the small flower buds that compose the head, as in broccoli.

GILLS: the numerous rows of paper-thin pink or light tan tissue seen underneath the mushroom cap when it opens.

GROUND COLOR: the basic or background color of the skin of a fruit before the sun's rays cause it to redden; the ground color may be seen beneath and around the red blush of the fruit.

HARD: the terms "hard," "firm," and "soft" are subjective terms used to describe the degrees of maturity or ripeness of a fruit; a "hard" texture will not give when pressed; a "firm" texture will give slightly to pressure; a "soft" texture is just that; the term "mature green" is sometimes used instead of "hard."

JACKET LEAVES: the heavy outer covering, as in the cauliflower.

MATURE: describes a fruit that is ready to be picked, whether or not it is ripe at this time; if a fruit is picked when mature, it is capable of ripening properly, but if picked when immature, will not ripen properly.

MID-RIBS: the center of the leaves, as in a head of lettuce.

NETTING: the veinlike network of lines running randomly across the rind of some melons.

PIP: one of the segments of a pineapple's surface; sometimes called an eye.

RIPE: ready to be eaten.

RUSSETING: a lacy, brownish, blemish-type coating on top of the skin.

SCALD: a blemish, or brownish discoloration, that occasionally develops in the skin of apples or other fruits in cold storage.

SILK END: the end opposite the stem end, as in an ear of corn.

SPIKE: pointed leaves growing from the top of the pineapple.

STEM END: the end from which the stem protrudes; it will have a scar or the remains of the stem to identify it.

SUNBURN: a green discoloration under the skin, as in the potato.

TAPROOT: the primary root that grows vertically downward, giving off small lateral roots.

TIPBURN: the tan or brown area, signifying dead tissue, around the margins of the leaves, as in lettuce.

TOPPED VEGETABLES: vegetables sold with the tops or leaves removed.

TUBER: a short, fleshy, usually underground stem or shoot bearing minute scale leaves with buds or "eyes," like the potato.

WRAPPER LEAVES: the green outer leaves, as in lettuce or cabbage.

A Dictionary of Fresh Fruits
and Vegetables

FRUITS

Apples

Tasty tree-borne fruits of many varieties differing widely in appearance, flesh characteristics, seasonal availability, and suitability for different uses: *For eating raw and in salads:* Cortland, Delicious, Golden Delicious, McIntosh, Stayman, Winesap, Jonathan. *For pies and apple sauce:* tart, slightly acid varieties: Gravenstein, Grimes Golden, Jonathan, Newton. *For baking:* the firmer-fleshed types — Rome Beauty, Northern Spy, Rhode Island Greening, Winesap, York Imperial.

BUY: Firm, crisp, well-colored (for the variety) apples; apples must be mature when picked to have good flavor, texture, and storing ability.

DO NOT BUY: Bruised, wilted, shriveled, or punctured apples lacking color; this indicates immature fruit and poor flavor; avoid also overripe apples (indicated by a yielding to slight pressure on the skin and soft mealy flesh); and apples affected by freeze (indicated by internal breakdown and bruised areas). Scald on apples may not seriously affect the eating quality of the apple.

AVAILABLE: Year round.

HOW TO STORE: Refrigerate eating apples to keep and use as desired; if the bite test shows that apples for eating raw need ripening, leave them at room temperature for a day or two more; then refrigerate. Apples do very well in cold and high humidity. Those coming from cold storage have flavor superior to those coming direct from tree to consumer.

Apricots

A delicate fruit that develops its flavor and sweetness on the tree; they should be picked when matured, but they must be firm, as they cannot be shipped when fully ripe.

BUY: Ripe, plump, relatively soft (though not damaged), juicy-looking apricots with a uniform orange-yellow color. Ripe apricots will yield to gentle pressure on the skin.

DO NOT BUY: Dull-looking, either mushy or very firm fruit with a pale yellow or greenish-yellow color (indications of overmaturity or immaturity respectively).

AVAILABLE: Mainly in June and July although a limited supply of imported apricots is marketed in large cities, in December and January also (domestic apricots are grown principally in California, Washington, and Utah).

HOW TO STORE: Keep cold and humid; use within 3 or 4 days.

Avocados

A fruit — usually pear-shaped, although sometimes almost spherical — of two general types with several varieties of each grown domestically in California and Florida. Depending on type and variety, avocados vary considerably in shape, size and color; some have rough or leathery textured skin, while others have smooth skin. The skin color of most varieties is green but can range to maroon, brown, or purplish-black as the fruit ripens. Avocados weighing under ½ pound are the most commonly available. They are picked according to percentage of oil content and are put on the market mature but not necessarily ripe.

BUY: Bright, fresh-appearing fruit heavy for its size; irregular light brown "scab" marks on the outside skin are superficial and do not affect the quality. *For immediate use:* slightly soft avocados which yield to gentle pressure on the skin; if the inner large pit rattles loosely when fruit is shaken, this is a secondary indication of ripeness. *For use within a few days:* firm avocados that do not yield to finger pressure (allow to ripen at room temperature).

DO NOT BUY: Wilted or bruised fruit with dark sunken spots in irregular patches or cracks or breaks in the surface.

AVAILABLE: Year round.

HOW TO STORE: Avocados are of good eating quality when they have been properly ripened. If quite firm, allow to ripen at room temperature 3 to 5 days. If ripe, refrigerate until ready to use. Refrigeration before fruit is soft will slow down the ripening process. *Note:* to prevent the peeled flesh from turning brown when exposed to the air, place in or sprinkle with lemon juice until ready to use (this adds greatly to the flavor, too).

Bananas

Unlike most other fruit, the banana develops its best eating quality after harvesting, thus allowing it to be safely shipped great distances; thus because bananas ripen ideally off the plant, they are harvested green even for consumption where they are grown. At the retail level, good-quality bananas may be anything from partly green to all yellow with brown spots.

BUY: Plump, firm fruit, bright in appearance and free from bruises or other injury. The stage of ripeness is indicated by the skin color, and many believe the best eating quality has been reached when the solid yellow color is speckled with brown. Although it is true the flesh is mellow and the flavor is fully developed at this stage, it is really a matter of personal preference.

DO NOT BUY: Split or bruised fruit with discolored skins (a sign of decay); a dull, grayish, aged appearance is also to be avoided; this shows the bananas have been exposed to cold and will not ripen properly.

AVAILABLE: Year round in abundance.

HOW TO STORE: Bananas are sensitive to cool temperatures and will be injured for ripening in temperatures below 55°. Therefore, do not store them in the refrigerator. The ideal temperature for ripening bananas is between 60° and 70° (higher temperatures cause them to ripen too quickly). Place them on a dish and allow them to ripen at room temperature to the stage you prefer. They do not have to have brown spots before being edible. Some like them yellow with a green tip, some all yellow, some all spotted. Indeed, occasionally the skin may be entirely brown with the flesh still in prime condition. If you store the bananas in a film bag, be sure it is open to the air. When the bananas have reached the stage of ripeness that you prefer, you can refrigerate them for a few days. The skin will turn brown but the flesh will keep well for a short time after ripening.

Berries

Although differing somewhat from one another in color and shape, they are similar in general structure. The same quality factors apply to them all.

Raspberries. The aggregate fruit of any of various brambles of the rose family, smaller and rounder than the blackberry and easily separated from the receptacle when ripe. The mass of drupelets composing the fruit are red, purple, black, or yellow. Numerous garden varieties are derived from the red raspberry of America and the black raspberry, or blackcap, more specifically from eastern America.

Blackberries. The larger berrylike fruit of any of various brambles of the rose family, usually black or dark purple when ripe.

Blackberries (⅘ natural size)

Boysenberries. A huge blackberrylike fruit with raspberrylike flavor; from the trailing bramble plant developed in California by crossing certain blackberries and raspberries.

Dewberries. The fruit of certain brambles; a variety of blackberry.

Loganberries. A red berrylike fruit regarded as a variety of the western dewberry or as a hybrid between it and the red raspberry.

Youngberries. A large sweet reddish-black fruit of a hybrid between a trailing variety of blackberry and a southern dewberry; grown in the western and southern states.

BUY: Fresh-looking, cold dry berries with a bright clean appearance and a uniform good color for the species: the individual cells making up the berry should be plump and tender but not mushy; look for berries that are fully ripened, with no attached stem caps.

DO NOT BUY: Bruised, leaky or moldy berries: Check this by carefully looking through the openings in ventilated plastic containers; also check for wet or stained spots on wood or fiber containers as possible signs of poor quality or spoiled berries.

AVAILABLE: June through August.

HOW TO STORE: Keep cold and covered; use as soon as possible.

Blueberries

A colorful and delicious fruit; the larger berries are usually cultivated varieties while the smaller ones are the wild varieties.

BUY: Plump, fresh, dry, dark blue berries with a waxy bloom; this silvery bloom is a natural, protective waxy coating; they should be firm, uniform in size, and free of stems and leaves. Larger ones are preferable for good flavor.

DO NOT BUY: Shriveled or very small berries of lighter blue. A good blue color and silvery bloom is the best indication of quality.

AVAILABLE: June to September.

HOW TO STORE: Keep berries cold and covered to avoid their drying out. Use within 2 or 3 days.

Cantaloupes

A fruit of the muskmelon family. If picked at the right maturity it will have a smoothly rounded depressed scar at the stem end and will ripen well for full flavor. This is called the "full slip" condition. Cantaloupes at the retail level are rarely ready to eat. If they have been shipped a long way, as most are, they must be picked while firm. Yet at full slip they have developed their full sugar content and need only soften.

BUY: Cantaloupes with the three major signs of full maturity: 1. *The stem should be gone,* leaving a smooth and symmetrical shallow basin at the stem end — full slip condition. (If all or part of the stem base remains, or if the stem end is rough, with a jagged or torn scar and has portions of the stem adhering, then the cantaloupe is probably not full mature and was picked when not fully mature.) 2. *The veining or netting should be thick,* coarse, and corky, and should stand out in bold relief over some part of the surface. 3. *The skin color (ground color) between the netting should have changed from green* to a yellowish-buff, yellowish-gray, or pale yellow.

Also look for signs of ripeness (a melon may be mature but not ripe for eating). Ripe cantaloupes have a yellowish cast to the rind, a pleasant cantaloupe odor when held to the nose, and will yield slightly to light finger pressure on the blossom end of the melon.

DO NOT BUY: Overripe melons, a condition shown by a pronounced yellow rind, a softening over the entire rind, and soft, watery, and insipid flesh. Small bruises normally have no effect on the quality of the fruit, but large bruised areas should be avoided as they generally cause soft, watersoaked areas underneath the rind. Do not buy melons with mold growth on them, especially in the stem scar. This and soft wet tissue under the mold are signs of decay.

AVAILABLE: May through September; produced mainly in Arizona, Texas, and California, with some imported early in the season.

HOW TO STORE: Since most cantaloupes are quite firm when freshly displayed in retail stores, they should be held from 2 to 4 days at room temperature to complete the ripening process. When ripe, refrigerate if they are not to be eaten immediately, or refrigerate for a few hours before serving.

Casabas

Large heavy normally pumpkin-shaped melon, sometimes very slightly pointed at the stem end; the rind is hard and marked with deep wrinkles running from the stem end to the blossom end and is light green to yellow, deepening to definite yellow when ripe.

BUY: Ripe melons with a gold yellow rind and a slight softening at the blossom end. The flesh should be soft, creamy white, sweet and juicy and *without* aroma.

DO NOT BUY: Melons marked by dark, sunken, watersoaked spots; this indicates decay.

AVAILABLE: July through November, with peak supply in September and October.

HOW TO STORE: Keep cool (50°–60°), and avoid drying out, in hydrator compartment or in a film bag in refrigerator.

Cherries

A fruit eaten raw or used in cooked desserts. Red tart cherries, also called sour or pie cherries, have a soft flesh, a lighter red color, and a more tart flavor than the sweet eating cherries found in the market. They are generally shipped to processing plants and then sold canned or frozen. Bing, Black Tartarian, Schmidt, Chapman, and Republican varieties of sweet cherries range from deep maroon or mahogany red to black. Lambert cherries are dark red.

BUY: Cherries with bright, firm, glassy, plump-looking surfaces and fresh-looking stems; a very dark color is the most important indication of good flavor and maturity in sweet cherries.

DO NOT BUY: Sticky, shriveled cherries and dried stems and a generally dull appearance indicating overmaturity. Immature fruit, equally undesirable, is hard, light in color, small, acid, and dry and will not ripen. Also reject cherries displaying any decay — fairly common at times on sweet cherries but often overlooked because of the normal dark color. Soft, leaking flesh, brown discoloration, and mold growth indicate decay.

AVAILABLE: May through August; produced mainly in the western states.

HOW TO STORE: Keep cold and humid; use within 2 or 3 days.

Coconuts

The fruit of the tropical coconut palm tree.

BUY: Coconuts that are heavy for their size and full of liquid; shake the nut to be sure the juice sloshes around.

DO NOT BUY: Dry coconuts, i.e., those with no liquid sound within when shaken are considered to be spoiled; nuts with moldy or wet "eyes" should also be rejected.

AVAILABLE: Year round, with a more abundant supply September through December.

HOW TO STORE: Keep cold; use as soon as possible.

Cranberries

Succulent red berries generally of good quality as they reach the market (packing houses have a method of rejecting berries of poor color and texture). A number of varieties are marketed, differing somewhat in size and color, but are not identified by variety names in food stores.

BUY: Fresh, plump, lustrous, firm berries with a red to reddish-black color.

DO NOT BUY: Soft, dull, shriveled, spongy, or leaky berries.

AVAILABLE: September to January.

HOW TO STORE: Refrigerate and use within a week or two, or freeze in the original package and use anytime.

Crenshaws

A hybrid muskmelon easily identifiable by its large size and distinctive shape: it usually weighs between 7 and 9 pounds, is rounded at the base or blossom end and pointed at the stem end. The rind is gold and green, relatively smooth with very shallow furrows running lengthwise, no netting, and little ribbing. The flesh runs from pale orange to bright salmon and is thick and juicy when ripe.

BUY: Melons with these signs of ripeness: 1. The rind should generally be a deep golden yellow, sometimes with small areas of lighter yellow. 2. The surface yields to light finger pressure, especially at the blossom end. 3. A pleasant melony aroma.

DO NOT BUY: Melons with slightly sunken, watersoaked areas on the rind, a sign of decay that will spread rapidly through the melon.

AVAILABLE: July to October, with a peak during August and September; grown in California.

HOW TO STORE: Keep at room temperature until ripe, then keep cool and use soon.

Dates

The fruit of the date palm tree; prepackaged and marketed with or without pits.

BUY: Soft, lustrous brown dates.

DO NOT BUY: Hard, dried-out fruit.

AVAILABLE: Year round.

HOW TO STORE: When package is opened, refrigerate; keep well wrapped and use as desired.

Figs

The oblong or pear-shaped fruit of the fig tree; pulpy when ripe and eaten raw or preserved or dried with sugar.

BUY: Soft-ripe figs with the characteristic color, ranging from greenish-yellow to purple or black, depending on the variety.

DO NOT BUY: Figs that give off a sour odor; this indicates overripeness.

AVAILABLE: In very small amounts from August to October.

HOW TO STORE: Keep cold and use immediately; they are extremely perishable.

Grapefruit

A citrus fruit; the principal distinction of varieties is between the seedless (having few or no seeds) and the seeded types, the seedless variety having a larger edible portion. Another distinction is the color of the flesh, pink or white, with the white being the most common and stronger in flavor.

BUY: Firm, well-shaped globular fruits that are springy to the touch and heavy for their size (heaviness denotes thin skins and more juice). Russeting, scars, and bronze-colored skin do *not* affect the eating quality.

DO NOT BUY: Soft, wilted, flabby, puffy, or loose-skinned fruit with dis-colored areas on the peel at the stem end; fruit with watersoaked areas, loss of bright color, or tender peel that breaks with finger pressure.

AVAILABLE: Year round, with the most abundant supply from January through May.

HOW TO STORE: May be kept at room temperature or refrigerated. Grape-fruits are picked "tree ripe" and are always ready to eat when bought.

Grapes

Smooth-skinned, juicy, vine-grown edible berries; most table grapes are of the European type, grown principally in California; only small quantities of eastern-grown American-type grapes are sold for table use. The major European-types are firm-fleshed, have an excellent flavor when well matured, and generally have a high sugar content. Common varieties are: Thompson seedless, an early green grape; Tokay and Cardinal, early bright-red grapes; Emperor, late, deep-red grape. The American-type grapes have softer flesh and are juicier than the European types. The outstanding variety for flavor is the Concord, blue-black when fully matured. Delaware and Catawba are also popular.

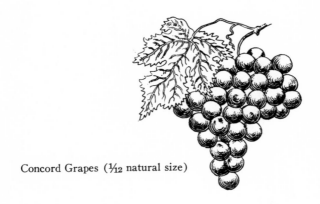

Concord Grapes (1/12 natural size)

BUY: Fresh, smooth, plump grapes firmly attached to the stem; they should be well colored for the variety: Thompson seedless, amber-green; Cardinals, cherry-red; Tokays, flame-red; Emperors, light red to red-purple; Ribiers, purple-black; Almerias and Calmerias, greenish-white. White or green grapes are sweetest when the color has a yellowish cast or the grape is straw color with a tinge of amber. Red varieties are better when a good red color predominates on all or most of the berries. Bunches are more likely to hold together if the stems are generally green and pliable.

DO NOT BUY: Sticky, soft, or wrinkled grapes, which show the effects of freezing or drying; grapes with dry and brittle stems or bleached areas around the stem end, which indicate injury and poor quality; or leaking berries, a sign of decay.

AVAILABLE: Thompsons — June through October; Cardinals — June and July; Tokays — August through November; Emperors — October through March; Ribiers — July through January; Almerias and Calmerias — October through March.

HOW TO STORE: All grapes are as ripe when bought as they will be — only ready-to-eat grapes are shipped to the markets; keep them cool and humid and eat within a week or so.

Guavas

A subtropical fruit; they may be round, oval, oblong, or pear-shaped and are usually 1 to 4 inches in diameter. They have a thin skin and are green to bright yellow in color, often with a pink blush.

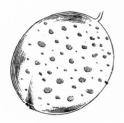

Guava (⅓ natural size)

BUY: Fully ripe guavas for a sweet and only mildly acid flavor.

DO NOT BUY: Dull, shriveled, or dry-looking fruit.

AVAILABLE: Most guavas are processed into preserves and jellies; cultivated to a small extent in Florida; and on the market occasionally, mostly in specialty stores.

HOW TO STORE: Keep cool and humid; use as soon as possible.

Honey Balls

A melon very similar to the honeydew melon, except that it is much smaller, is very round, and is slightly and irregularly netted over the surface. Use the same buying tips as for the honeydew melon.

Honeydews

A smooth-skinned, large, green-fleshed variety of the muskmelon family. They are from 4 to 8 pounds, bluntly oval in shape, and generally very smooth with only occasional traces of surface netting. The rind is firm and ranges from creamy white to creamy yellow, depending on its ripeness. The stem does not separate from the fruit and must be cut for harvesting.

BUY: Mature honeydews that have a soft velvety feel and ripe melons, as shown by a slight softening of the blossom end, with a faint pleasant fruit aroma and a yellowish white or creamy rind color.

DO NOT BUY: Dead-white melons, especially if they have a greenish tinge and a hard, smooth surface; these are unripe and immature and will not sweeten; honeydews with large watersoaked bruised areas, a sign of injury; or melons with cuts or punctures through the rind, which usually lead to decay. *Note:* Small, superficial, sunken spots will not damage the melon for immediate use, but large decayed spots will.

AVAILABLE: February through October, in greatest abundance June through October and in March; chief sources are California, Texas, and Arizona, with some imports.

HOW TO STORE: Unless honeydews are obviously ripe, it is well to hold them at room temperature for a few days before serving just to be sure; when ripe, keep them cool and humid if not immediately used. *Note:* Honeydews present their best flavor when served at room temperature.

Kiwi

A small, fuzzy, cylindrical fruit from New Zealand.

BUY: Firm fruit, to be ripened at home.

DO NOT BUY: Bruised or mushy fruits.

AVAILABLE: June to December.

HOW TO STORE: Ripen at room temperature until they yield to gentle pressure; after ripening, if not used immediately, refrigerate and serve within a day or two.

Kumquats

The smallest of the citrus group, they are often marketed with some green leaves. They are edible and make a fine holiday display.

BUY: Orange-colored oblong fruits, 1¼ × 1½ inches.

DO NOT BUY: Bruised or mushy fruits.

AVAILABLE: November through March.

HOW TO STORE: Keep at room temperature or refrigerate.

Lemons

A tree-borne citrus fruit related to the orange.

BUY: Lemons with a rich yellow color, a reasonably thin and smooth-textured skin, and a slight gloss. They should be heavy for their size and moderately firm (signs of juiciness). A pale or greenish-yellow color means very fresh fruit with slightly higher acidity. Coarse or rough skin texture is a sign of thick skin and not much flesh.

DO NOT BUY: Fruit with a darker yellow or dull color; or with hardened or shriveled skin (signs of age); or with soft spots, mold on the surface; or punctures of the skin (signs of decay).

AVAILABLE: Year round in large amounts; most of the nation's commercial supply comes from California and Arizona.

HOW TO STORE: Lemons need not be refrigerated if used within a few days or a week (room temperature is better for them).

Limes

A small globular, greenish, tree-borne citrus fruit. Most green limes, sometimes called Persian or Tahitian limes, are produced in Florida and are marketed when mature; the Mexican or key lime is smaller and light yellow when ripe.

BUY: Bright green domestic Persian limes with glossy skins and heavy weight for their size — yellow fruit lacks acidity; Mexican or key limes that are light yellow.

DO NOT BUY: Limes with a dull, dry skin (a sign of aging and loss of acid flavor), or fruit with purple to brown irregular-shaped spots that indicate undesirable scalding, or those showing evidence of decay by soft spots, mold, and skin punctures.

AVAILABLE: Year round, with peak supply June through August.

HOW TO STORE: Keep at room temperature if used within a few days; otherwise refrigerate.

Lychees

The fruit of a subtropical tree native to South China and cultivated in Florida. The fruit is round to oval, 1 to 1½ inches in diameter, with a bright leathery skin and small conical protuberances. The edible portion is the translucent white to pale cream covering of the seed, with about the same consistency as a fresh grape. It has an interesting subacid flavor.

AVAILABLE: The bulk of the Florida crop matures between mid-June and early July and is marketed as maturity permits.

HOW TO STORE: Refrigerate; use as soon as possible.

Mangoes

A luscious and unique tropical fruit; they are round to oval in shape, varying considerably in size, weighing from ½ to 1 pound.

BUY: Mangoes with a smooth outer skin of green color with yellowish to red areas. The red and yellow increase as the fruit ripens. The pulp should be yellow, delicate, and juicy with an apricot/pineapple flavor.

DO NOT BUY: Mangoes that are wilted or have grayish discolorations of the skin or pitting, black spots, or other signs of decay.

AVAILABLE: May through August.

HOW TO STORE: Keep at room temperature until very soft, then eat as soon as possible. When fully soft they may be refrigerated. *Note:* The pulp of an unripened mango has the flavor of turpentine.

Nectarines

A tangy, sweet, smooth-skinned variety of peach, combining the characteristics of both the peach and plum. Most varieties have an orange-yellow ground color between the red areas, although some varieties have a greenish ground color.

BUY: Unblemished, smooth fruit of rich color and plumpness with a slight softening along the "seam." Like the peach, the nectarine does not gain sugar after harvest and must be picked well matured to be satisfactory. Mature fruit will soften readily and become juicy. *Russeting or staining of the skin may affect the appearance but will not affect the eating quality.*

DO NOT BUY: Hard, dull fruits or slightly shriveled nectarines that may be immature, picked too soon, and of poor eating quality; also avoid soft or overripe fruits or those with cracked or punctured skin or displaying any other signs of decay. Considerably green fruit is also likely to be unsatisfactory.

AVAILABLE: June into September; produced in California.

HOW TO STORE: Give nectarines plenty of time to soften at room temperature. Then keep them cold and humid and use as soon as possible.

Oranges

The globular citrus fruit of an evergreen tree of the rue family of many varieties. The leading varieties from California and Arizona are the Washington Navel and Valencia, both characterized by a rich orange skin. The Navel orange has the thicker, more pebbled skin, which is easily removed by hand, and segments that separate more readily. It is ideally suited to eating whole or as segments in salads. The western Valencia orange is excellent for either juicing or slicing in salads. Parson Brown and Hamlin are early varieties of the Florida and Texas orange crops, and the Pineapple orange is an important, high-quality fruit good for eating whole. Florida and Texas Valencias are later varieties. The Florida Temple orange, like the California Navel, peels easily, separates into segments readily, and has excellent flavor.

Oranges are required by strict state regulations to be well matured before being harvested and shipped out of the producing state. Thus the skin color is not a reliable indication of quality, and green spots or a greenish cast do not mean immaturity. Often fully matured oranges turn greenish (called regreening) late in the marketing season. Some Florida oranges may have artificial color added. It has no effect on the eating quality but must be labeled "color added."

BUY: Firm, heavy oranges with a bright, fresh, fine-textured skin having few or no seeds (the seedier the orange, the less juice and edible pulp). "Russeting," a tan-brown or blackish mottling or speckling of the skin, is often found on Florida and Texas oranges (not on California varieties) and has absolutely no effect on eating quality. In fact, it often occurs on oranges with thin skin and superior eating flavor.

DO NOT BUY: Lightweight, puffy, or spongy oranges that will lack juice and flesh content; very rough skin texture indicates abnormally thick skin and less flesh, too, while dull, dry skin indicates aging and deteriorated eating quality. Also avoid decay as shown by cuts, skin punctures, soft spots on the surface, and discolored, weakened areas of the skin around the stem end or button.

AVAILABLE: Year round from California, Florida, Texas, and Arizona: the Washington Navel from November to early May; the western Valencia from late April through October; Parson Brown and Hamlin from early October until June; the Pineapple orange from late November through March; Florida and Texas Valencias from late March through June; the Florida Temple orange from early December until early March.

HOW TO STORE: Keep at room temperature or refrigerate.

Papayas

The large oblong yellow fruit of a tropical American tree.

BUY: Papayas of moderate size, i.e., bigger than a large pear, as very large fruit may not have as much flavor as the medium sizes. Well-colored fruit, at least half yellowish with no large amount of green and smooth unbroken skin. Papayas should have somewhat the shape of a pear, and if not ripe should be yellow and yielding to slight pressure between the palms.

DO NOT BUY: Large, green fruit that is hard, or that is bruised, punctured, shriveled, or showing any other signs of deterioration.

AVAILABLE: Year round in small amounts, with peak quantities in May or June.

HOW TO STORE: Ripen at room temperature, then refrigerate and use as soon as possible.

Peaches

A sweet, juicy tree-borne fruit of many difficult-to-distinguish varieties; they fall into two general types: the freestone, whose flesh readily separates from the pit, and the clingstone, whose flesh clings tightly to the pit. Freestones are usually preferred for eating or for freezing, while clingstones are used primarily for canning, although occasionally sold fresh.

BUY: Only mature peaches — *no green* ones. (A peach does not gain sugar after picking since it has no starch to convert to sugar. Therefore it is desirable to obtain peaches as near tree-ripe as possible. Full tree-ripeness is not commercially feasible because of damage in marketing, but fruit can be picked well matured. Hydrocooled fruit is preferable since it can be picked nearer to the ripe stage and given an ice-cold bath soon after harvest to slow respiration.) Maturity is indicated by a yellowish ground color with a red blush and a general absence of greenness. They should be fairly firm or becoming a trifle soft.

DO NOT BUY: Very firm or hard peaches with a distinctly green ground color; also avoid overripe fruit that is very soft. Peaches with large flattened bruises will have large areas of discolored flesh underneath; or fruit showing any sign of decay, which starts as a pale tan spot and expands in a circle, gradually turning darker in color.

AVAILABLE: June through September.

HOW TO STORE: Keep at room temperature until soft enough to eat; then refrigerate and use as soon as possible. If any sign of brown rot appears, use at once as it will develop rapidly.

Pears

Luscious tree-borne fruits produced in quantity and available in the following varieties: Bartlett, Anjou, Bosc, Winter Nellis, and Comice; picked mature but hard, they reach ideal ripeness off the tree.

BUY: Pears of standard varieties: Bartletts, pale yellow to rich golden yellow; Anjou or Comice, light green to yellowish green; Bosc, greenish yellow to brownish yellow (the brown cast caused by skin russeting, characteristic of this variety); Winter Nellis, medium to light green. In general, big plump pears are best; they should be clean, free of blemishes, and not misshapen, firm but beginning to soften.

DO NOT BUY: Wilted, shriveled pears with dull skin and slight weakening of flesh near stem; this indicates immaturity and these pears will not ripen. Also avoid those with spots on the sides or blossom ends indicating corky tissue beneath.

AVAILABLE: Bartlett, August through November; Anjou, Bosc, Winter Nellis, and Comice, November through April.

HOW TO STORE: Ripen pears at room temperature; if in film bag, open a little. The Bartlett is yellowish with a red blush when ripe and develops a delightful perfume when ready to eat. The other varieties do not noticeably change color. When ripe, keep cold and humid (in hydrator compartment or film bag in refrigerator) and eat as soon as possible. *Note:* Pears ripen from the inside out and should not be held until soft on the outside. At that stage, the inside may be too soft and tasteless to eat. Eat while still firm but not hard.

Persian Melons

A globe-shaped muskmelon, averaging about 7½ inches in diameter and weighing about 7 pounds; they resemble cantaloupes, but are more nearly round, have finer netting, and are about the same size as honeydews; the rind is dark green covered with a fine netting and the flesh is orange, very thick, and fine-textured.

BUY: Fruit with a pleasant melon aroma that yields to slight pressure. As they ripen, the rind under the netting turns a lighter green; they do not gain sugar after harvesting but will soften and become juicy.

DO NOT BUY: Melons that are too soft and overripe, badly bruised, or bearing signs of mold.

AVAILABLE: July into October.

HOW TO STORE: Allow plenty of time for softening and becoming juicy; then keep cold and humid and use as soon as possible.

Persimmons

A sweet, plumlike, palatable fruit of trees of the ebony family; the oriental or Japanese persimmon, grown in California, is larger than a plum, oblong

Persimmon (⅔ natural size)

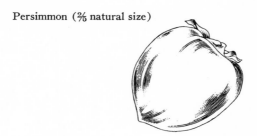

and conic with a rounded apex — the green cap should be in place. It is bright orange and seedless.

BUY: Fruit that is plump with smooth, highly colored skin.

DO NOT BUY: Fruit that is bruised or in any way visibly damaged.

AVAILABLE: October through December.

HOW TO STORE: Keep at room temperature until they are as soft as jelly; at this stage they will have a rich, sweet flavor. When ripe, keep cold and humid and use as soon as possible.

Pineapples

A succulent, unusual-looking fruit of a tropical plant coming principally from Puerto Rico, Hawaii, and Mexico.

BUY: Firm fruit heavy for its size and as large as possible — the larger the fruit, the greater proportion of edible flesh. Look for freshness and especially crown leaves that are fresh and deep green; fragrance (a pineapple aroma) is a good sign (usually pineapples are kept too cold to give off an aroma). There should be a slight separation of the eyes or pips and they should be plump and glossy; the "spike" or leaves should be easy to pull out from the top, although this last alone is not a reliable test.

Pineapples are usually dark green in mature hard stage. As the more popular varieties (such as Red Spanish and Smooth Cayenne) ripen, the green color fades and orange and yellow take its place. When fully ripe, pineapples are golden yellow, orange-yellow or reddish-brown — depending on the variety, although one seldom-seen pineapple, the Sugar Loaf, remains green even when ripe. However, shell color is not a good indication of maturity for the shopper. The grower relies on a test of sugar content and most pineapples are ready for eating when they reach the American market.

DO NOT BUY: Pineapples with sunken or slightly pointed pips, discolored or soft spots, or brown leaves and a dried appearance. Traces of mold, an unpleasant odor, and eyes that turn watery and darker in color are signs of decay that will spread rapidly through the fruit.

AVAILABLE: Year round, with peak supply March through June.

HOW TO STORE: Most pineapples are ready for eating by the time they reach the market, so holding it only results in deterioration. Keep it cold and humid; use as soon as possible.

Plantains

A variety of banana; usually thought of as a larger, starchy, acid, and gummy type of banana that will not sweeten. (However, there are bananas that do not sweeten and plantains that do.) Generally speaking, plantains imported into this country are of the cooking type and are cooked before reaching full ripeness.

BUY: Use the same criteria as for selecting unripe bananas.

AVAILABLE: Year round in small amounts in some areas.

HOW TO STORE: Use immediately for cooked dishes.

Plums and Italian Prunes

The fruit of various species of trees of the peach family and allied to the cherry. Quality characteristics of both are very similar, and the same buying tips apply to both.

BUY: Fruit that is plump, clean, and fresh-appearing, full-colored for the variety and fairly soft.

DO NOT BUY: Fruit with skin breaks, punctures, or brownish discoloration; also avoid immature fruits — they are relatively hard, poorly colored, very tart, and sometimes shriveled. Avoid overmature fruits that are excessively soft, leaking, or decaying.

AVAILABLE: *Plums*. Some varieties of plums are produced in California and are available from June to September; varieties differ widely in appearance and flavor, so it is wise to experiment.

Prunes. Only a few varieties are commonly marketed; they are all very similar. Prunes are purplish-black or bluish-black, with a moderately firm flesh that separates freely from the pit. Most commercial production is in the northwestern states. Fresh prunes are available from August through October.

HOW TO STORE: Should be beginning to soften when displayed in the market; however, they must be picked firm to survive the marketing period. If picked mature with adequate sugar content, they need only be allowed to soften at room temperature for 3 or 4 days. Then keep cold and humid; use as soon as possible.

Pomegranates

A thick-skinned, several-celled reddish berry the size of an orange, having many seeds in a crimson pulp of agreeable acid flavor and borne on a tropical African and Asiatic tree.

BUY: Fruit about the size of an apple, with a tough pink or bright red rind and crimson flesh. There should be a large number of seeds, each surrounded by juicy pulp with a spicy flavor.

DO NOT BUY: Fruit that looks hard and dry.

AVAILABLE: Late September into November, with two-thirds of the annual total in October.

HOW TO STORE: Keep cold and humid until used.

Pumpkins

A round, deep-yellow, vine-bearing fruit of the gourd family.

BUY: Fruit of a good orange-golden color that has a hard rind and is heavy in relation to its size.

DO NOT BUY: Cut or severely bruised pumpkins.

AVAILABLE: Late October.

HOW TO STORE: Keep cool until ready to use.

Strawberries

The juicy, edible, red fruit of a genus of plant in the rose family.

BUY: Fresh, dry, clean, bright-looking berries with a full solid red color or very little white or green. They should have firm flesh, a bright luster *with the cap stem still attached.* Medium-sized berries will have the best flavor as a rule — small, misshapen berries and extremely large berries both lack flavor.

DO NOT BUY: Berries with large uncolored areas or with large seedy areas; these will be poor in flavor and texture. Avoid very soft berries with a dull shrunken appearance; these are signs of overripeness and decay. Moist or moldy berries are also to be avoided, as mold will spread rapidly from one berry to another. Be sure to look for stained containers, which usually indicate leakage and spoilage; it is also wise to try to see berries toward the bottom of the container to check for defects.

AVAILABLE: Year round, with peak supply April through June: first shipments come from southern Florida in January, and then production gradually spreads north and west into many parts of the country before tapering off in the fall.

HOW TO STORE: Keep cold and humid and use as soon as possible; they are highly perishable.

Tangelos

A citrus fruit, hybrids of mandarin oranges and grapefruit, with an excellent and distinctive flavor of their own.

BUY: Firm fruit heavy for its size, thin-skinned with a light orange peel; like other citrus fruits, quality is determined at the grove by tests of acids and soluble solids, not external appearance alone.

DO NOT BUY: Soft or badly blemished fruit.

AVAILABLE: Late October through January.

HOW TO STORE: Keep at room temperature for a few days only; for a longer storage period keep cold and humid.

Tangerines

A special variety of the orange family.

BUY: Deep yellow-orange or almost red fruit with bright luster, indicating freshness, maturity, and good flavor. They should be heavy for size, inindicating ample juice; a puffy appearance and less than firm feel is normal because of the typically loose nature of the skin, which zips off readily.

DO NOT BUY: Very pale yellow or overall greenish fruits — these have less flavor; or tangerines with cut or punctured skins or very soft or water-soaked areas or moldy spots — all these signs indicate decay that spreads rapidly. *Note:* Small green areas on otherwise highly colored fruit are not a problem.

AVAILABLE: November through February, peaking in December and January. Florida is the chief source; considerable quantities are also produced in California and Arizona, some in Texas, and a few are imported.

HOW TO STORE: Keep cold and humid and use as soon as possible; they are highly perishable.

Ugli Fruit

A specialty fruit, possibly a form of tangelo, that lives up to its name. An uncommon variety that appeals to those liking the unusual, it has an extremely rough peel ordinarily distinguished with blemishes; it has 1 to 6 seeds and 11 sections and is very juicy with an interesting orangelike flavor.

BUY: When mature, ugli fruit has an orange color with blotches of light green.

AVAILABLE: Irregularly, in specialty stores.

HOW TO STORE: Keep at room temperature or refrigerate.

Watermelons

The large oblong or roundish fruit of a vine of the cucumber family having a hard green or white rind and a pink or red pulp with a very sweet juice. Judging the quality of a watermelon is very difficult unless it is plugged and tested. Generally, the essential factors of quality are maturity and size. The larger melons have proportionally more edible flesh than the smaller ones. However, it is safest to buy a melon that has been cut at the retail store.

BUY: Melons (cut) with firm, juicy flesh of a good red color, relatively free of white streaks or "white heart," and with dark brown or black seeds.

The following are some appearance factors that may help in selecting an uncut melon, but are not wholly reliable: The surface should be relatively smooth; ripe melons of good quality are firm, symmetrical, and fresh-looking with a waxy bloom (the rind should be neither shiny nor dull); the ends of the melon should be filled out and rounded; the "belly" or underside (where it has been in contact with the soil) should be a creamy yellow. If the melon is very hard, white, or very pale green on the underside, it is probably immature. *Do not expect to ripen it.* Total sugar does not increase after the watermelon comes off the vine. Thumping is useless — it is for the watermelon expert, not the average consumer.

DO NOT BUY: Melons (cut) with pale-colored flesh and white streaks or "white heart" and whitish seeds, which indicate immaturity; with dry mealy flesh or watery, stringy flesh, which indicates overmaturity or aging after harvest.

AVAILABLE: Mostly May into September, with peak supply in June, July, and August.

HOW TO STORE: Keep at room temperature or refrigerate — be sure to refrigerate immediately after cutting.

VEGETABLES

Anise

Properly an herb of the carrot family with carminative and aromatic seeds; a salad and cooking vegetable with a bulb and a feathery top.

BUY: Anise with fresh, green foliage; the stalk and bulb should be a light greenish-white.

DO NOT BUY: Dry, brownish, droopy vegetable.

AVAILABLE: October through April.

HOW TO STORE: Keep cold and humid; use within a few days.

Artichokes

Large unopened flower bud of an herb plant belonging to the thistle family. The many leaflike parts making up the bud are called scales. This globe artichoke is no relation of the Jerusalem artichoke.

BUY: Plump, heavy, compact globular artichokes with thick, large, clinging, fleshy, fresh-looking leaf scales of a good green color.

DO NOT BUY: Artichokes with large areas of brown on the scales or with spreading scales — a sign of aging that indicates drying and toughening of the edible portions; vegetables with grayish-black discolorations, caused by bruises or mold growth on the scales; also avoid signs of worm injury.

AVAILABLE: Year round in limited amounts; peak supply in April and May. Produced only in California.

HOW TO STORE: Keep cool and humid; use within a few days.

Asparagus

Large species of Old World perennial plants of the lily-of-the-valley family, having much-branched stems and minute scalelike leaves; the tender shoots of one species of these plants are used as food.

BUY: Fresh, firm stalks with *compact closed* tips (open tips are a sign of overmaturity); spears should be *round* and *smooth* (angular or flat stalks are apt to be woody). A rich green color should cover most of the spear — only the green portion of fresh asparagus is tender, so select stalks with the largest amount of green running down the stalk.

DO NOT BUY: Asparagus with tips that are open and spread out, moldy, or decayed; or with ribbed spears (spears with up-and-down ridges) or spears that are not fairly round — these are all signs of aging and mean tough asparagus with poor flavor. Also avoid excessively sandy asparagus; sand grains can easily lodge beneath the scales or in the tips of the spears and are difficult to remove in washing. Reject warm asparagus; it is likely to be turning fibrous — asparagus should be kept cold all the way to the consumer. Never buy asparagus that has its butt soaking in water or appears to have been soaked; among other objections, the stalk may absorb dirty water.

AVAILABLE: Mid-February through June, with peak supplies from April to June. Chief sources are California, Michigan, Washington, and New Jersey.

HOW TO STORE: Keep cold and humid; use as soon as possible.

Beans, Green or Wax

Certain varieties of bean grown for the pods; related to the plants of the pea family and edible when young.

BUY: Fresh, bright-appearing beans of good green (or yellow, for wax beans) color; they should break with a snap and have no strings. Seeds should be immature; young tender beans with pods in a firm, crisp condition.

DO NOT BUY: Scarred or discolored beans; avoid wilted or flabby bean pods. Thick tough fibrous pods indicate overmaturing.

AVAILABLE: Year round, with abundant supplies May through August.

HOW TO STORE: Keep cold and humid; use as soon as possible.

Beans, Lima

A common variety of bean, its flat seed much used for food.

BUY: Young, tender beans with pods in a firm, crisp condition. In the pod, the pods should be fresh, well filled, bright, and dark green; shelled limas should be plump with a tender skin of a good green or greenish-white color.

DO NOT BUY: Wilted or flabby bean pods or vegetables with serious blemishes and decay; thick, tough, fibrous pods indicate overmaturity.

AVAILABLE: Mostly May into October.

HOW TO STORE: Keep cold and humid and use as soon as possible; they are highly perishable.

Beets

Biennial plant of the goosefoot family with oval-stalked leaves and juicy root, cultivated as a garden vegetable. Early beets are often sold in bunches with tops still attached, while others (usually late-crop beets) are sold on the basis of weight with tops removed. If the tops are fresh and reasonably unblemished, they make good eating.

BUY: Round and firm small to medium-sized beets with a generally smooth surface of good deep red color and a slender tap root (the large main root); large beets may be woody. If beets are bunched, you can judge their freshness fairly accurately by the condition of the top — although occasionally badly wilted tops indicate a lack of freshness, the roots may still be satisfactory if they are firm.

DO NOT BUY: Elongated beets with round scaly areas around the top surface will be tough, fibrous and strong-tasting; avoid flabby, rough, wilted or shriveled beets that have been exposed to the air too long.

AVAILABLE: Year round, with the peak supply June through October. Major growing areas are in California, Colorado, Ohio, New York, New Jersey, Texas.

HOW TO STORE: Keep cold and humid; remove greens and use as soon as possible; use roots within a week.

Broccoli

A hardy type of cauliflower and member of the cabbage family.

BUY: Fresh, green broccoli in a firm compact cluster of small flower buds that are still tightly closed and do not reveal the bright yellow flowers; bud clusters should be dark green, sage green, or purplish-green in color, depending on variety; stems should not be thick or tough.

DO NOT BUY: Broccoli with spread bud clusters, enlarged or open buds or wilted and yellowish leaves; these are signs of overlong display and old age. Also avoid broccoli with soft, slippery, watersoaked spots on the bud cluster — these are signs of decay.

AVAILABLE: Year round, with peak supply October through May; since broccoli grows best in cool weather, it is least abundant during July and August.

HOW TO STORE: Keep cold and humid and use as soon as possible.

Brussels Sprouts

The edible small green heads borne on the stem of a plant in the cabbage family. They develop as enlarged buds on a tall stem, one sprout appearing where each main leaf is attached; the "sprouts" are cut off and are usually packed in small containers.

BUY: Firm, fresh, compact, and unblemished sprouts of a bright green color with tight-fitting outer leaves.

DO NOT BUY: Sprouts with wilted yellowish or yellowish-green leaves or leaves that are loose, soft or wilted — this indicates aging; puffy or soft sprouts, which mean poor eating; or sprouts with small holes or ragged leaves, indicating possible worm injury.

AVAILABLE: September through February, with peak supply October through December; most are produced in California, New York and Oregon, with a few imported.

HOW TO STORE: Keep cold and humid; use as soon as possible.

Cabbage

A leafy vegetable of many varieties derived from a European plant of the mustard family. Three major groups of cabbage varieties are available: smoothleaved green cabbage, crinkly leaved Savoy green cabbage, and red cabbage; all types are suitable for any use, although the Savoy and red varieties are more in demand for use in salads and slaws. *Note:* "New cabbage," cabbage sold fresh; "old cabbage," cabbage sold from storage.

BUY: Firm, hard, solid heads of cabbage that are heavy for their size; they should be closely trimmed, with stems cut close to the head and only 3 or 4 outer or wrapper leaves — and preferably no loose leaves. (Outer leaves fit loosely on the head and are usually discarded, but too many loose wrapper leaves on a head cause extra waste.) *Outer leaves should be green* (or, if red cabbage, a good red). They should be fresh and free from serious blemishes. Remember, green cabbage is more nutritious than white; some early-crop cabbage may be soft or only fairly firm, but is suitable for immediate use if the leaves are fresh and crisp. Cabbage out of storage is usually trimmed of all outer leaves and lacks green color, but is satisfactory if not wilted or discolored.

DO NOT BUY: New cabbage with wilted, decayed, or yellowing leaves; heads with splits, softness, or scuffiness; cabbage with worm-eaten outer leaves which often indicates worm injury that has penetrated into the head. Avoid heads with some outer leaves separated from the stem — these may have undesirably strong flavor and coarse texture, and indicate overage.

AVAILABLE: Year round in large amounts; grown in many states, with California, Texas, and Florida marketing most new cabbage in winter, while many northern states grow cabbage for late summer and fall shipment or to be held in storage for winter sale.

HOW TO STORE: Keep cold and humid; use within a week or two.

Carrots

The orange-colored, spindle-shaped edible root of a biennial plant.

BUY: Well-formed, smooth, firm, fresh carrots of a good orange color; the modern packs of topped carrots in film bags are usually of very good quality — most are marketed when relatively young, tender and mild-flavored, an ideal stage for raw carrot sticks. Larger carrots are packed separately and are used primarily for cooking or shredding.

DO NOT BUY: Wilted, flabby, soft or shriveled carrots or those with large green "sunburned" areas at the top that must be trimmed. Avoid carrots showing spots of soft decay; also avoid excessively forked, rough or cracked carrots — these will be wasteful.

AVAILABLE: Year round. California and Texas market most carrots, but many other states produce large quantities.

HOW TO STORE: Keep cold and humid.

Cauliflower

An annual variety of the cabbage in which the head consists of the thickened flower cluster instead of the leaves. The white edible portion is called the curd, and the heavy outer leaf covering, the jacket leaves.

BUY: White or creamy-white, clean, compact, firm curds — this indicates good quality. Nearly all cauliflower is now shipped with most of the jacket leaves removed, but if there are any, they should be fresh and green. Size has no relation to quality; a slightly granular or "ricey" texture of the curd will not hurt the eating quality if the surface is compact. Also ignore small green leaflets extending through the curd.

DO NOT BUY: Cauliflower with a spreading curd — loose, open flower clusters — which indicates aging and overmaturity; wilted, spotted or speckled curds or those with brown, bruised areas — this is a sign of insect injury, mold growth, or decay.

AVAILABLE: Year round; most abundant from September through January. California, Texas, Oregon, New York, and Michigan are major sources.

HOW TO STORE: Keep cold and humid; use as soon as possible.

Celeriac

A variety of celery often referred to as celery root or knob celery.

BUY: Fresh, firm celeriac that is clean and healthy-looking.

DO NOT BUY: Bruised or in any way damaged celeriac.

AVAILABLE: Year round; most abundantly from October through April.

HOW TO STORE: Keep it cold and humid.

Celery

A European plant of the carrot family whose blanched leafstalks are eaten raw or cooked; most celery on the market is of the "Pascal" type, which has thick branched green outer stalks.

BUY: Fresh, crisp, clean celery of standard clipped length with stalks that are solid, rigid, and thick, with good heart formation and fresh-looking leaflets. Stalks should be of light or medium green with a glossy surface and mostly green leaflets.

DO NOT BUY: Soft, wilted, pliable celery with flabby upper branches or leaf stems — this indicates pithiness and lack of freshness; excessively hard branches, on the other hand, may be stringy or woody. Celery with seedstems is undesirably mature; such seedstems may appear as solid, somewhat round stems replacing the heart formation. Avoid celery with hollow or discolored centers in the branches; celery with internal discoloration will show some gray or brown on the inside surface of the larger branches near where they are attached to the base of the stalk. Therefore, *reject:* 1. Celery with "blackheart," a brown or black discoloration of the small center branches. 2. Insect injury in the center branches or the insides of outer branches. 3. Long, thick seedstem in place of the usually small, tender heart branches.

AVAILABLE: Year round; production is concentrated in California, New York, and Michigan.

HOW TO STORE: Keep cold and humid. *Note:* celery can be somewhat revived and freshened by placing the butt end in cold water, but badly wilted celery will never become really fresh again.

Chayotes

A relative of the cucumber, producing pear-shaped fruit 3 to 5 inches long, ranging from dark green to ivory white; it is sometimes called the vegetable pear.

BUY: Fresh-appearing fruit of good typical color.

DO NOT BUY: Deeply wrinkled, bruised, or damaged chayotes.

AVAILABLE: In very small quantity, November through May.

HOW TO STORE: Keep cool and humid.

Chard

See Greens.

Chicory

See Endive, escarole.

Chinese Cabbage

Primarily a salad vegetable; Chinese cabbage plants are elongated, with some varieties developing a firm head and others an open leafy form.

BUY: Compact, conical heads with fresh, crisp, clean, green leaves free from blemishes and decay.

DO NOT BUY: Wilted or yellowed plants.

AVAILABLE: Year round.

HOW TO STORE: Keep cold and humid; use within a week or so.

Chives

A relative of the onion, but milder in flavor and sold growing in pots. If given good care, chive plants will supply fresh leaves for several weeks to be snipped off with scissors, washed, and used. The "season" is whenever the buyer can find them.

Collards

See Greens.

Corn

Most corn supplies now on the market are yellow-kernel corn and should

34 *A Dictionary of Fresh Fruits and Vegetables*

be, but some white corn is sold; yellow corn contains considerable Vitamin A, while white corn has none. It is important to try to obtain true "sweet" corn, not immature field corn, which has a starchy flavor instead of a really sweet taste; to be good, sweet corn should be refrigerated immediately after harvesting and kept cold all the way to the kitchen kettle — it will retain fairly good quality for a number of days if it has been kept cold and moist from the time it was picked.

BUY: Corn with fresh-looking husks of a good green color, silk ends that are free from decay or worm injury, and stem ends (opposite from the silk) that are not too discolored or dried; ears should be well covered with plump, not too mature kernels.

DO NOT BUY: Ears with underdeveloped kernels that lack yellow color (in yellow corn); old ears with very large kernels; ears with dark yellow kernels with depressed areas on the outer surface. Also avoid ears of corn with yellowed, wilted, or dried "straw-colored" husks, or discolored and dried-out stem ends. Reject corn that is warm to the touch — it will surely taste starchy, and the kernels will probably be tough. (The sugar in corn turns to starch with time and warmth, and it doesn't take long.)

AVAILABLE: Almost year round; most plentiful from early May until mid-September. Sweet corn is produced in many states during the spring and summer; most midwinter supplies come from south Florida.

HOW TO STORE: Keep cold and humid; use as soon as possible. *Note:* It is not unusual for corn in abundant supply during spring and summer to be unsatisfactory, even though grown near its actual marketplace. This is because of failure to cool it quickly and keep it cold until purchase.

Cucumbers

The long, succulent fruit of a vine of the gourd family, cultivated as a garden vegetable that is usually eaten raw in salad. The young fruit are substantially used for pickles.

BUY: Cukes with good green color that are firm over their entire length; they should be well shaped and well developed but not too large in diameter. Good cucumbers often have many small lumps on their surfaces, and a white or greenish-white color in no way indicates poor quality. Cucumbers should have soft and immature seeds.

DO NOT BUY: Overgrown cucumbers that are large in diameter and have a dull yellowish color — the seeds are likely to be hard; very large cucumbers will also have hard seeds. Avoid puffy cucumbers with withered or shriveled ends, signs of toughness and bitter flavor.

A Dictionary of Fresh Fruits and Vegetables 35

AVAILABLE: Year round; most abundant May through August. Produced at various times in many states and imported during the colder months.

HOW TO STORE: Keep cool and humid; use within a few days.

Dasheens

A tropical plant with edible corms and tubers, it was formerly called the Oriental taro.

BUY: Ovoid and smooth tubers that weigh from 4 to 8 ounces — these are first grade; the corms are somewhat spherical; the tubers are ovoid-cylindrical.

AVAILABLE: Year round in New York City; in specialty shops now and then in major cities; grown to a small extent in the South.

HOW TO STORE: Tubers keep better than corms; both need to be cool and dry.

Eggplant

The large, smooth ovoid fruit of a widely cultivated herb plant allied to the potato and used as a vegetable.

Round Purple eggplant
(⅛ natural size)

BUY: Firm, smooth eggplants, heavy for their size, with a uniformly dark purple to purple-black skin (there are light-colored eggplants, but they are seldom seen on the market); they should be free of scars and cuts.

DO NOT BUY: Wilted, cut, shriveled, soft, or flabby eggplants; they will be bitter, poor in flavor, and very wasteful. Also avoid eggplants with worm injury on the surface or that show decay in the form of irregular dark brown spots, or are otherwise poorly colored.

AVAILABLE: Year round to some extent; most plentiful August and September.

HOW TO STORE: Keep cool and humid; use as soon as possible.

Endive, Escarole, Chicory

Leafy vegetables used mainly in salads. Chicory or endive has narrow, notched edges and crinkly leaves resembling the dandelion leaf; chicory plants often have blanched yellowish leaves in the center, which are considered highly desirable by many; escarole leaves are much broader and less crinkly than those of chicory. *Note:* Witloof, or Belgian, endive is a compact, cigar-shaped plant that is creamy white from blanching. The small shoots are kept from becoming green by being grown in complete darkness.

BUY: Fresh, clean, crisp, cold, and tender salad vegetables with outer leaves of a good green color.

DO NOT BUY: Plants with dry or yellowing leaves and seedstems — signs of old age; flabby and wilted leaves can also mean old age or poor care. Avoid plants with leaves showing brownish discolorations or insect injury; the bunches should not show black or otherwise discolored leaf margins or reddish discolorations of the hearts.

AVAILABLE: Year round; most abundant in winter and spring.

HOW TO STORE: Keep cold and humid; use as soon as possible.

Greens

A large number of widely differing species of plants grown for uses as cooking greens; the better-known kinds are beet greens, broccoli, cabbage sprouts, collards, dandelions, Swiss chard, kale, turnip tops, mustard greens, rabe, cress, sorrel, spinach, chicory, endive and escarole.

BUY: Greens with crisp, fresh, young, tender leaves that are free from blemish and have a good healthy green color; beet tops and ruby chard should show a reddish color.

DO NOT BUY: Greens that display insect injury, fibrous coarse stems, seedstems, dry or yellowing leaves, dirt or poor development; greens that are wilted or flabby. Softness is a sign of decay. Greens that are warm when sold should be suspect. *Note:* In checking greens for evidence of insect injury, doublecheck for aphids, which are sometimes hard to see and equally hard to wash away.

A Dictionary of Fresh Fruits and Vegetables 37

AVAILABLE: Year round in one form or another.

HOW TO STORE: Keep cold and moist.

Horseradish Root

The pungent root of a tall, coarse, white-flowered herb plant of the mustard family, most often used as a condiment.

BUY: Firm roots with no soft spots or shriveling.

DO NOT BUY: Soft, wilted, flabby, shriveled roots; roots dug when the plant is still growing do not keep as well as those conditioned by cold weather before harvest.

AVAILABLE: Year round.

HOW TO STORE: Keep cold and humid.

Jerusalem Artichokes

A tuber of the perennial American sunflower plant used as a vegetable; it is not an artichoke and has nothing to do with Jerusalem.

BUY: Tubers that vary to 3 inches in diameter — this is the edible part of the plant; fresh, nonflabby, firm tubers.

DO NOT BUY: Soft, shriveled tubers; they shrivel readily when exposed to the air, so keep them in a film bag.

AVAILABLE: Planting is irregular, and the marketing season and supply is uncertain; specialty food shops are thus the best source.

HOW TO STORE: Keep in film bag in refrigerator.

Kohlrabi

A member of the cabbage family in which the stem is greatly enlarged and is eaten like cauliflower. Its stem is swollen just above the ground into a globe 3 or 4 inches in diameter; its leaves are similar to those of a turnip. When young, both stems and leaves can be eaten after being boiled or steamed.

BUY: Kohlrabi with a firm, crisp stem that is not too large; tops should be crisp and green.

DO NOT BUY: Flabby, wilted vegetables.

AVAILABLE: May through November, with peak in June and July; supply is always small.

HOW TO STORE: Keep cold; use within a few days.

Leeks

A cultivated biennial of the lily family, much like the closely related onion and having similar culinary uses, but distinguished by having smaller bulbs and broad, flat, succulent, dark green leaves. Although similar in appearance, leeks are usually milder in flavor than green onions and larger than shallots.

BUY: Leeks with green, fresh tops and medium-sized necks that are well blanched for at least 2 or 3 inches from the root. They should be young, crisp and tender for good quality; slight bruising of the tops is not important.

DO NOT BUY: Yellowed, wilted, or otherwise damaged tops — may indicate old age — and flabby, tough, fibrous necks.

AVAILABLE: Year round to some extent, but always in small supply; most plentiful September through November and in the spring. Usually sold in small tied bunches.

HOW TO STORE: Keep cold and humid, in film bag in refrigerator hydrator compartment; use within a week or so.

Lettuce

The common garden species of a genus of plants of the chicory family, with crisp, succulent leaves, and used for salad. There are various kinds of lettuce, including some with red leaves; however, four types are generally sold: Iceberg, Butterhead, Romaine, and Leaf.

Iceberg lettuce is the major group — heads are large, round, and solid, with medium-green outer leaves and lighter or pale green inner leaves.

Butterhead lettuce, including the Bibb and Boston varieties, has a smaller head than Iceberg; it is slightly flat on top and has soft, succulent light green leaves in a rosette pattern in the center.

Romaine lettuce plants are tall and cylindrical with crisp, dark green leaves in a loosely folded head.

Leaf lettuce includes many varieties — none have a compact head. Leaves are broad, tender, fairly smooth, succulent and vary in color according to variety; it is grown mainly in greenhouses or on truck farms and sold locally.

BUY: Iceberg lettuce that is clean, crisp and tender, with heads fairly firm to firm, free from seedstems and leaves with ragged brown areas and with no excessive outer leaves. Butterhead, Romaine, Bibb and loose-leaf lettuce should be clean, fresh and tender — these will have a softer texture, but leaves should not be wilted. All lettuce should have a good bright color, medium to light green.

DO NOT BUY: Iceberg lettuce with heads that are very hard and that lack green color — signs of overmaturity; heads that have developed discoloration in the center of the leaves (the mid-ribs) will not be as flavorful. Also avoid heads with irregular shapes and hard bumps on top — this indicates the presence of an overgrown central stem. Check for tipburn, a tan or brown dead tissue area, around the margins of the leaves, especially on the edges of the head leaves. Slight discoloration of the outer or wrapper leaves will usually not hurt the quality of the lettuce, but serious discoloration or soft decay definitely should be avoided.

AVAILABLE: Iceberg, year round in large amounts, the others in smaller and less certain supplies; at various seasons from California, Arizona, New York, New Jersey, Texas, Colorado, New Mexico, Wisconsin, and several other states.

HOW TO STORE: Keep cold and humid; use within a few days.

Mushrooms

An edible fleshy fungus. Only one species is cultivated in the United States, *Agaricus campestris,* the common field mushroom, modified somewhat in cultivation. The wide upper portion is called the cap, the numerous rows of paper-thin tissue seen underneath when it opens are called the gills, and the vertical protuberance, the stem.

BUY: Clean and fresh-looking young mushrooms small to medium in size; caps should be either closed around the stem or moderately open with pink or light tan gills. The surface of the cap should be white or creamy (occasionally light brown from some producing areas); the flesh should be firm, thick and creamy white. Sizes ranging from ¾ inch to 3 inches in diameter are usually preferred.

DO NOT BUY: Overripe or wilted mushrooms with wide-open caps, pitted, dark, discolored gills or caps. Brown or black gills indicate old age.

AVAILABLE: Year round, with peak supply November through April; produced mostly in Pennsylvania with a substantial supply from California, New York, Ohio, Illinois, and several other states.

HOW TO STORE: Keep cold and humid; use as soon as possible.

Okra

A tall annual of the mallow family, cultivated for its immature mucilaginous green seed pods and used as a basis for soups and stews.

BUY: Fresh, clean, young tender pods — the tips will bend with very slight pressure. They should be 2 to 4½ inches long and have a bright green color. They should snap easily when broken and be easily punctured and should be free from blemishes.

DO NOT BUY: Tough, fibrous pods — tips are stiff and resist bending; dull, dry, hard pods will be unpalatable; shriveled, pale, faded green and discolored pods lack flavor.

AVAILABLE: May into October; most plentifully grown and marketed locally in the southern states.

HOW TO STORE: Keep cold and humid; use as soon as possible.

Onions, Dry

An Asiatic plant of the lily family with an edible bulb of pungent taste and odor; the many varieties of onions grown commercially fall into three general classes: globe onions, Granex-Grano onions, and Spanish onions.

Globe onions are the most common and are primarily cooking onions; most have yellow skins, but some are white or red-skinned. They are predominantly round to oval and have a rather pungent flavor; most are medium-sized — the smaller onions are sometimes packed and sold separately.

Danver's Yellow Onion
(⅓ natural size)

Granex-Grano onions are mostly yellow-skinned — a few are white. They are less round and less symmetrical than the globes, ranging from somewhat flattened to top-shaped. They are mild in flavor and considered ideal for slicing and eating raw as well as for cooking; they range in size from medium to large.

Spanish onions are similar to globes in shape but generally much larger; most varieties are yellow-skinned, with some white-skinned types. They are mild in flavor (often called "Sweet Spanish") and are perfect for slicing or salads; medium sizes are sometimes packed separately from the large ones — 3 inches or more in diameter.

BUY: Bright, clean, hard or firm onions that are well shaped with dry skins that crackle and have no seedstems or sprouts; they should be reasonably free of green sunburn spots and other blemishes.

DO NOT BUY: Onions with wet or very soft necks; moisture at the neck indicates either immaturity or decay. Avoid onions with a thick, tough, woody, hollow center in the neck or with fresh sprouts; this indicates seedstem development. Shape is not too important, except that for some uses there may be excessive waste in preparation of off-shape bulbs, such as splits, doubles and bottlenecks. *Note:* Neither color, shape, nor size indicates pungency.

AVAILABLE: Year round. Globe onions — in quantity in late summer, fall, and winter. Granex-Grano onions — in spring and summer; they come from the warmer growing areas. Spanish onions — in moderate supply in fall and winter. Major growing areas are California, New York, Texas, Michigan, Colorado, Oregon, and Idaho.

HOW TO STORE: Refrigerate or keep at room temperature, but *keep them dry.*

Onions, Green

Ordinary onions harvested very young, with little or no bulb formation and tubular tops. A number of types are similar in appearance though somewhat different in nature. Shallots and leeks also come under this classification; they are sometimes called scallions. They are sold in small bunches.

BUY: Onions with fresh tops of a good green color, medium-sized necks that are well blanched (white) for 2 to 3 inches from the root; they should be young, tender, and crisp.

DO NOT BUY: Onions with yellowing, wilted, discolored, or decayed tops — signs of a tough, fibrous, and flabby condition affecting the edible portions; bruised tops will not affect the eating quality of the bulbs if the tops are removed.

AVAILABLE: Year round; more abundant May through August.

HOW TO STORE: Keep cold and humid; use as soon as possible.

Parsley

A European aromatic garden herb-plant of the carrot family whose leaves are used as flavoring for soups and stews or as a garnish. It ranks at the top

Common, or Plain, Parsley (⅙ natural size)

of vegetables with Vitamin A and should be considered a valuable addition to the diet.

BUY: Crisp, fresh, bright green leaves free from yellow leaves and dirt.

DO NOT BUY: Wilted or yellowing parsley, which indicates old age or damage.

AVAILABLE: Year round.

HOW TO STORE: Keep cold and humid (parsley root, sold separately, also keeps well when cold and humid). Opinion is divided on freshening slightly wilted parsley leaves by trimming off the stem ends and placing the parsley in cold water; there is no advantage to generally storing parsley that way for any length of time (it is not stored that way commercially).

Parsnips

A European biennial herb-plant of the carrot family, with large pinnate leaves and yellow flowers; its long, tapered root, poisonous in the wild state, is made palatable and nutritious through cultivation. Parsnips do not develop their full flavor until after prolonged exposure to cold temperatures of about 40° or lower, therefore, they are primarily a late winter vegetable. They should come to the retail consumer after a period of commercial storage, not direct from the field.

BUY: Parsnips of small or medium width, smooth, firm, clean, well formed, and free from serious blemishes or decay.

DO NOT BUY: Large, coarse roots that probably have woody, fibrous or pithy cores; wilted, shriveled or flabby roots will be tough when cooked. Softness may be a sign of decay and discoloration an indication of freezing.

AVAILABLE: To a small extent throughout the year, with peak supply October through April.

HOW TO STORE: Keep cold and humid.

Peas, Green

The round, smooth, or wrinkled edible seed borne severally in pods by a vine of a family of leguminous plants; fresh green pleas are rarely on the market today because few people care to shell them and because high quality is hard to find.

BUY: Pods that are uniformly green and well filled; the peas must be young to be good and must be cooled quickly after harvest and kept cold at all times.

DO NOT BUY: Dry, wilted, warm, scanty pods; if allowed to warm, they lose sugar and tenderness quickly.

AVAILABLE: Formerly year round, with peak March through July — now difficult to find outside major city specialty stores.

HOW TO STORE: Keep cold and humid; use as soon as possible.

Peppers, Sweet

The many-seeded fruit of a tropical herb plant of the nightshade family; the green pepper or sweet pepper is the unripe fruit of the red pepper species, eaten as a vegetable. Often called bell peppers.

BUY: Fresh, firm, and thick-fleshed peppers that are bright medium to dark green. They should be of relatively heavy weight with a glossy sheen. The best are 4 to 5 inches long, with 3 or 4 lobes, and taper only slightly toward the blossom end.

DO NOT BUY: Soft, dull-looking, immature peppers, that are wilted or flabby, with cuts or punctures through the walls; peppers with soft watery spots on the sides, indicating decay; lightweight peppers with flimsy walls and thin sides.

AVAILABLE: Year round; most plentiful May through October.

HOW TO STORE: Keep cool and humid; use within a few days.

Potatoes

The edible starchy tubers of an American plant of the nightshade family. *Note:* Cooking quality varies by type and production areas; aside from size, some types from some areas are known to be good bakers and French friers — this is because of their high content of dry matter; for boiling and salads, a potato of slightly higher moisture content is desirable. For practical purposes, potatoes can be divided into three groups, although the distinctions between them are not clear and there is much overlapping:

"New potatoes" are freshly harvested and marketed during the late winter or early spring; the term is also used for later crop-producing areas to designate freshly dug potatoes that are not quite fully matured. Their best use is for boiling and creaming. They vary widely in size and shape, depending on variety. They are likely to be affected by "skinning" or "feathering" of the outer layer of skin; however, this usually only affects their appearance.

"General purpose" potatoes include the great majority of potatoes of both long and round types in the markets. They may be used for boiling, frying or baking, although several of the common varieties are not the best bakers. By means of air-cooled commercial storage facilities, they are amply available year round.

"Baking" potatoes: both the variety and the growing area are important factors affecting baking quality. The Russet Burbank, a long variety of potato with fine, scaly netting on the skin, is the most widely grown and best known in this group; Idaho potatoes, another variety of long baking potato, are also well known.

BUY: Firm, relatively smooth, clean, well-shaped potatoes, no matter what kind or size; some amount of skinned surface is normal in new potatoes, but large skinned or discolored areas are undesirable. General purpose potatoes and baking potatoes should be free from blemishes, sunburn, and decay.

DO NOT BUY: Badly cut or bruised potatoes (that mean waste in peeling); potatoes with a green color, probably caused by sunburn or exposure to light in the store; wilted, shriveled, or sprouted potatoes or those showing any sign of decay; they should also be relatively free from skinned surfaces.

AVAILABLE: Year round.

HOW TO STORE: *Do not refrigerate!* Low temperatures cause conversion of starch to sugar; keep at room temperature in the dark and away from undue heat or cold.

Radishes

The pungent fleshy root of a plant of the mustard family, usually eaten raw as a relish. Various types are the globular red and white, the globular white, the long red, the long white, and the long black.

BUY: Fresh, well-formed, smooth, firm, crisp radishes of medium size (¾–1⅛ inches in diameter); the desirable globular red radishes should be plump, round, and of a good red color. Most radishes are now sold topped and bagged, but if tops are on they should be fresh and green and can be cooked and eaten.

DO NOT BUY: Very large or flabby radishes, which are likely to have pithy centers; radishes with yellow or decayed tops (signs of overage). Also avoid radishes that are spongy, wilted, or showing a large number of cuts, black spots, or pits.

AVAILABLE: Year round; most plentiful from May through July. California and Florida produce most of our winter and spring supplies; several northern states provide radishes the rest of the year.

HOW TO STORE: Remove tops, if any; keep the roots cold and humid.

Rhubarb

The common garden rhubarb is a species of plant of the buckwheat family; the acid leaf stalks are traditionally boiled with sugar and eaten as a sauce or made into pies.

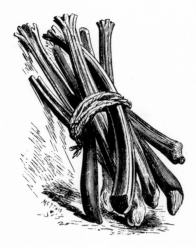

Rhubarb Stalks (⅓ natural size)

BUY: Fresh, firm, crisp, tender stems with a bright, glossy appearance; stalks should not be excessively thin. In general, mainly pink and red stems will be most flavorful, although some varieties from some soils, which are predominantly light green, are of good quality; the younger stems, having immature leaves, are usually the most tender and delicate in flavor. *Do not eat the leaves.*

DO NOT BUY: Very thin or very thick stalks — they are likely to be fibrous, tough, and stringy. Wilted or flabby stems indicate lack of freshness and poor flavor; tenderness and crispness can be tested by puncturing the stalk.

AVAILABLE: January through June; in very limited supply during the rest of the year.

HOW TO STORE: Keep cold and humid.

Rutabagas

A variety of turnip with a very large elongated yellowish root, an edible root of a biennial herb-plant of the mustard family. They are higher in total dry matter and total digestible nutrients than turnips. They are virtually all yellow-fleshed as opposed to the white-fleshed turnips, and are more elongated with a thick neck.

BUY: Rutabagas that are heavy in weight for their size, firm, fresh-looking, generally smooth, round or moderately elongated in shape (size is not a quality factor). Rutabagas stored for winter marketing are often coated with wax to prevent loss of moisture and shriveling — such a coated root is usually preferable.

DO NOT BUY: Rutabagas with skin punctures, deep cuts, or any signs of decay.

AVAILABLE: Year round; most plentiful during the cold months of fall and winter.

HOW TO STORE: Keep cold and humid. *Note:* Remove the thin layer of wax coating with the peeling just before cooking.

Shallots

An onionlike plant producing small clustered bulbs used generally like garlic for flavoring; they are distinguished from green onions by the bulb made up of cloves like garlic with no swelling at the base. Unlike garlic, the individual clove is covered by a membrane.

BUY: Young, crisp, tender shallots. Good-quality shallots have fresh green tops and medium-sized necks that are well blanched for at least 2 or 3 inches from the root.

DO NOT BUY: Shallots with wilted and yellowing tops — an indication of old age.

AVAILABLE: Fresh, from November through April.

HOW TO STORE: Keep cold and humid.

Spinach

A potherb of the goosefoot family, cultivated for its edible leaves.

BUY: If clipped leaves, spinach with fresh, clean, tender leaves of a good green color; if plants, fresh-looking spinach that is well developed and relatively stocky. Most spinach is of the savory or crumpled-leaf type, but whether savory or smooth is not important.

DO NOT BUY: Spinach whose larger leaves are yellow, discolored, wilted, bruised, or crushed — small, yellowish-green undeveloped heart leaves are not objectionable; plants that are overgrown and straggly or plants with seedstems.

AVAILABLE: Year round; more abundant January through May.

HOW TO STORE: Keep cold and humid and use as soon as possible; it is very perishable.

Squash

The fruit of a plant or vine of the gourd family. Squashes may be conveniently grouped into: 1. the soft-skinned, immature, and small group — to be eaten skin and all, including the seeds — commonly known as summer squash; 2. hard-shelled, mature, and small winter squash; 3. hard-shelled, mature, and large winter squash.

Warted Marrow Squash (⅛ natural size)

Summer squash includes those varieties that are harvested while still immature and when the entire squash is tender and edible; they include the yellow Crookneck, the large yellow Straightneck, the greenish-white Patty Pan, and the slender green Zucchini and Italian Marrow.

BUY: Crisp, young, relatively heavy, tender, and well-formed squash that is fresh-appearing, firm, and well developed; a tender squash can be identified by a glossy skin.

DO NOT BUY: Stale or overmature squash that has a dull skin and a hard, tough surface; it will have enlarged seeds and dry, stringy flesh.

AVAILABLE: Year round, in one variety or another.

HOW TO STORE: Keep cold and humid; use within a few days.

Winter squash includes those varieties marketed only when fully mature; some of the most important are the small corrugated Acorn, Butternut, Buttercup, green and blue Hubbard, green and gold Delicious, and Banana.

BUY: Only fully mature squash that is identified by a hard, tough rind; squash that is heavy for its size, i.e., with a thick wall, affording more edible flesh. Slight variations in skin color do not affect the flavor.

DO NOT BUY: Squash with any softness of the rind, indicating immaturity, thin flesh, and poor eating quality; squash with cuts, punctures, sunken or moldy spots on the rind — all signs of decay.

AVAILABLE: Most plentiful from early fall to late winter.

HOW TO STORE: Keep at room temperature. *Note:* They cannot be kept for extended periods in unduly warm temperatures.

Sweet Potatoes

A tropical vine related to the morning glory, having variously shaped leaves, purplish flowers, and a large, thick, sweet, and mealy tuberous root that is cooked and eaten as a vegetable; they are divided generally into two groups.

Moist sweet potatoes (often called yams) are the most common type; they have orange-colored flesh and are very sweet (true yams are tropical and are not grown commercially in the U.S.).

Dry sweet potatoes have a pale-colored flesh and are low in moisture; their production has dwindled rapidly.

BUY: Well-shaped, clean, firm, smooth sweet potatoes with bright, uniformly colored skins free from decay; the copper-skinned kinds with orange flesh are softer than the generally firm, light tan–skinned tubers with yellow flesh. However, selection should depend on individual taste and choice.

DO NOT BUY: Sweet potatoes with wormholes, grub injury, cuts, punctures, or any defects that penetrate the skin, which indicate the beginning of decay and causes waste; even if you pare away the injured areas, the rest of the potato flesh that may appear healthy will probably have a bad flavor. *Note:* Great care should be taken in the selection of sweet potatoes, as they are far more perishable than Irish potatoes. Decay is a serious problem with sweet potatoes and can be detected in three forms: wet, soft decay; dry, firm decay that begins at the end of the potato, making it discolored and shriveled; and dry rot in the form of sunken, discolored areas on the sides of the potato.

AVAILABLE: Year round, with peak October through April. Most are grown in the southern and eastern states from Texas to New Jersey, with California also a heavy producer.

HOW TO STORE: *Cold is harmful to sweet potatoes.* Keep them dry and *do not refrigerate* except after cooking.

Tomatoes

A South American perennial herb-plant of the nightshade family, widely cultivated for its fruit, a large, rounded, pulpy, edible berry usuallly red (or sometimes yellow) when ripe. "Homegrown" tomatoes produced on nearby farms are generally thought to provide the best flavor, because they are allowed to ripen completely before being picked. However, some areas now ship tomatoes that have been commercially picked after the color has begun to change from green to pink ("vine-ripe"); these can develop flavor and texture almost as satisfying as the home-grown ones. *Note:* Selection is a problem, as even tomatoes picked at an immature green will redden completely, but will not attain *good* flavor or juiciness; in addition, a tomato picked pink or red, if shipped or held at too cold a temperature, will chill and then not ripen properly. Consequently, there is no foolproof formula for selection. It is best to find a retailer whose tomatoes are usually satisfactory and follow the general tips listed below.

BUY: Fairly firm, smooth, well-formed tomatoes, free from blemishes and reasonably ripe; fully ripe tomatoes have an overall rich red color and a slight softness; *handle tomatoes gently* to test for texture! It is best to buy tomatoes slightly less than fully ripe — these will be of firm texture with a color range from pink to light red — and ripen at home to desired stage.

DO NOT BUY: Overripe and bruised tomatoes, which will be soft and watery; tomatoes with sunburn — green or yellow areas near the stem scar; or decayed tomatoes, which will have soft, watersoaked spots, depressed areas, or surface mold.

AVAILABLE: Year round. Major producers include Florida, California, and Texas, while an imported supply supplements regular domestic crops from late winter to early spring.

HOW TO STORE: Keep tomatoes that require further ripening in a warm place to ripen, i.e., room temperature protected from cold drafts; then refrigerate; they will keep for some time. Very cold temperatures will turn tomatoes mushy and prevent them from ripening later on.

Turnips

The thick edible roots of a biennial herb-plant of the mustard family. The most popular turnip has white flesh and a purple top, with a reddish-purple tincting of the upper surface; it may be sold with the leaves removed (topped) or in bunches with the tops still on. Although there is some difference in shape and skin color, the different varieties have much the same flavor.

BUY: Smooth, firm, fairly round turnips of small or medium size; they should have few leaf scars around the crown or fibrous roots at the base. If tops are on, they should be fresh, green, crisp, and young.

DO NOT BUY: Large, coarse, wilted turnips, or turnips with too many leaf scars around the top and with obvious fibrous roots. If tops are on and are yellowed or wilted, old age is indicated.

AVAILABLE: Almost year round in some stores.

HOW TO STORE: Topped turnips should be kept cold and humid; if tops are on and good enough to eat, they should be removed and used as soon as possible.

Watercress

A white-flowered perennial of the mustard family, growing naturally in clear running water, with moderately pungent leaves used in salads and as garnishes; it may also be cultivated along the banks of freshwater streams and ponds. This small round-leaved plant is highly prized not only for its pleasant, spicy flavor, but also for its very high Vitamin A content. There is only one variety of true watercress, although there are other cresses that grow wild in marshy areas, and land cresses as well.

BUY: Fresh, crisp, young, tender watercress of rich medium green, free from dirt and yellowish leaves.

DO NOT BUY: Bunches of watercress with yellow, wilted, or decayed leaves, indicating old age.

AVAILABLE: Year round, in limited quantities.

HOW TO STORE: Keep cold and humid and use as soon as possible — it is highly perishable; it is best to place it in a film bag with ice. *Do not soak in water.*

A Storage Chart

FRUITS

Store in refrigerator and use within the time specified.

Apples, eating, ripe	1 week
Apricots	3 to 5 days
Avocados	3 to 5 days
Blackberries (unwashed)	1 to 2 days
Blueberries (unwashed)	3 to 5 days
Cherries (unwashed with stems attached)	1 to 2 days
Cranberries	1 week
Figs	1 to 2 days
Grapes	3 to 5 days
Melons (only if ripe)	1 to 2 days
Nectarines	3 to 5 days
Peaches	3 to 5 days
Pears	3 to 5 days
Pineapples	1 to 2 days
Plums	3 to 5 days
Raspberries (unwashed)	1 to 2 days
Rhubarb	3 to 5 days
Strawberries (unwashed with caps on)	1 to 2 days
Watermelon	3 to 5 days

Store at room temperature.

Bananas (fully ripe)	1 to 2 days
Bananas (green-tipped)	3 to 5 days
Melons (if not ripe)	until ripe

VEGETABLES

Store in film bags in the refrigerator or in the hydrator compartment and use with the time specified.

Asparagus	1 to 2 days
Beans, lima (uncovered in pods)	1 to 2 days
Beans, snap (green or wax)	3 to 5 days
Beets (remove tops)	1 to 2 weeks
Broccoli	1 to 2 days
Brussels sprouts	1 to 2 days
Cabbage	1 to 2 weeks
Carrots (remove tops)	1 to 2 weeks
Cauliflower	3 to 5 days
Celery	3 to 5 days
Corn (unhusked and uncovered)	1 to 2 days
Cucumbers	3 to 5 days
Greens: spinach, kale, collards, chard, beet, turnip and mustard greens	1 to 2 days
Lettuce and other salad greens	1 to 2 days
Mushrooms	1 to 2 days
Okra	3 to 5 days
Onions, green	1 to 2 days
Parsnips	1 to 2 weeks
Peas (uncovered in pods)	1 to 2 days
Peppers	3 to 5 days
Radishes (remove tops)	1 to 2 weeks
Squash, summer	3 to 5 days
Tomatoes (store only ripe tomatoes in refrigerator)	3 to 5 days

Store at cool room temperature and use within the time specified.

Eggplant (about 60°; if air is dry keep in film bag)	1 to 2 days
Onions, mature (60° and dry; keep in open mesh container)	Several months
Potatoes (dark, dry, well ventilated and about 45° to 50°)	Several months
Rutabagas (about 60°)	Several months
Sweet potatoes (about 60°)	Several months
Squash, winter (cool, dry, about 60°)	Several months

Cooking

White Curled Swiss Chard
(1/10 natural size)

Preparation

F R U I T S

Fresh fruits must be carefully washed whether they are to be served raw or cooked. Small bruises and injured areas should be trimmed away and soft or decayed fruits immediately discarded.

Berries and cherries should not be washed until just before serving and then in a colander under a thin, gently running stream of cold water.

Apples and pears should be pared as thinly as possible. Peaches and apricots, which have tightly adhering skins when ripe, should be dipped into boiling water for about 45 seconds and then into cold water before peeling. This will loosen the skins to permit easy peeling, using the dull edge of a knife.

Orange and grapefruit halves are best prepared for serving by running a sharp-bladed knife (preferably curved, with a serrated edge) around each section to loosen it from the membrane and skin. If the whole fruit is to be peeled, be sure to remove all of the white inner peel with a sharp knife.

Don't forget that discoloration of peeled fruits such as avocados, apples, peaches, pears, and bananas can be avoided or at least minimized by dipping them into citrus fruit juice — lemon, lime, orange, grapefruit, or pineapple juice.

Two cardinal rules for preparing fresh vegetables are: *wash thoroughly* and *pare sparingly*.

In order to wash vegetables thoroughly before cooking, it is necessary to use a lot of water and often many rinses. Be sure to lift leafy greens from the water several times to let the sand and grit settle to the bottom.

Soaking vegetables like broccoli and Brussels sprouts in cold salt water for a little while will remove insects that can't be seen on the surface leaves.

Allowing potatoes to stand in water to cover will prevent them from darkening if they cannot be cooked immediately after paring. However, it is not a good idea generally to soak most fresh vegetables for any length of time as there is a substantial loss of food value, as nutrients are dissolved in the water.

To prepare vegetables for cooking or serving raw, be sure to remove bruised, wilted, yellowed, or tough portions. But pare and trim sparingly, keeping in mind the loss of nutrients as well as edible food, especially when paring potatoes and root vegetables before cooking.

The dark green outer leaves of leafy vegetables like lettuce and cabbage are high in nutrients and should *not* be discarded *unless* they are wilted or tough.

On the other hand, the woody mid-ribs of kale leaves may (and should be) removed for better flavor with little loss of nutritive value.

Artichokes, Globe

Wash; cut ½ inch off the top. Cut off the stem. With a scissors, cut off the sharp tips of the leaves. Stand upright in a deep kettle to cook in 1½ inches of boiling water with 1 thick lemon slice and ¼ teaspoon salt per artichoke. Cover and cook about 30 minutes, or until outside leaf pulls off easily. Remove each artichoke from cooking pan with two large spoons. Drain upside down until cool. Be sure to remove the fuzzy center "choke" before serving. This can be done easily with a teaspoon. *1 artichoke per serving.*

Asparagus

Cut or break off each stalk as far down as it snaps easily. Remove scales with a knife. Then wash thoroughly, using a brush.

To cook whole stalks in an upright position: Tie 5 to 6 stalks in a bundle with a string. Stand it upright in the bottom part of a double boiler. Sprinkle with 1 teaspoon salt. Pour in 1 to 1½ inches boiling water. Cover with the top part of the double boiler inverted. Boil 15 to 20 minutes or until just crisp-tender. The boiling water cooks the stalks while the rising steam cooks the tender heads; thus the whole stalk is uniformly cooked. Lift out by catching tines of fork in the string. Place drained asparagus on a platter; cut the strings.

To cook in a skillet or large-bottomed saucepan: Place asparagus in two layers in a 9- or 10-inch skillet or saucepan. Sprinkle with 1 teaspoon salt. Pour in boiling water to a depth of 1 inch. Cover. Boil 12 to 15 minutes, or until the lower part of the stalks are crisp-tender. Lift out with a pancake turner or two forks.

Avocados

Wash; cut in half; remove pit. Serve in halves or cut in bite-sized pieces.

Beans, Snap, Green, or Wax

Wash; remove strings and break off both ends. Cook whole, cut in 1-inch pieces, or in strips cut lengthwise (French style). Boil, pan, steam, cream, glaze, or bake in casserole.

Beans, Lima

Shell just before using and wash. Boil, cream, scallop, pan, steam, or bake in casserole.

Beets

Cut off tops (may be cooked separately) and all but 1 inch of stems and roots. Wash and scrub well but do not pare. Cook beets in their skins. Boil, steam, glaze, or bake in casserole for best results.

Broccoli

Remove only the tough outer leaves. Trim off a slice from the bottom part of the stalk, then cut lengthwise slits up the stem almost to the flowerets. This will enable the vegetable to cook more evenly. Unless this is done, the delicate flowerets tend to get cooked ahead of the stem. Soak in cold, salted water for 10 to 15 minutes. Boil, steam, or bake in casserole.

Common Celeriac or Turnip-rooted Celery
(⅛ natural size)

Brussels Sprouts

Cut off bruised and wilted leaves. Wash carefully and soak in cold, salted water for 10 to 15 minutes. Boil, steam or bake in casserole.

Cabbage

Remove separated and wilted outer leaves; wash and cut in wedges or shred. Boil, steam, pan or bake in casserole.

Carrots

Remove green tops immediately; wash and scrape. Leave whole, cut in quarters lengthwise, slice or dice. Boil, steam, cream, fry, scallop, glaze, pan, or bake in casserole.

Cauliflower

Remove leaves and woody stalk. Wash thoroughly and soak in cold salted water. May be cooked whole or separated into flowerets. Boil, steam, cream, scallop, fry, or bake in casserole.

Celeriac

Cut off root fibers and leaves. Scrub but do not peel. Boil, steam, or bake in casserole.

Celery

Separate stalks, cutting through the heart lengthwise; remove leaves, trim roots and scrub. Slice or dice. Boil, steam, pan, braise, fry, cream, scallop, glaze or bake in casserole.

Chard, Swiss

Wash well; if not young and tender, remove tough mid-ribs from the leaves. *See* Greens for cooking methods.

Chives

Clip and wash. Use as seasoning and garnish.

Coconuts

Shelled easily. After draining out the milk, place the coconut in the freezer for about an hour or in a moderate (350°) oven for a short time. Then rap sharply with a hammer; the shell will shatter and the meat will come away easily.

Corn

Remove husks, strip off silk, and cut off undeveloped ends. Do *not* put salt in the cooking water as it will toughen the corn. Cook *immediately.* Boil, steam, pan, or barbecue.

Eggplant

Wash; pare only if skin is bruised or tough. Cut in ½-inch slices. Fry or bake in casserole.

Greens (*kale, collards, chicory, endive, escarole, beets, turnip, mustard, and dandelion*)

Cut off yellowed, bruised, and wilted leaves; wash thoroughly in 5 or 6 rinse waters, lifting often to allow sand and grit to settle. Boil, steam, or pan.

Jerusalem Artichokes

Scrub; pare very thinly for boiling as potatoes.

Kohlrabi

Remove leaves, wash well, pare, and cut into small cubes; or dice or slice. When young, both stem and leaves can be eaten after boiling or steaming.

Broad, or London, Flag Leek

Leeks

Cut off green tops to within 1½ inches of white stalk. Wash. Boil or steam.

Lettuce

Break or gently cut out center heart; remove wilted outer leaves. Wash thoroughly in several rinses of cold water. Drain and pat dry. Tear into serving portions; do not cut with a knife. May also be braised.

Mushrooms

Scrub gently; cut off base of stem. Cook whole or sliced. Sauté in butter or margarine.

Okra

Wash pods thoroughly; cut off stems. Cook small pods whole and cut large pods into ½- or ¾-inch slices. Boil, steam, or pan.

Onions

Wash and peel under cold running water. Leave whole or cook quartered, sliced, diced, or minced (in combination with other foods). Whole onions may be cooked unpeeled, to be peeled immediately after cooking. Boil onions whole, sauté them sliced or diced, fry them in rings, bake them creamed or scalloped or glazed.

Parsley

Wash in cold water; drain and break into small sprigs. Use as garnish.

Parsnips

Wash; pare thinly or scrape. May be cooked whole, in halves, or quartered lengthwise or crosswise. Boil, steam, or fry.

Peas

Shell just before cooking and rinse in cold water. Boil or steam.

Peppers

Rinse in cold water; remove stem end and seed core. Cook whole or slice side walls into strips for sautéing, frying, or to serve raw in salad. Steam whole or bake stuffed with meat or other vegetables.

Pineapple

Cut off the crown and stem end. Stand the pineapple upright and cut off the rind in lengthwise strips. Remove the eyes with a pointed knife. Cut into quarters, cut away the core, then cut into chunks or spears.

Potatoes

"New" — scrub; boil in skins. "General purpose" — wash, peel thinly; fry, boil, or bake in skins. "Baking" — scrub; cook whole in jackets.

Rhubarb

Wash; trim away coarse or leafy portions. Cut stalks into 1-inch slices. Boil or steam.

Rutabagas

Wash; pare thinly; slice or cut in cubes. Boil or steam.

Spinach

Cut off tough root stems and wilted leaves; wash thoroughly in large quantities of cool water several times, lifting vegetable out of water each time to allow sand and grit to settle. Drain. Boil, steam, or pan only in water clinging to leaves.

Squash

Acorn — wash; cut in half; remove seeds and bake. Summer — wash; if skin is tender, do *not* peel. Cut in slices or cubes and boil, steam, fry, pan, or bake in casserole. Winter — wash; cut in quarters, remove seeds and pulp. Pare rind thinly; cube or cut in serving pieces and boil, bake, or steam.

Sweet Potatoes

Scrub; bake in jackets.

Tomatoes

Wash; plunge into boiling water 1 minute; quickly cool in cold water. Drain; cut out stem ends; skins should slip off. Cut up or cook whole in its own juice. Boil, steam, broil, or fry.

Turnips

Scrub and pare thinly; cook whole if small or cut in quarters, cubes, slices, or dice. Boil or steam.

Watercress

Remove yellowed or wilted leaves. Rinse thoroughly in cold water several times, lifting from water often to allow sand and grit to settle. Break into sprigs. Pan, or serve raw as garnish or salad green.

Number of Servings

A serving is generally measured as one medium-sized apple, banana, orange, peach, or pear; two or three apricots, figs, or plums; or ½ cup fruit plus liquid.

Be sure to allow for the waste of inedible portions such as peelings, cores, trimmings, and pits when using the guide below to gauge servings per purchase unit.

FRESH RAW FRUIT	NUMBER OF SERVINGS
Apples, bananas, figs, peaches, pears, or plums	3 or 4 per pound
Apricots, sweet cherries, dates, or seedless grapes	4 or 5 per pound
Blueberries or raspberries	4 or 5 per pint
Strawberries	7 or 8 per quart

See the Guide to Simmering Fruits (page 77) to estimate the number of servings from fresh cooked fruits.

The pods, trimmings, parings, and husks and other inedible portions of vegetables must be considered when figuring the yield in servings.

Keep in mind also that some vegetables absorb water during cooking and swell, while others lose water and shrink.

See the Boiling Guide for Vegetables for the purchase quantities necessary to make 6 half-cup servings.

Figs (natural size)

Remember that dried fruits increase substantially in volume and weight during cooking due to their absorption of water. See the Guide to Simmering Dried Fruits (page 80) for estimated numbers of servings from a family-sized package.

Leftovers

Similarly, leftover fruits that will darken and lose flavor in a matter of hours after they are cut, peeled, or pared should be quickly consigned to the oven for baking, to the pan for simmering, or added to salads or desserts. *Note:* Do not add fresh pineapple to gelatin as it contains an enzyme that will prevent gelling.

V E G E T A B L E S

Leftover vegetables lend themselves to interesting and imaginative combinations and should never be wasted.

Try adding them to your stock pot or directly to soups, casseroles or egg, meat, gelatin and tossed green salads. Leftover vegetables are particularly handy for recipes that call for cooked vegetables.

They may be creamed, scalloped, glazed, fried or pureed for cream soups in just the same way you would use freshly cooked vegetables.

Tomatoes are a great addition to hamburgers and meat loaves, while com-

True Shallot (½ natural size)

binations of yesterday's leftovers and today's freshly cooked vegetables can stretch the budget as well as add interest to your meal.

Finally, don't forget old-fashioned vegetable soup and meat and vegetable stews, favorites in most families, and a fail-safe catchall for most of your leftover vegetables.

Methods

To preserve nutrients and to promote fine eating quality and attractive appearance, the U.S. Department of Agriculture recommends the 3 R's of cooking fresh fruits and vegetables:

1. Reduce the amount of water used.
2. Reduce the length of cooking time.
3. Reduce the amount of surface area exposed.

In addition, it wise to use the cooking water, if palatable, which contains dissolved nutrients; to avoid keeping foods hot for long periods; and to avoid long exposure to air, especially in the case of mashed or chopped foods.

BOILING VEGETABLES

Cook vegetables only until they are tender to insure the best flavor, color, texture and food value. Use as little cooking water as possible — the less water, the more nutrients retained. Vegetables cooked whole in their skins retain most of their nutritive value. To shorten cooking time, cut, slice, dice, or coarsely shred vegetables.

— ½ to 1 cup of water with ½ to 1 teaspoon salt is usually sufficient cooking liquid for 6 servings if the vegetables are reasonably young and tender.

— Older root vegetables usually require water to cover and longer cooking.

— It is best to cook fresh spinach and similar greens in only the water remaining on their leaves after washing, over low heat, and in a pan with a tight-fitting lid.

— Tomatoes can be cooked in their own juices.

Follow these general directions for boiling fresh vegetables and use the guide that follows for specific cooking times and buying quantities:

1. Bring salted water to a boil.
2. Add the vegetable; cover and quickly bring water back to a boil.
3. Reduce heat and cook gently until the vegetable is crisp and just tender.
4. Serve immediately; vegetables that are allowed to stand will lose nutritive value as well as flavor.

Vegetable Boiling Guide

VEGETABLE	BUYING QUANTITY (POUNDS) *for 6 half-cup servings*	COOKING TIME (MINUTES) *after water returns to boil*
Asparagus	2½ for spears 1¾ for cuts and tips	10 to 20 (whole spears) 5 to 15 (cuts & tips)
Beans, lima	2¾ in pods	25 to 30
Beans, snap (green or wax)	1	12 to 16 (1-inch pieces)
Beets	2½ with tops 1½ without tops	30 to 45 (young, whole) 45 to 90 (older, whole) 15 to 25 (sliced or diced)
Broccoli	2	10 to 15 (heavy stalk split)
Brussels sprouts	1½	15 to 20
Cabbage	1¼	3 to 10 (shredded) 10 to 15 (wedges)

VEGETABLE	BUYING QUANTITY (POUNDS) *for 6 half-cup-servings*	COOKING TIME (MINUTES) *after water returns to boil*
Carrots	1½ without tops	15 to 20 (young, whole) 20 to 30 (older, whole) 10 to 20 (sliced or diced)
Cauliflower	2	8 to 15 (separated) 15 to 25 (whole)
Celery	1½	15 to 18 (cut up)
Corn	3 in husks	5 to 15 (on cob)
Kale	1¼ untrimmed	10 to 15
Okra	1¼	10 to 15
Onions, mature	1¾	15 to 30
Parsnips	1½	20 to 40 (whole) 8 to 15 (quartered)
Peas	3 in pods	12 to 16
Potatoes	1½ 1¼	25 to 40 (whole, medium) 20 to 25 (quartered) 10 to 15 (diced)
Spinach	1½ prepackaged	3 to 10
Squash, summer	1½	8 to 15 (sliced)
Squash, winter	2½	15 to 20 (cut up)
Sweet potatoes	2	35 to 55 (whole)
Tomatoes	1¼	7 to 15 (cut up)
Turnip greens	2¾ prepackaged	10 to 30
Turnips	1¾ without tops	20 to 30 (whole) 10 to 20 (cut up)

VARIATIONS: 1. Sprinkle lemon juice or herb vinegar on boiled vegetables for a delightfully tart and low-calorie touch.

2. Add a pinch of herbs or a tablespoon of minced onion, green pepper, or chives before cooking for flavor without calories.

3. Mash vegetables, beat in a little hot milk, add butter or margarine to taste, and season with salt and pepper.

4. Season after cooking with a flavorful fat — bacon drippings, butter or

margarine — or with salad oil to which a little lemon juice, horseradish, or garlic has been added.

5. Serve with basic sauces.

BASIC SAUCES FOR BOILED VEGETABLES

White Sauce

This simple sauce is not only a satisfying accompaniment to many cooked vegetables, but it also serves as a basis for several other vegetable sauces. Thin white sauce is usually preferred with starchy vegetables like peas or lima beans and soups; medium white sauce for other vegetables, casseroles, and sauces; thick white sauce for croquettes and soufflés.

For a smooth white sauce, blend the flour with fat or cold liquid, then combine with remaining liquid, stirring constantly over low heat until thickened. For ingredients and quantities, see the table below.

The fat may be omitted if the white sauce is to be used in cream soups, casseroles or other recipes where fat is not needed for flavor or texture.

White Sauce Ingredients

FOR 1 CUP	THIN SAUCE		MEDIUM SAUCE	
	standard	*low fat*	*standard*	*low fat*
Butter or other fat	1 tablespoon	2 teaspoons	2 tablespoons	1 tablespoon
All-purpose flour	1 tablespoon	1 tablespoon	2 tablespoons	2 tablespoons
Salt	¼ teaspoon	¼ teaspoon	¼ teaspoon	¼ teaspoon
Milk *	1 cup	1 cup †	1 cup	1 cup †
Calories in 1 cup white sauce	290	180	420	245

Cheese Sauce

Make 1 cup of thin or medium white sauce. Remove from heat; stir in 1 cup shredded Cheddar cheese. Blend well. Delicious with asparagus, broccoli, cabbage, cauliflower, potatoes, and summer squash.

* Vegetable liquid may be used in place of part of the milk.
† Use skim milk or reconstituted nonfat dry milk for low-fat white sauce.

Mock Hollandaise

Make 1 cup of medium white sauce. Beat 2 egg yolks and stir a little hot sauce into them; then stir mixture into the rest of the sauce. Stir in 2 tablespoons butter or margarine. Cook over hot water about 1 minute. Remove from heat and stir in 1 tablespoon lemon juice. Serve at once. Especially good over asparagus and broccoli.

Note. Use only clean eggs with no cracks in the shell for this recipe.

Mushroom Sauce

Use proportions of fat and flour for 1 cup medium white sauce. Cook 1 cup small whole or sliced mushrooms in fat. Add the flour. A splendid topping for green beans, peas, or asparagus.

Mushrooms (⅞ natural size)

Onion or Celery Sauce

Use proportions of fat and flour for 1 cup thin white sauce. Cook ½ cup finely chopped onion or celery in the fat until tender, stir in flour and salt, and slowly blend in liquid. Cook over low heat stirring constantly until thickened. Add 1 teaspoon Worcestershire sauce before serving. Serve over carrots, green beans, or peas.

For 6 half-cup servings, add 3 cups cooked, drained vegetables to 1 cup hot white sauce; heat to serving temperature.

Use any cooked vegetable or try some of the following combinations:

cauliflower and peas
carrots and peas
corn and green beans
Brussels sprouts and celery

carrots and lima beans
celery and asparagus
onions and carrots

SCALLOPING

Preheat oven to 350° and grease a 1-quart casserole. Combine 3 cups cooked, drained vegetables and 1½ cups medium white sauce (either the standard or low-fat recipe) in the casserole.

Top with 3 tablespoons fine dry bread crumbs mixed with 2 teaspoons melted butter or margarine. Bake 25 to 30 minutes. Makes 6 half-cup servings.

VARIATIONS: 1. Sprinkle grated cheese, finely chopped onion or parsley, or cooked mushrooms between the layers.

2. Use crushed prepared cereal in place of bread crumbs as a topping.

3. Alternate layers and sauce.

4. Add a pinch of marjoram, thyme, or oregano to the sauce before combining with vegetables.

VEGETABLES AU GRATIN

To 1 cup medium white sauce, add 1 cup shredded sharp process American cheese and blend. Combine cheese mixture with 4 cups hot cooked and drained vegetables. Pour into a 1-quart casserole. Toss ½ cup fine soft bread crumbs with 1 tablespoon melted butter or margarine and sprinkle on top of vegetables. Bake at 350° for 20 to 25 minutes or until browned. Makes 6 to 8 servings.

Cut cooked vegetable(s) into strips or large pieces to make 3 cups. Blend 2 tablespoons butter or margarine with ¼ cup packed brown sugar and 1 tablespoon water in a heavy frying pan over low heat. Add the vegetable(s).

Cook over low heat, turning vegetable(s) several times until syrup is very thick and vegetable(s) are well coated, about 5 to 10 minutes. Keep heat *low* to prevent scorching.

VARIATIONS: 1. Use honey or maple syrup instead of brown sugar and omit water.

2. Substitute frozen orange juice concentrate for water.

BROILING FRUITS

This is a quick method of cooking fruit that makes an easy supplement to your meat courses. Since cooking time is short and the heat very high, watch the fruit carefully to prevent scorching. Be sure, too, to place the broiler rack at the height recommended by the manufacturer of your range.

Broiled Apple Rings

Wash and core 3 apples; slice ¼ inch thick. Arrange slices in foil-lined broiler pan. Brush with fresh lemon juice, and with melted butter or margarine, if desired. Broil about 4 minutes. Turn and brush the other side with lemon juice and, if desired, with melted butter or margarine. Sprinkle with mixture of 1 tablespoon sugar and ¼ teaspoon cinnamon. Broil about 2 minutes longer. Makes 6 servings.

Broiled Bananas

Peel 6 all-yellow or green-tipped bananas; leave whole. Proceed as for broiled apple rings. Broil about 2 minutes on each side. Makes 6 servings.

VARIATION: Sprinkle bananas with finely chopped peanuts before broiling the second side.

Broiled Peach Halves

Wash, peel, halve, and pit 6 peaches. Proceed as for broiled apple rings. Broil about 8 minutes on first side and 3 to 5 minutes on second side, or until golden brown.

VARIATION: Broil rounded side of the peach halves first; then put ½ teaspoon jelly in each hollow before broiling the second side.

Broiled Grapefruit

Wash and dry 3 medium-sized grapefruits. Cut in halves. With sharp knife (preferably with curved serrated blade) cut around each section of fruit close to membrane. Remove seeds. Sprinkle each half with brown sugar. Broil 10 minutes or until golden. Flavor with sherry or rum before serving and garnish with cherries.

VARIATION: Drizzle grapefruit with honey instead of brown sugar before broiling; or fill center with jam before serving.

Broiled Tomato Halves

Remove hard stem ends of 3 large, firm tomatoes and cut in halves. Place on baking sheet and season with salt, pepper, and garlic, onion powder, rosemary, basil, thyme or dill.

Broil under moderate heat — *do not overcook* — until singed around edges. Garnish with chopped parsley, crisp bacon crumbles, anchovies, mayonaise, or sliced mushrooms sautéed in butter. Makes 6 servings.

SIMMERING FRUITS

This is a most satisfactory method of cooking fruits quickly in a sugar and water syrup to preserve color, flavor, and nutrients. Be sure to use only enough sugar to bring out the flavor of the fruit; too much sugar will mask delicate natural fruit flavors.

In order to help the fruit keep its shape, add sugar before cooking. This will prevent the fruit from absorbing moisture and becoming too soft. Firm varieties of fruits, however, should be cooked in plain water rather than syrup, with the sugar added during the last few minutes of cooking time.

Cook the fruit only until tender. Do not overcook or color, flavor and nutrients will be lost.

Follow the general directions listed below and refer to the guide that follows for specific ingredient amounts and cooking time.

To prepare fruits for simmering:

apples — wash; pare, core and slice.

apricots — wash; halve and pit apricots or leave whole; peel, if desired.

peaches — wash; peel and pit peaches; halve or slice.

pears — wash; pare, core and halve or slice.

plums — wash but do *not* peel; halve and pit plums or leave them whole.

1. Combine sugar and water and bring to a boil.

2. Add fruit to boiling syrup; cover and return to boiling; then reduce heat until syrup just simmers.

3. Cook until fruit is tender but not mushy. Stir as little as possible to avoid breaking fruit.

Note. When cooking firm varieties of pears, do not add sugar until the last 10 minutes of cooking.

Guide to Simmering Fruits

FRUIT	BUYING QUANTITY (*pounds*)	WATER (*cup*)	SUGAR * (*cup*)	COOKING TIME (*minutes*)	SERVINGS (½ *cup*)
Apples	2	½	¼	8 to 10	6
Apricots	1½	½	¾	5	6
Peaches	1½	¾	¾	5	6
Pears:					
soft varieties	2	⅔	⅓	10	6
firm varieties	2	⅔	⅓	20 to 25	6
Plums	1	½	⅔	5	6

VARIATIONS: 1. Add a few cinnamon candies to the syrup when cooking apples or pears.

2. Add a teaspoon of grated or dried orange or lemon peel during the last few minutes of cooking.

3. Add a stick of cinnamon or a few cloves to cooking syrup. Delicious with apples, pears, peaches.

* For fruits of medium tartness; for very tart fruits add more sugar.

Fruit sauces are easy to make, require relatively little cooking time, and serve a variety of uses. Applesauce or rhubarb sauce stand alone as simple desserts. Cranberry sauce and applesauce are delicious adjuncts to meat and poultry, while cherry sauce and peach sauce are colorful toppings for puddings, ice cream, sponge cake, pound cake or angelfood cake.

Follow the directions given below, adjusting the amounts of water and sugar in the guide to the individual juiciness and tartness of the fruit. (The amounts given are based on fruits of medium juciness and tartness.)

Applesauce

Wash apples; core and slice. If you do not plan to strain sauce, pare the apples. If you want a pink sauce, use red apples and leave the skins on.

Add the apples to boiling water. Cover and return to boiling; then reduce heat until water just simmers. Cook over low heat until the apples are tender. Stir occasionally to prevent sticking. Remove them from the heat. For a very smooth sauce, put the apples through a strainer or food mill. Add sugar and mix well.

Cherry Sauce

Use either sweet or sour cherries for this sauce, adjusting the quantity of sugar according to the tartness of the fruit.

Wash, sort, stem, and pit the cherries. Bring water to a boil. Add the cherries, cover, and return to boiling. Reduce the heat until water just simmers.

Cook over low heat, stirring occasionally, until the cherries are tender. Stir in the sugar; simmer 1 minute longer.

Cranberry Sauce

Wash and sort berries. Combine sugar and water. Bring to a boil. Add the berries to the boiling sugar syrup. Cook over low heat until the berries pop. Put sauce through a strainer or food mill or leave berries whole, as desired.

Peach Sauce

Wash, peel, pit, and slice peaches. Bring water to a boil. Add the peaches, cover, and return to boiling. Reduce heat until water just simmers. Cook over low heat, stirring occasionally, until peaches are tender. Stir in sugar; simmer 1 minute longer.

Rhubarb Sauce

Wash rhubarb; trim away coarse or leafy portions. Cut stalks into 1-inch slices. Bring water to a boil; add rhubarb, cover, and return to boiling. Reduce heat until water just simmers. Cook over low heat, stirring occasionally, until rhubarb is tender. Stir in sugar; simmer 1 minute longer.

Guide to Making Fruit Sauces

	BUYING QUANTITY	WATER	SUGAR *	COOKING TIME (MINUTES)	YIELD
FRUIT	(*pounds*)	(*cups*)	(*cups*)	(*after adding fruit*)	(*cups*)
Apples	2	⅓	¼	12 to 15	3
Cherries	1	⅔	½	5	2
Cranberries	1	2	2	15	4 whole 3 strained
Peaches	1	⅔	½	5 to 8	2
Rhubarb	1½	¾	⅔	2 to 5	3

VARIATIONS: 1. Add a little ground cinnamon or nutmeg to apple, peach, or cherry sauce.

2. One-half teaspoon of grated lemon rind is a tangy addition to apple, sweet cherry, cranberry, or peach sauce.

3. Add 2 or 3 tablespoons of thawed frozen raspberry-lemon concentrate to applesauce.

SIMMERING DRIED FRUITS

Dried fruits may be cooked before serving. Some should be carefully washed

* For fruits of medium tartness; for very tart fruits, add more sugar.

before they are used; see washing instructions on various packages. As a rule, dried fruits need no longer be soaked before cooking, but they will be plumper and more flavorful if they are refrigerated for several hours after they are cooked and before they are served.

Follow the general directions given below and see the Guide to Simmering Dried Fruits that follows for specific information.

1. Wash fruit, place in a saucepan, and add water. Bring to a boil.

2. Simmer fruit until plump and tender. Be sure to check labels on packages as some processed fruits take less cooking time than recommended in the Guide.

3. If more sweetening is needed, add sugar at the end of the cooking period. (Adding sugar at the beginning makes the fruit less able to absorb moisture and become tender.)

Guide to Simmering Dried Fruits

FRUIT	QUANTITY (ounces)	WATER (cups)	SUGAR (cups)	COOKING TIME (minutes)	SERVINGS (½ cup)
Apples	8	3½	⅓	10	8
Apricots	8	2¼	⅓	10	6
	11	3	½	10	8
Mixed Fruits	8	2¼	⅓	20	6
	11	3	½	20	8
Peaches	8	3	⅓	25	7
	11	4	½	25	9 or 10
Pears	8	2	⅛	25	4
	11	3	¼	25	6
Prunes	16	4	¼ to ½ (optional)	25	8 or 9

VARIATIONS: 1. Add a stick of cinnamon and a few cloves at the beginning of the cooking period.

2. Add 1 teaspoon of grated lemon or orange rind at the beginning, or ¼ cup of frozen orange juice concentrate near the end, of the cooking period.

3. Add ½ cup of raisins to dried apples, apricots, or mixed fruits before cooking.

Panning is a method of cooking shredded or sliced vegetables in the minimum amount of water and fat on top of the range. In addition, it is a method often used to best retain the color, flavor, and nutrients of certain vegetables — a method often used by the Chinese. It is an especially good way of preparing cabbage, carrots, corn, snap beans, spinach and summer squash.

Follow these general rules for panning fresh vegetables and see the guide that follows for specific cooking times, quantities, and ingredients needed to make 6 servings:

1. Shred or slice vegetable, removing tough stems and ribs; e.g., leafy vegetables should be shredded, green beans cut lengthwise.

2. Heat fat (butter, margarine, or drippings) in heavy frying pan over moderate heat.

3. Add vegetable and sprinkle with salt.

4. Add water, stir gently; cover with a tight lid to hold in the steam.

5. Cook over low heat, stirring occasionally to prevent sticking, until vegetable is just tender. Slow-cooking vegetables may require the addition of a few tablespoons of water while the faster-cooking ones will probably contain sufficient moisture to prevent sticking.

Vegetable Planning Guide

	QUANTITIES OF				
VEGETABLE	VEGETABLE (*quarts*)	FAT (*tblspn*)	SALT (*tspn*)	WATER	COOKING TIME (*minutes*)
Beans, snap green or wax sliced in 1-inch pieces	1	1½	½	⅔ cup	20 to 25
Cabbage, finely shredded	1½	1½	¾	3 tablespoons	6 to 8
Carrots, thinly sliced	1	2	½	3 tablespoons	10
Corn, cut	1	1½	½	⅓ cup	15 to 18
Spinach, finely shredded	3	2	½	none	6 to 8
Summer squash, thinly sliced	1	½	½	3 tablespoons	12 to 15

VARIATIONS: 1. Add finely chopped onion or onion juice before cooking. 2. Add bits of crumbled crisp bacon or diced ham to cooked vegetables.

STEAMING

This is a method of cooking particularly suited to mild-flavored vegetables, which also will conserve more of the nutrients in these vegetables than if they were boiled.

Prepare the vegetables as if for boiling and place them in a colander over boiling water or in the perforated upper part of a steamer. Cover tightly and steam until the vegetables are crisp-tender, allowing about 10 to 15 minutes more cooking time than in boiling. Season and serve as you would a boiled vegetable.

FRENCH FRYING

French frying is a method of cooking vegetables in deep fat at a medium-high temperature that is particularly suited to potatoes, sweet potatoes, batter-dipped onion rings, eggplant sticks, parsnips, breaded green pepper rings, tomato and squash slices, and cauliflowerets.

Follow these general directions for successful French frying; for detailed instructions see the one- and two-stage procedures outlined below.

1. Rinse potatoes and sweet potatoes quickly in cold water before frying to remove surface starch.

2. To prevent spattering, pat dry all vegetables thoroughly to completely remove moisture before frying.

3. Keep cooking pan or container in which fat or oil is stored free of moisture.

4. Be sure to use a well-balanced and deep heavy pan or kettle of substantial size.

5. Keep pan handles turned away from the edge of the range.

6. Never cover pan while heating oil or fat.

7. Cut foods into uniform pieces so that they will cook and brown evenly.

8. After frying, drain food thoroughly by placing it on absorbent paper such as paper towels or unglazed brown paper.

9. A frying basket for lowering foods into the oil and for draining is helpful.

10. Do not overload your frying basket. If too much food is put into it at one time, the temperature of the fat will drop excessively, cooking will slow down, and the vegetables will absorb more fat.

11. A long-handled fork, a slotted spoon, or tongs are handy for turning foods during frying.

12. For accuracy, use a deep-fry thermometer; read it at eye level or as manufacturer directs.

13. Wait until oil has reached the correct temperature before adding the food.

14. Maintain the frying temperature at all times.

15. It is a good practice to fry only one layer of food at a time.

16. When frying fritters, keep them well separated.

17. For frying large quantities of potatoes, it is best to use the two-stage procedure: fry the potatoes ahead, one layer at a time; then just before serving, brown them in much larger batches in hotter fat.

ONE-STAGE PROCEDURE: 1. Fill kettle a third full of fat or oil and heat to 370° to 385°. Have frying basket in the fat.

2. Raise basket and add enough vegetables to cover the bottom of the basket.

3. Lower the basket gently into the fat. If the fat bubbles a good bit, lift and lower the basket several times until the bubbling subsides.

4. Fry until vegetable is cooked through and golden brown.

5. Lift basket from fat. Drain a few seconds; pour vegetable onto absorbent paper.

6. Season. Spread fried vegetable on a cookie sheet and place in a warm oven to retain heat while frying additional vegetables.

TWO-STAGE PROCEDURE: A good way to partially prepare French-fried potatoes and sweet potatoes ahead of time.

A. Proceed as for one-stage method except fry only until food is cooked, but not brown. (Do NOT hold parfries longer than 1 or 2 hours at room temperature or 24 hours in covered container in refrigerator. To hold parfries longer than 24 hours, freeze them.)

B. 1. Heat fat to 375° with frying basket in the fat.

2. Raise the basket and add about two layers of parfries.

3. Fry until golden brown.

4. Lift basket from fat. Drain for a few seconds; then pour vegetable onto absorbent paper.

5. Season and serve.

Dipping Batter

Sift together 1 cup flour, 1 teaspoon baking powder, and ½ teaspoon salt. Combine 1 slightly beaten egg, ¼ cup corn oil, and 1 cup milk. Add to dry ingredients and beat until smooth.

Corn Meal Batter

Sift together 1 cup flour, 1½ teaspoons baking powder, and 1 teaspoon salt. Add ½ cup corn meal. Combine 2 slightly beaten eggs, 2 tablespoons corn oil, and ¾ cup milk. Add to dry ingredients and mix until smooth.

Bread Crumb Coating

Coat foods to be fried with seasoned, fine, dry bread crumbs. Then dip in beaten egg and coat again with the crumbs.

1. Arrange foods to be coated for frying as in an assembly line. Starting at the left, place the food to be fried, then the seasoned crumbs (on waxed paper), the egg or milk in a shallow bowl, more crumbs (on waxed paper); and, at the far right, something to hold the coated food.

2. Keep the fingers of the left hand dry for rolling the food in the crumbs; use the right hand for dipping it in the egg or milk.

3. Dust the food with flour prior to batter-dipping. Use tongs to dip food into batter and to place it in hot oil.

4. Let coated vegetable croquettes stand for a while before frying them. This gives the crumbs a chance to adhere.

Vegetables

Cauliflower, tomato, eggplant, summer squash or zucchini, onions, green pepper, parsnips. Separate cauliflower into flowerets. Cut tomato and eggplant into ½-inch slices. Cut squash into ¼-inch slices. Slice and separate onions and green peppers into rings. Pare parsnips. Dust with flour, dip in Dipping Batter or Corn Meal Batter or coat with Bread Crumb Coating. Fry 2 to 5 minutes or until tender and brown.

Fruit Fritters

Peel and cut into slices or halves. Dry, dust with flour, dunk in Dipping Batter. Fry 2 to 5 minutes.

FRYING

Preparation varies for various fruits and vegetables but the two following methods are generally applicable.

PAN FRYING: Cooking in a pan with the addition of very little fat, just enough to keep the food from sticking; also called pan broiling or sautéing (a term usually associated with such foods as onions, peppers, and mushrooms). To pan fry, use enough oil or fat to cover the bottom of the pan. Heat oil or fat over medium heat before adding the food to be fried. To test, add a small piece of food; if it sizzles, the oil or fat is hot enough.

Large Bell Pepper or Capsicum (⅓ natural size)

SHALLOW FRYING: Frying in a frying pan or skillet in fat about 1 inch deep. Almost anything you deep fry may be shallow-fried. To shallow fry, pour corn oil or other fat into a skillet or frying pan to a 1-inch depth. Heat over medium heat to 375° on a deep-fry thermometer.

Parsnips, Potatoes, Sweet Potatoes

Use about 3 cups sliced or diced cooked vegetable for 6 half-cup servings. Heat 2 or 3 tablespoons butter, margarine, drippings, corn oil, or other fat in a heavy frying pan over moderate heat. Add vegetable and cook 5 to 10 minutes, or until lightly browned. Turn vegetable during cooking to insure even browning. Add a little diced ham or crumbled bacon and diced onion for specially good flavor.

FRYING VEGETABLES

Carrots, Onions, Potatoes

Use 3 cups sliced raw vegetable to make 6 half-cup servings of potatoes or carrots, or 6 quarter-cup servings of onions.

Heat 3 tablespoons fat or oil in a heavy frying pan over moderate heat. Add sliced vegetable and cook 15 to 25 minutes, or until vegetable is tender and lightly browned. Turn vegetable frequently.

Eggplant or Tomatoes

Use 1 medium eggplant or 4 medium-sized, firm tomatoes for 6 servings. Pare eggplant. Cut eggplant or tomatoes into ½-inch slices. Dip vegetable slices into flour or fine dry bread crumbs. Heat ¼ cup fat or oil in a heavy frying pan over moderate heat. Add vegetable and cook over low heat 2 to 4 minutes, or until tender and lightly browned. Add more fat or oil if necessary to prevent sticking.

FRYING FRUITS

Apple rings, bananas, peaches, or pineapple rings make delicious pan-fried fruits when lightly browned in butter or margarine.

Pan-fried Apple Rings

Wash and core 3 large apples for 6 servings. Slice ½ inch thick. Melt 3 tablespoons butter or margarine in frying pan. Fry apples over moderately low heat until tender, turning to brown evenly, about 10 to 12 minutes.

Sprinkle apples with mixture of 1 tablespoon sugar and ¼ teaspoon cinnamon before serving.

Pan-fried Bananas

Peel 6 all-yellow or green-tipped bananas (for 6 servings) and cut in half crosswise. Cook as directed for apple rings, about 8 to 10 minutes. Sprinkle lightly with salt.

Pan-fried Peaches

Wash, peel, halve, and pit 6 peaches for 6 servings. Cook as directed above for apple rings, about 12 to 15 minutes. Sprinkle with mixture of 1 tablespoon sugar and ¼ teaspoon cinnamon.

Pan-fried Pineapple

Pare, slice, and core fresh pineapple. For 6 servings use 6 slices of pineapple. Cook as directed for apple slices, about 10 to 12 minutes. Sprinkle with 2 tablespoons brown sugar.

BAKING VEGETABLES

Baked potatoes, baked sweet potatoes, and baked acorn squash are their own raison d'être for this method of cooking fresh vegetables. However, if you are using your oven for the balance of the meal or other oven-cooked dishes, it is economical to bake your vegetables at the same time.

Wash them, pare as outlined below, cut them up or leave them whole, and place in a casserole with a small amount of water and seasonings. Cover and bake.

Potatoes and Sweet Potatoes

Preheat oven to 425°. Wash and dry vegetables. Rub with a little fat to soften the skins. Prick with a fork to allow steam to escape during baking (this will prevent bursting). Bake until tender: 50 to 60 minutes for medium-sized white potatoes; 35 to 60 minutes for sweet potatoes. *Note.* if other foods are to be cooked at 350° or 375°, potatoes or sweet potatoes may be baked along with them. Allow 10 to 20 minutes longer than times given above.

VARIATIONS: *White Potatoes.* After baking, cut potatoes in halves; remove the potatoes from their skins, carefully preserving the skins. Mash the potato pulp with butter or margarine and a little warm milk; stuff back into skins and sprinkle with grated cheese, or spread generously with sour cream and chopped chives. Return to the oven for 10 minutes or until lightly browned.

Sweet Potatoes. Cut baked sweet potatoes in halves; scoop out sweet potato pulp from skins, carefully preserving the skins. Mash with butter or margarine and a little warm milk. Or use 1 tablespoon peanut butter for each sweet potato in place of butter or margarine and/or orange juice and a little grated orange rind in place of the milk. Stuff mixture back into the skins and return to the oven for 10 minutes.

Carrots

Preheat oven to 375°. Grease a 1½-quart casserole or baking dish. Wash and scrape carrots; cut in half lengthwise. Place in a casserole. Add ¼ cup hot water. Dot with 2 or 3 tablespoons butter or margarine. Sprinkle with salt and pepper. Cover. Bake until tender, about 45 minutes. *1½ pounds medium-sized carrots for 6 servings.*

Onions

Preheat oven to 375°. Grease a 1½-quart casserole. Peel onions; cut in half crosswise. Arrange with cut side up in casserole. Add just enough water to cover the bottom of the casserole. Sprinkle with salt and pepper. Cover. Bake 30 minutes. Top with 1 cup buttered bread cubes and bake uncovered 15 to 20 minutes longer, until cubes are brown and onions are tender. *2 pounds medium-sized onions for 6 servings.*

Tomatoes

Preheat oven to 375°. Wash tomatoes and cut off stem ends. Place tomatoes in a casserole. Sprinkle with salt and pepper. Top with 1 cup buttered bread cubes. Add just enough water to cover the bottom of the casserole. Cover. Bake 15 minutes. Uncover and bake 10 to 15 minutes longer until the tomatoes are soft and the bread cubes are browned. *6 medium-sized tomatoes for 6 servings.*

VARIATION: Top tomatoes with onion slices and crisscross with green pepper strips before baking. Omit buttered bread cubes.

Winter Squash

Preheat oven to 400°. Cut acorn squash in half or Hubbard squash into 3- or 4-inch cubes. Arrange in a baking pan. Brush with melted butter or margarine and sprinkle with salt and brown sugar. Add just enough water to cover the bottom of the baking pan. Cover. Bake acorn squash 30 minutes, uncover; bake Hubbard squash 45 minutes, uncover. Continue baking until squash is tender — 20 to 30 minutes for acorn squash; about 30 minutes for Hubbard squash. For special flavor, sprinkle a little cinnamon or nutmeg on squash before baking. *3 acorn squash or 3 pounds Hubbard squash for 6 servings.*

Italian Vegetable Marrow or Zucchini
(⅛ natural size)

Summer Squash

Preheat oven to 400°. Slice squash into ½-inch slices and place in a casserole. Dot with butter or margarine; sprinkle with salt and 1 tablespoon finely chopped onion. Add just enough water to cover the bottom of the casserole. Cover. Bake 50 minutes to 1 hour, until squash is tender. *3 pounds summer squash for 6 servings.*

Baked Apples

Preheat oven to 400°. Wash and core apples. Apples may be baked whole with skins on or halved and pared. If apples are baked in their skins, pare them a third of the way down or slit skins around apples about halfway down (this helps to keep them from bursting). Arrange apples in baking dish. Add 1 tablespoon sugar to each apple and top with 1 teaspoon butter or margarine. Sprinkle with cinnamon. Pour ½ cup water around apples to prevent sticking. Bake, *uncovered,* until tender — about 45 to 60 minutes. *6 apples for 6 servings.*

VARIATIONS: *Cranberry Baked Apples.* Stuff 6 whole apples with mixture of ¾ cup chopped raw cranberries, ½ cup sugar, and 3 tablespoons chopped nuts. Omit butter or margarine.

Almond-Raisin Stuffed Apples. Stuff 6 whole apples with mixture of ¼ cup raisins and ¼ cup slivered blanched almonds. Use honey in place of sugar.

Baked Apricots or Peaches

Preheat oven to 400°. Wash and peel fruit. Halve fruit and remove pits. Arrange fruit, hollow side up, in a shallow baking dish. Combine ½ cup boiling water, ¼ cup sugar, and 2 teaspoons lemon juice. Pour over fruit and sprinkle with 2 tablespoons brown sugar. Bake, *uncovered,* until tender. Apricots require approximately 20 minutes; peaches, 30 minutes. *Use 12 apricots or 6 peaches for 6 servings.*

Baked Pears

Preheat oven to 400°. Wash, pare, halve, and core firm pears. Arrange pears, hollow side up, in a shallow baking dish. Combine ½ cup boiling water, ¼ cup brown sugar, and 2 teaspoons lemon juice. Pour over pears and sprinkle with 2 tablespoons brown sugar and ½ teaspoon cinnamon. Bake, *uncovered,* until tender — 45 to 60 minutes. *Use 6 pears for 6 servings.*

Brown vegetable in a small amount of hot fat, then add a small amount of liquid and cook slowly in a tightly covered pan on top of the range or in the oven.

This method is most often used for meats but it also may be employed to great advantage with certain vegetables.

Braised Celery

Cut 1 bunch celery stalks into 2-inch pieces and sauté in 3 tablespoons butter or margarine in a heavy skillet until golden brown. Add 1 cube bouillon dissolved in ½ cup boiling water and continue cooking slowly until celery is tender. *Makes 4 to 6 servings.*

Braised Endive

Melt 2 tablespoons butter or margarine in skillet, add 8 small heads endive, and brown lightly. Add ¼ cup consommé or bouillon and salt and pepper to taste. Cover tightly and cook over low heat 15 minutes, or until tender. *Makes 4 servings.*

BARBECUING

This method of outdoor grilling over live charcoal briquettes with a spicy sauce is most often associated with hamburgers, frankfurters, and steaks, but may also be used effectively to cook fruits and vegetables.

Indian-style Roast Corn

Turn back the husks and strip off the silk of 6 ears of corn. Dip in salted water. Draw husks back up and lay cobs on top of coals. Cook 8 to 10 minutes, turning frequently to prevent burning. Husks should be dry and brown when done. Break off husks with barbecue glove and serve with butter. *Makes 6 servings.*

Vegetable Kebabs

Cut cooked white and sweet potatoes and sliced bacon into 1-inch pieces. Pierce whole mushrooms, small cooked onions, small whole cherry tomatoes, and the white and sweet potato pieces alternately with the bacon pieces on skewers. Sprinkle with salt and pepper and dip into melted butter or margarine. Brown over grill, turning skewers to cook all sides evenly.

Fruit Kebabs

Cut apples into 1-inch chunks; peel bananas and cut into 1-inch pieces. Remove pits from whole apricots; prepare 1-inch chunks of fresh pineapple. Thread fruit alternately on skewers, repeating pattern until skewer is filled. Brush with melted butter or margarine and brown quickly and carefully, turning frequently to toast fruit evenly.

Honey-cured Bananas

Make a 3-inch-long shallow slit in the banana skins, leaving the peels on the bananas. Force 1 tablespoon of honey into the opening and let stand for about an hour. Place on grill and cook 8 minutes, turning frequently.

A Basic Guide to Herbs and Spices

Herbs and spices, if carefully used, add a unique and distinctive flavor to any dish. They are particularly good combined with vegetables and can transform a bland, uninspired meal into a memorable culinary occasion. However, they are meant to enhance the basic ingredient, not overpower it. Therefore, be sure to use them sparingly.

Experiment cautiously to determine your personal preferences. These general rules should help prevent real disasters, while the basic guide that follows will provide a framework for the development of individual tastes as well as some new suggestions for the more experienced palate.

General Tips

1. In untested recipes, use only ¼ teaspoon dried herb or spice for every 4 servings.

2. Add herbs during the last hour of long-cooking dishes like soups, stews, and sauces.

3. Add herbs to uncooked foods like fruits, juices, salad dressings, and desserts at least several hours before serving, to allow the flavors to "marry," or mingle and set. If time is limited, steep the herbs in a hot liquid for a few minutes before adding.

4. Do not combine too many herbs or spices at one time unless following a tested recipe.

5. "Serve only one herb course to a meal" is a good rule for the novice.

6. Buy herbs and spices in small quantities and keep containers tightly sealed to prevent loss of fragrance and flavor.

7. Chop fresh herbs with kitchen shears instead of a knife to preserve flavor and vitamin content of the leaves.

8. Garden-fresh herbs should be cut early in the morning after the dew has dried and before the plants have been touched by the midday sun. They can be stored in the refrigerator for a couple of days wrapped in waxed paper.

9. Chop fresh herbs very fine to allow some of the flavoring oils to escape.

10. Fast freezing will preserve the flavor of fresh herbs; although they will look wilted when defrosted, they are safe for cooking.

11. Most herbs and spices have a low sodium content and, therefore, are especially useful for restricted diets.

12. For a simple and delicious use of herbs with vegetables: heat chopped herbs in melted butter and add to the vegetable after it has been cooked.

Equivalents

1. ¼ teaspoon powdered herb = ½ teaspoon dried herb (crumbled) = 2 teaspoons fresh chopped herb.

Note. Dried herbs are more concentrated and stronger than fresh herbs.

2. *Onion:* 1 tablespoon onion powder = 1 medium raw onion. 1 tablespoon instant (dry) minced onion = ¼ cup minced raw onion. 1 tablespoon onion flakes = ¼ cup minced raw onion. ¼ cup instant chopped onion = 1 cup chopped raw onion.

3. *Garlic:* ⅛ teaspoon garlic powder, instant minced garlic, or garlic chips = 1 average-sized clove fresh garlic. ½ teaspoon garlic salt = 1 average-sized clove fresh garlic.

In the list below, italics indicate the generally preferred seasoning in each case; however, do experiment with the other seasonings for personal preferences.

Fruits

APPLES: *cinnamon,* cloves, or nutmeg

BANANAS: *nutmeg*

BERRIES: *cinnamon* or nutmeg

CHERRIES: mace

FRUIT CUP: *anise seed* or rosemary

GRAPEFRUIT : *mace,* cinnamon, or cloves

LEMONS : rosemary

MELONS : cardamom seed

ORANGES : *rosemary*

PEACHES : cinnamon or *mace*

PEARS : *ginger* or coriander seed

PINEAPPLE : nutmeg

PUMPKIN : cardamom seed

RHUBARB : nutmeg

STEWED FRUITS : anise seed or *peppermint*

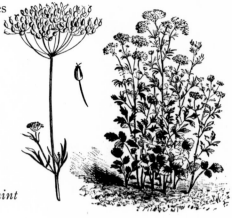

Anise (⅙ natural size)

Vegetables

ASPARAGUS : *marjoram,* mustard seed, sesame seed, or tarragon

BEANS, BAKED : cumin seed, mustard seed, or *thyme*

BEANS, LIMA : marjoram, oregano, *sage,* savory, tarragon, or thyme

BEANS, SNAP : basil, dill, marjoram, mint, mustard seed, oregano, *savory,* tarragon, or thyme

BEETS : allspice, *bay leaf,* caraway seed, cloves, dill, ginger, mustard seed, savory, or thyme

BEETS, PICKLED : *cloves,* coriander seed, or dill

BROCCOLI : caraway seed, dill, mustard seed, *oregano,* or tarragon

BRUSSELS SPROUTS : basil, caraway seed, *celery seed,* dill, mustard seed, sage, or thyme

CABBAGE : *caraway seed,* celery seed, dill, mint, mustard seed, nutmeg, savory, or tarragon

CARROTS : allspice, bay leaf, caraway seed, dill, fennel, ginger, mace, marjoram, mint, *nutmeg,* or thyme

CAULIFLOWER : caraway seed, celery salt, dill, *mace,* or tarragon

CORN : *paprika,* parsley, or thyme

CUCUMBERS : basil, dill, mint, or *tarragon*

EGGPLANT : marjoram or *oregano*

MUSHROOMS : tarragon

KOHLRABI : mace or *nutmeg*

LENTILS : curry powder, *oregano,* or savory

ONIONS: caraway seed, *mustard seed,* nutmeg, oregano, sage, or thyme

PEAS: basil, dill, marjoram, *mint,* oregano, poppy seed, rosemary, sage, or savory

POTATOES: basil, bay leaf, caraway seed, celery seed, *chives,* dill, mustard seed, oregano, parsley, poppy seed, or thyme

    MASHED: oregano. BOILED: parsley. FRIED: rosemary.

SALAD GREENS: basil, chives, dill, or *tarragon*

SAUERKRAUT: *caraway seed,* cloves, or fennel

SPINACH: *basil,* mace, marjoram, nutmeg, oregano, rosemary

SQUASH: *allspice,* basil, cinnamon, cloves, fennel, ginger, mustard seed, nutmeg, or rosemary

SUCCOTASH: *mace, mustard seed,* or paprika

SWEET POTATOES: allspice, cardamom, *cinnamon,* cloves, or nutmeg

TOMATOES: *basil,* bay leaf, celery seed, oregano, sage, sesame seed, tarragon, or *thyme*

TURNIPS: *dill seed* or rosemary

ZUCCHINI: marjoram, paprika, or *shallots*

Pepper and parsley may be added to any of the above vegetables for good taste; curry powder adds a special flavor to creamed vegetables.

Soups

BEET: bay leaf or dill.

BOUILLABAISSE: celery seed, parsley, or saffron

CABBAGE: anise seed or caraway seed

CELERY AND TOMATO: bay leaf or thyme

CHICKEN GUMBO: oregano

CHOWDERS: tarragon

CREAM OF ARTICHOKE: mace, nutmeg, or paprika

CREAM OF ASPARAGUS: chives, paprika, or sage

MINESTRONE: basil

MOCK TURTLE: basil or marjoram

MULLIGATAWNY: curry powder

ONION: marjoram or thyme

Chives (¼ natural size)

PEA: cardamom, rosemary, or thyme

TOMATO: dill seed, oregano, or thyme

VEGETABLE: anise, basil, bay leaf, dill, or sage

VICHYSSOISE: chives

Salads

ASPARAGUS SALAD: tarragon

ASPIC: bay leaf or celery seed

AVOCADO SALAD: dill or oregano

BEET SALAD: caraway seed or chervil

CARROT SALAD: basil

CAULIFLOWER SALAD: tarragon

CHICKEN SALAD: nutmeg or thyme

COLE SLAW: celery seed or dill seed

EGG SALAD: dill weed

FISH SALAD: bay leaf or oregano

FRUIT SALAD: mace

MIXED GREEN SALAD: tarragon

POTATO SALAD: oregano or parsley

SALMON SALAD: tarragon

SARDINE SALAD: tarragon

SEAFOOD SALAD: basil

STRING BEAN SALAD: savory

TOMATO SALAD: basil or thyme

TUNA SALAD: rue or tarragon

VEGETABLE SALAD: basil or dill

Serving:
The Recipes

Very Early Dandelion (⅛ natural size)

Appetizers

Stuffed Artichokes

6 medium artichokes
3 tablespoons lemon juice
1 ¼ teaspoons salt
¼ cup butter or margarine
½ cup water
2 cups herb-seasoned stuffing

1 tablespoon finely chopped onion
¼ cup finely chopped parsley
2 tablespoons Parmesan cheese
1 clove garlic, minced
1 tablespoon pine nuts
½ teaspoon oregano

Wash the artichokes. With a sharp knife, cut off the stem and top third. Remove center young leaves and choke, scraping until the heart is exposed and clean. Rub the cut surfaces with the lemon juice. Place the artichokes in a snug-fitting saucepan. Add remaining lemon juice, 1 teaspoon of the salt and 1 inch boiling water. Cook uncovered 5 minutes; cover and cook 30 to 35 minutes or until base of stem can be easily pierced with a fork. Preheat oven to 350°. Prepare stuffing by heating the butter or margarine and the water in a saucepan until the oil melts. Stir in the remaining ingredients. Spoon the stuffing into the artichokes; place close together in a baking dish. Add ½ inch boiling water and bake for 20 minutes. Serve with melted butter, if desired. *Makes 6 servings.*

Artichoke-Crab California

1 can (10½ ounces) chicken gravy
1 pound cooked crab, flaked
¼ cup heavy cream
2 tablespoons sherry
Dash cayenne pepper
Dash white pepper

½ cup cut-up, cooked artichoke hearts
¼ cup chopped, toasted almonds
¼ cup sliced ripe olives
¼ cup buttered bread crumbs
Paprika

Preheat oven to 350°. Combine all the ingredients except the bread crumbs and paprika. Spoon into 4 individual baking dishes or large seashells. Sprinkle with the bread crumbs and paprika. Bake for 20 minutes or until lightly browned. *Makes 4 servings.*

Asparagus Vinaigrette

2 pounds asparagus
1 teaspoon Accent (optional)
⅔ cup olive oil
⅓ cup vinegar

2 tablespoons capers
¼ cup diced pimiento
1 can (2 ounces) anchovy fillets

Wash the asparagus; break off each stalk as far down as it snaps easily. Discard the woody end. Cook, covered, in boiling salted water in a large skillet 5 to 10 minutes, just until crisp-tender. Drain; sprinkle with Accent. Place in a shallow dish. Beat together the oil and vinegar; stir in the remaining ingredients. Pour over the asparagus. Refrigerate several hours or overnight. *Makes 6 servings.*

Avocado Tomato Dip

1 medium to large ripe avocado
   (⅔ cup puree)
¼ cup finely diced tomato
¼ cup dairy sour cream

½ teaspoon salt
⅛ teaspoon black pepper
2 wedges tomato

Wash, peel, and dice avocado. Mash and put through very fine sieve twice. Combine puree with diced tomato, sour cream, salt, and pepper. Pour into a small serving dish; garnish with tomato wedges. Serve with fresh carrot and celery sticks, crackers, and potato chips. *Makes approximately 1 cup.*

Avocado-stuffed Celery

½ large ripe avocado
1 teaspoon lemon or lime juice
¾ teaspoon salt or salt to taste

1/16 teaspoon cayenne
21 ribs of celery, 3 inches long
Paprika

Mash the avocado until smooth. Add the lemon or lime juice, salt, and cayenne. Stuff the mixture into the celery ribs. Garnish with paprika. Serve as an hors d'oeuvre, or as you would any other kind of stuffed celery. *Makes 21 pieces.*

Lenormand's Cauliflower (1/12 natural size)

Spiced Cauliflower Canapés

1 medium head cauliflower
1 teaspoon salt
1 clove garlic, cut in half
1 teaspoon mixed pickling spice
1 tablespoon lemon juice

TARTAR SAUCE
1 cup mayonnaise
1 tablespoon chopped capers
1 tablespoon chopped green olives
1 tablespoon chopped mixed sweet
   pickles
1 tablespoon chopped parsley

Cut off the outside leaves of the cauliflower and break head into flowerets. Place them in a saucepan with the salt, garlic, pickling spice, lemon juice, and 1 cup boiling water. Cook, uncovered, 5 minutes. Cover and cook 10 minutes or only until barely crisp-tender. *Do not overcook.* Serve plain as a canapé or dip in Tartar Sauce for a snack or hors d'oeuvre.

SAUCE: Combine all ingredients and mix well. Serve as a dip for cauliflower. *Makes 1¼ cups.*

Cauliflower Cocktail Dips

Trim off the outside leaves of 1 medium-sized cauliflower head. Wash and break into flowerets. Serve with one of the following cocktail dips:

HORSERADISH SOUR CREAM DIP

2 packages (3 ounces *each*) cream cheese
¼ cup dairy sour cream
2 tablespoons horseradish sauce
½ teaspoon salt

1 teaspoon paprika
Dash cayenne
2 tablespoons chopped parsley
¾ teaspoon finely chopped onion

Combine the cream cheese and sour cream. Mix until smooth. Blend in the horseradish, salt, paprika, cayenne, and 1 tablespoon of the parsley. Turn the mixture into a serving dish. Sprinkle with the remaining parsley. Serve as a dip for raw cauliflowerets. *Makes 1¼ cups.*

COTTAGE CHEESE—ONION DIP

1 cup (½ pound) small curd cottage cheese
¼ cup dairy sour cream
2 teaspoons finely chopped onion

¾ teaspoon salt
¼ teaspoon black pepper
Dash cayenne
2 tablespoons finely chopped parsley

Combine all the ingredients. Spoon into a small bowl. Serve as a dip for raw cauliflowerets. *Makes 1⅓ cups.*

Cantaloupe Supreme

3 cantaloupes
1 pint strawberries
2 cups watermelon balls
2 cups honeydew balls
¼ bunch mint

1 tablespoon lemon juice
2 tablespoons orange juice
2 tablespoons water
1½ tablespoons sugar
⅓ head Romaine lettuce

Halve the cantaloupes; remove the seeds and scoop melon balls from each half. Remove the remaining melon, leaving the shells intact. Dice into small pieces and reserve. Hull, wash, and halve ¾ of the strawberries. Combine with the melon. Remove the leaves from ⅓ of the mint. Chop fine and combine with the next four ingredients. Mix well, bring to a boil. Cool, pour over the combined fruit, and refrigerate. When ready to serve, line the melon shells with leaves of Romaine and fill with marinated fruit. Top with a whole strawberry and a mint leaf and place in a dessert dish. *Makes 6 servings.*

Note. Delicious served with double-decker or finger sandwiches of sliced ham, cream cheese, and chives.

Mushroom Canapés

4 dozen whole mushrooms, about 1 inch in diameter
1 tablespoon butter or margarine
½ teaspoon salt
1 tablespoon finely chopped onion
1 tablespoon oil drained from canned tuna fish

1 tablespoon fresh lemon juice
7-ounce can tuna fish, flaked
¼ teaspoon salt
¹⁄₁₆ teaspoon black pepper
¾ cup grated sharp American cheese
Fresh parsley

Preheat broiler. Wash the mushrooms; remove stems and chop finely. Sauté the whole caps in the butter or margarine with the salt. In another pan, sauté the chopped mushroom stems and the onion in the tuna fish oil until all liquid is absorbed. Add the lemon juice, tuna fish, salt, pepper, and ½ cup of the cheese. Spoon into the mushroom caps. Sprinkle each cap with ¼ teaspoon grated cheese. Broil 1 or 2 minutes. Garnish with the parsley. Spear with toothpicks and serve as a hot hors d'oeuvre. *Makes 4 dozen.*

Roquefort-stuffed Mushrooms

1 cup crumbled (¼ pound) Roquefort cheese
1 package (3 ounces) cream cheese
About 24 mushrooms, 1 inch in

diameter
Green pepper strips, cut thin and narrow, or parsley leaves

Blend the two cheeses. Wash and drain the mushrooms; pat dry. Fill with the cheese mixture, using a pastry bag fitted with a star tube, if desired. Stick 3 slivers green pepper or a leaf of parsley in the center of each mushroom as a garnish. Serve as an hors d'oeuvre. *Makes about 2 dozen.*

Pickled Fish Fillets with Mushrooms

1 pound small mushrooms

3 cups chopped onions

½ cup water
½ cup flour
1 teaspoon salt
¹⁄₁₆ teaspoon black pepper
1 ½ pounds flounder fillets
¼ cup cooking oil

1 large "banana" pepper, seeded and
thinly sliced
2 tablespoons diced pimiento
1 bay leaf
½ cup white vinegar

Rinse, pat dry, and trim the mushrooms. Place 1 inch water in a large sauce-pan and bring to a boil. Add the mushrooms; return to a boil. Reduce heat and simmer two minutes; drain and set mushrooms aside. In same sauce-pan combine the onions with the water; cover and simmer for 5 minutes or until soft; set aside. Combine the flour, salt and pepper in a paper or plastic bag. Add the fish and shake gently to coat thoroughly. Heat the oil in a large skillet. Add the fish, a few pieces at a time; sauté on both sides until golden. Arrange the fish in a 12" x 9" x 2" casserole. Add to oil remain-ing in skillet the reserved mushrooms, onion, pepper, pimiento, bay leaf and vinegar; stir gently. Bring to a boil; pour over fish in casserole. Cool, cover, and refrigerate. Serve as an hors d'oeuvre, appetizer, or as a salad with lemon wedges. *Makes 6 to 12 servings.*

Happy Hour Pop-Ups for Dieters

1 can (3 to 4 ounces) chopped
mushrooms
2 envelopes unflavored gelatin
2 cups water
Nonnutritive sweetener equivalent to
4 teaspoons sugar
1 teaspoon salt

¾ cup lemon juice
½ cup finely chopped green pepper
½ cup finely chopped cucumber
½ cup finely chopped radishes
1 cup finely chopped cauliflower
1 cup finely chopped celery

Drain the mushrooms, reserving liquid. Set the mushrooms aside. Add enough water to liquid to measure ½ cup. Pour into a saucepan and sprinkle with the gelatin. Place over low heat and stir until gelatin dissolves, about 3 minutes. Remove from heat; stir in the water, sweetener, salt, and lemon juice. Chill to the consistency of unbeaten egg white. Fold in the vegetables. Turn out into two sectioned ice-cube trays with sections in place. Chill until firm. Unmold and serve three or four cubes on individual lettuce-lined salad dishes or keep the cubes, covered, in refrigerator for snacking. *Makes 6 cups, about 3 dozen cubes.*

Tangerine Seafood Cocktail

3 cups diced avocado
3 tablespoons lemon juice
1 ½ cups diced tangerines
3 cups diced cooked lobster, shrimp,
  or crabmeat, or all three
½ cup catsup

⅛ teaspoon black pepper
½ teaspoon salt
½ teaspoon horseradish
1 teaspoon grated lemon peel
30 tangerine sections
Watercress or shredded lettuce

Marinate the avocado in 1 tablespoon of the lemon juice. Add the diced tangerines, seafood, catsup, the remaining 2 tablespoons lemon juice, the

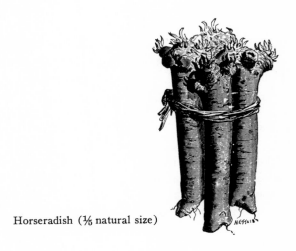

Horseradish (⅙ natural size)

pepper, salt, horseradish, and lemon peel. Toss lightly. Chill. Serve in tall sherbet glasses, garnished with tangerine sections and watercress or shredded lettuce. *Makes 6 servings.*

Low-Calorie Fresh Fruit Cup

1 ½ cups strawberries
1 ½ cups pineapple, diced
1 ½ cups honeydew melon balls
½ cup orange juice

1 tablespoon lemon juice
2 teaspoons pure vanilla extract
6 sprigs mint

Wash and hull the berries. Combine with the pineapple and melon balls.

Combine the orange juice, lemon juice, and vanilla. Pour over the fruit. Turn the mixture over once or twice and place in sherbet glasses topped with a sprig of fresh mint. Serve very cold. *Makes 6 servings.*

Note. Only 51 calories per generous half-cup portion.

Deviled Seafood

¼ cup finely chopped green pepper
¼ cup finely chopped onion
1 cup finely chopped celery
1 teaspoon Worcestershire sauce
½ teaspoon salt
1 cup mayonnaise

1 can (6 to 7 ounces) shrimp, drained
1 can (6 to 7 ounces) crabmeat, flaked
2 cups herb-seasoned stuffing, crushed

Preheat oven to 350°. Stir together all the ingredients until blended. Spoon into a 1-quart shallow casserole or 8 ovenproof shells. Bake for 30 minutes or until lightly browned. *Makes 6 to 8 servings.*

Tabasco Curry Dip

1 cup dairy sour cream
1 tablespoon curry powder
½ teaspoon Tabasco
2 teaspoons minced onion

¾ teaspoon salt
1 tablespoon vinegar or lemon juice
Raw vegetables

Combine all ingredients, stirring until thoroughly blended. Serve with carrot and celery sticks, radishes, cucumber slices, scallions, cauliflowerets, or other raw vegetables. *Makes about 1 cup.*

Soups

Country Soup with Apple Knödel

¼ cup beef marrow (2 pounds beef bones)
½ cup cracker meal
¾ teaspoon salt
¾ teaspoon double-acting baking powder
¼ teaspoon ground mace
1½ cups finely chopped apple
2 tablespoons chopped parsley
2 large eggs, well-beaten
¼ cup (3 strips) diced bacon

½ cup finely chopped onion
⅛ teaspoon finely chopped garlic
2 medium-sized tomatoes
1½ quarts rich beef stock or bouillon
2 cups shredded white cabbage
1 cup shredded red cabbage
2 cups diced tart cooking apples
1 teaspoon salt
1 whole clove
⅛ teaspoon black pepper

Mix first 5 ingredients together until well blended. Add apples, parsley, and eggs, mixing until a soft dough is formed. Refrigerate at least one hour or until firm. In the meantime, fry bacon in a 2-quart saucepan until fat is rendered. Add onion and garlic; cook until onion is transparent and golden. Wash, peel, seed, and dice tomatoes; add to onion mixture. Stir in stock, cabbages, apples, and seasonings. Bring mixture to a boil; cover and simmer 15 minutes. Shape dough into 2-inch balls and drop into hot soup. Cover; simmer 15 minutes without lifting lid. Serve as a main course. If served as a first course, make knödels ½ inch in size. *Makes 6 servings.*

Creamed Asparagus Soup

1 pound asparagus
3½ cups chicken stock or 3 chicken
   bouillon cubes dissolved in 3½
   cups water
4 tablespoons butter or margarine

4 tablespoons flour
½ cup light cream
½ teaspoon salt
⅛ teaspoon black pepper
Pimiento

Trim off the coarse ends of the asparagus and cut into 1-inch pieces. Cook until tender, 12 to 15 minutes, in 1 cup of the stock. Melt the butter or margarine in a deep saucepan. Remove from heat and stir in the flour. Add remaining stock gradually and cook, stirring, until slightly thickened. Stir in the cream, seasonings, cooked asparagus and stock. Heat thoroughly. Serve hot, garnished with pimiento. *Makes 6 to 8 servings.*

Avocado Soup

2 cups (2 medium) soft-ripe
   avocados, diced
2 tablespoons lemon juice
2 tablespoons butter or margarine
2 tablespoons flour

2 cups chicken broth or bouillon
1 cup milk
¾ teaspoon salt
¼ teaspoon black pepper
Lemon slices

Beat the avocado and lemon juice to a pulp in a blender or force through a coarse sieve. Melt the butter or margarine in a saucepan. Stir in the flour until smooth. Add chicken bouillon gradually, stirring until smooth. Cook until thickened slightly and bubbling. Add milk and seasonings. Stir in avocado pulp and beat one minute longer. Serve hot or well chilled, garnished with slices of lemon. *Makes 6 servings.*

Cream of Broccoli Soup

3 cups broccoli cut into ½-inch
   pieces
1 teaspoon salt
½ cup chopped onion
3 tablespoons butter or margarine
3 tablespoons flour

1 cup broccoli liquid
3 cups milk
¾ teaspoon salt
¼ teaspoon black pepper
Paprika

Place the broccoli in a saucepan in 1 inch salted boiling water. Bring to a boil and cook, uncovered, 5 minutes. Cover and cook 15 minutes or until the broccoli is crisp-tender. Drain and reserve 1 cup liquid. Sauté the onion in the butter or margarine in a large pot until soft and transparent. Blend in the flour. Slowly blend in the broccoli water. Heat the milk; to the mixture add the broccoli, salt, and pepper. Cook until slightly thickened, about 5 minutes. Serve hot, garnished with a sprinkling of paprika. *Makes 2 quarts.*

Bisque of Brussels Sprouts

1½ pounds (1 quart) Brussels sprouts	½ teaspoon nutmeg
1 large bay leaf	½ teaspoon marjoram
1 thin slice garlic	1 teaspoon salt
1 whole clove	¼ teaspoon pepper
6 thin slices onion	1½ quarts beef stock or beef bouillon
3 sprigs parsley	½ cup medium cream
	3 well-beaten egg yolks

Wash and trim Brussels sprouts and cook, uncovered, in boiling salted water to cover. Add the bay leaf, garlic, clove, onion, and parsley and cook until sprouts are fork-tender. Drain thoroughly; press the vegetables through a fine sieve into another saucepan or kettle. Add the nutmeg, marjoram, salt,

Brussels Sprout (½ natural size)

and pepper. Stir in the beef stock and bring to a boil. Remove the soup from the heat. Combine the cream and egg yolks and briskly beat this into the soup mixture, working quickly and strenuously to prevent curdling. Return kettle to the heat and bring the soup to a boil, stirring constantly. Remove at once and serve immediately. *Makes 6 servings.*

Cabbage Soup, Scandinavian Style

3 cups medium fine–shredded cabbage	1 quart beef stock
2 tablespoons butter or margarine	¾ teaspoon salt
1 tablespoon brown sugar	⅛ teaspoon black pepper

Fry 2½ cups of the cabbage in butter or margarine until lightly browned. Add the sugar, stock, and salt. Cover and simmer one hour. *Do not boil.* Add remaining ½ cup cabbage and simmer 5 minutes. Season with pepper. Serve hot. *Makes 6 cups.*

Chinese Cabbage Soup

1 cooked chicken breast, about ¾
   pound
7 cups chicken stock or bouillon
6 cups sliced Chinese cabbage
   (celery-cabbage)

1¼ teaspoons salt
1¼ teaspoons black pepper
⅛ teaspoon soy sauce

Slice the chicken into very thin pieces about ⅛ inch wide and 1½ to 2 inches long. Combine with chicken stock and cook only until hot. Slice Chinese cabbage into strips ½ inch wide; add to the soup. Cook 3 to 4 minutes or only until cabbage is crisp-tender (*do not overcook*). Add salt, pepper, and soy sauce. Serve hot. *Makes 6 servings.*

If desired, replace Chinese cabbage with a head of lettuce. Reduce cooking time to 1 minute or only until lettuce is slightly wilted.

Cream of Carrot Soup

3 cups thinly sliced fresh carrots
2 tablespoons chopped onion
4 tablespoons butter or margarine
⅓ cup water
¾ teaspoon salt
½ teaspoon sugar

⅛ teaspoon freshly ground black
   pepper
1½ tablespoons flour
3 cups milk
1 tablespoon lemon juice
Finely chopped parsley

In a small saucepan combine the carrots, onions, 2 tablespoons of the butter or margarine, water, salt, sugar and pepper. Cover tightly and cook over very low heat 20 to 25 minutes or until the carrots are tender. Mash the mixture with a fork.

In the top of a double boiler, melt the remaining 2 tablespoons of butter or margarine. Blend in flour. Cook over low heat 5 minutes, stirring frequently. Add carrot mixture to milk mixture. Cook covered, over hot water 30 minutes, stirring frequently. Stir in the lemon juice. Serve hot, garnished with chopped parsley. *Makes 6 servings.*

Cream of Cauliflower Soup

2 cups cauliflowerets	¼ cup flour
4 cups boiling water	½ cup light cream or milk
½ teaspoon salt	1 teaspoon ground nutmeg
2 chicken or beef bouillon cubes	⅛ teaspoon black pepper
¼ cup butter or margarine	Chopped parsley

Cook the cauliflowerets in the boiling water and salt until tender, 5 to 8 minutes. Drain the water into a bowl. Add bouillon cubes and mix well. Reserve cauliflowerets. Melt butter or margarine in 2-quart saucepan. Blend in flour. Remove from heat and stir in the bouillon and cauliflower liquid, cream or milk, nutmeg, and pepper. Stir and cook over medium heat 4 to 5 minutes or until mixture begins to thicken. Add cooked cauliflowerets and heat 1 minute. Serve hot, garnished with parsley. *Makes 6 servings.*

Senegalese Celery Soup

3 tablespoons butter or margarine	1 cup milk combined with
½ cup finely chopped celery	1 cup light cream, or 2 cups half-and-
½ cup finely chopped onion	half
½ teaspoon curry powder	½ teaspoon salt
2 tablespoons flour	¾ cup heavy cream
¾ cup sweetened applesauce	⅛ teaspoon ground coriander
2 cups chicken broth	

Melt the butter or margarine; add the celery and onion and cook until soft. Blend in curry powder and flour. Stir constantly as mixture thickens. Gradually add applesauce, broth, milk and cream (or half-and-half), and salt. Heat to simmering and stir for 5 minutes. Pour into heatproof bowls. Whip cream and stir in coriander. Spoon cream onto soup in liberal dollops. Put bowls under broiler until cream browns. *Makes 4 to 6 servings.*

Corn and Cheese Soup

1 cup chopped onion	1½ teaspoons salt
1 clove garlic, chopped	2 cups hot water
1 cup diced celery	½ cup diced carrots
¼ cup butter or margarine	4 cups corn cut off the cob
¼ cup flour	4 cups milk

¼ teaspoon chili powder

¼ teaspoon black pepper

¹⁄₁₆ teaspoon cayenne

2 cups shredded American cheese

2 tablespoons lemon juice

Sauté the onion, garlic, and celery in butter or margarine until soft, about 10 minutes. Blend in the flour and salt. Remove from heat and add water. Stir and cook until mixture is smooth and of medium thickness. Add the carrots and corn. Simmer 15 minutes. Add the milk, seasonings, and cheese. Heat 5 minutes or only until the cheese melts. *Do not boil.* Stir in lemon juice just before serving. Add a little hot water if soup thickens on standing. *Makes 2 quarts.*

Cucumber Soup

3 cucumbers, peeled, seeded, and
    sliced

1 small onion, grated

2 cups water

3 tablespoons flour

½ teaspoon salt

¼ teaspoon black pepper

1 cup medium cream

Paprika

Combine the cucumbers and onion in a saucepan. Add water and cook until very soft. Remove from heat. Blend the flour in slowly and press through a fine sieve into a bowl. Add salt, pepper, and cream. Chill thoroughly and serve ice cold garnished with a sprinkling of paprika. *Makes 6 servings.*

Escarole Soup, Italian Style

5 pounds soup bones with marrow

3¼ teaspoons salt

1 can (6 ounces) tomato paste

2 quarts water

¾ pound ground chuck

¼ teaspoon finely chopped garlic

1 large egg, lightly beaten

½ teaspoon black pepper

3 tablespoons grated Parmesan
    cheese

1 pound chopped escarole

1 cup diced onion

1 cup diced celery

1 cup diced potato

2 tablespoons chopped parsley

Place the soup bones, 2½ teaspoons of the salt, the tomato paste and water in a 4-quart saucepan. Cover and simmer one hour. Combine the chuck, garlic, egg, the remaining ¾ teaspoon salt, ½ teaspoon of the pepper, and the cheese. Shape into ¾-inch balls. Add to hot soup and simmer 10 minutes. Add vegetables and simmer 30 minutes or until vegetables are tender. Remove bones and serve hot with the parsley sprinkled over the top. *Makes 8 servings.*

Bacon Cream of Kale Soup

1 pound kale
3 strips bacon
⅓ cup finely chopped onion
3 tablespoons flour

2 cups milk
2 teaspoons salt
⅛ teaspoon black pepper

Wash the kale; place it in a saucepan without water; cover and cook until tender. Remove the kale from the heat and press it through a sieve or mince it in a blender. Fry the bacon until crisp. Remove it from the pan, reserving the fat. Add onions to the fat and sauté until soft. Blend in flour. Add milk and kale puree and cook until slightly thickened. Add seasonings and serve at once with the bacon crumbled over the top. *Makes 4 servings.*

Florence, or Magnum Bonum, Cos Lettuce
(⅙ natural size)

Cream of Lettuce Soup

¼ cup butter
1 thin slice garlic, finely chopped
1 teaspoon finely chopped tarragon
½ teaspoon dried parsley
2 tablespoons finely chopped green
  pepper

3 tablespoons minced onion
1 large head Romaine lettuce, finely
  shredded
1 bunch watercress, chopped
1 quart beef stock or bouillon
Salt and pepper

1 cup scalded milk   1 cup heavy cream
2 egg yolks, slightly beaten

Cream the butter with the garlic, tarragon, and parsley until light and well blended. Heat in a large heavy kettle. Add the green pepper and onion. Stir constantly and cook for 3 to 5 minutes. Gradually add the lettuce and watercress; cook for 3 to 5 minutes more. Add the beef stock, continuing to stir until well mixed. Cook the mixture for 20 minutes. Add salt and pepper to taste and cook for an additional 20 minutes. Remove kettle from heat and stir in the scalded milk. Mix together the egg yolks and cream and, just before serving, add to the soup. *Makes 6 servings.*

Hungarian Mushroom Soup

4 cups coarsely chopped mushrooms   ¼ cup flour
   (about ¾ lb.)   ½ teaspoon chervil leaves (optional)
2 tablespoons bacon drippings   1 ½ quarts rich chicken stock
1 tablespoon finely chopped onion   1 large egg, slightly beaten
2 teaspoons salt   ½ cup sour cream
1 teaspoon paprika

Sauté the mushrooms in the bacon drippings with the onion, salt, and paprika. Blend in the flour and chervil, if used. Add stock and mix well. Stir and cook until soup has thickened slightly.

   Blend the egg with the sour cream and add to the soup tureen. Now pour the hot soup into the tureen, slowly at first, stirring constantly. Serve hot. *Makes about 2½ quarts.*

Cream of Parsley Soup

3 cups rich chicken stock   1 teaspoon lemon juice
2 cups milk   3 cups (1 large bunch) finely
2 large egg yolks, beaten   chopped parsley
1 ⅜ teaspoons salt   ½ cup heavy cream, whipped
1/16 teaspoon black pepper   (optional)
1/16 teaspoon cayenne   Parsley sprigs

Place the chicken stock in saucepan. Cover and heat slowly. Mix the milk with egg yolks and stir into the stock. Continue stirring and cook slowly (do not boil) 15 minutes or until slightly thickened. Add 1 ¼ teaspoons of the salt, the black pepper, cayenne, lemon juice and parsley. Heat ½ minute. Strain and serve hot or cold.

Add the remaining ⅛ teaspoon salt to the cream; drop a teaspoon of salted cream on top of each serving, if desired. Garnish with fresh parsley. *Makes 4 to 6 servings.*

Vichyssoise

4 leeks	1 tablespoon salt
1 medium-sized onion, sliced	2 cups milk
2 tablespoons butter	2 cups medium cream
5 medium-sized potatoes, peeled and sliced	Salt and pepper
1 quart chicken bouillon	1 cup heavy cream
	Chopped chives to taste

Slice very thin the white part of the leeks. In a large kettle, cook the leeks and the onion in the butter until soft and golden. Add the potatoes, bouillon and salt. Boil for 45 minutes. Press the mixture through a fine sieve. Return to medium heat and add the milk and medium cream. Add salt and pepper to taste and bring to a boil once again. Press the mixture through a fine sieve and cool. When the soup is cold, stir in the heavy cream. Chill thoroughly and sprinkle with chives just before serving. *Makes 8 servings.*

Low-Calorie Potato Soup

1 pound potatoes, peeled	⅓ cup nonfat dry milk
½ cup sliced onions	2 cups water or stock
2 cups water	1 tablespoon bacon fat
1 teaspoon salt	3 strips bacon, crumbled
⅛ teaspoon white pepper	1 tablespoon chopped chives

Cook the potatoes and onions in the water until soft. Drain and reserve the cooking water. Mash the potatoes well. Add the salt and pepper. Dissolve the dry milk in the other two cups of water or stock. Mix in the bacon fat. Add milk mixture to the potatoes and cooking liquid. Bring to a boil. Serve garnished with bacon and chives. *Makes 6 servings.*

Note. Only 124 calories per serving.

Gazpacho

4 cups finely diced tomatoes
1 cup finely diced green pepper
3 cups finely diced cucumbers
2 tablespoons grated carrot
2 tablespoons lemon juice

2 teaspoons minced onion
1¾ teaspoons salt
⅛ teaspoon black pepper
Dash cayenne
3 cups tomato juice

Mix vegetables with remaining ingredients. Serve well chilled. Garnish with leftover diced vegetables or croutons. *Makes 6 servings.*

Scandinavian Fruit Soup

1 cup pitted dry prunes
1 cup dried apricots
¼ cup raisins
½ lemon, sliced
1 teaspoon ground cardamom seed

¼ cup sugar
3 tablespoons quick-cooking tapioca
6 cups water
1 cup peeled, diced apple

In a 3-quart saucepan, combine all ingredients except the apple and add the water. Bring to a boil, stirring occasionally. Add the apple and simmer, covered, 5 minutes. Serve warm or cold, as an appetizer or a dessert. *Makes 8 servings.*

Old-Fashioned Vegetable Soup

3 pounds soup bones
2 quarts water
1 bay leaf
1 cup thinly sliced carrots
2 cups canned tomatoes, drained
1 cup chopped celery
2 cups diced potatoes
2 cups whole kernel corn (fresh or canned)

2 cups sliced okra
1 cup chopped onion
1 tablespoon powdered beef bouillon
1 tablespoon salt
1 teaspoon celery salt
½ teaspoon savory
½ teaspoon black pepper
¼ teaspoon thyme leaves or ⅛ teaspoon ground thyme

Combine the soup bones, water, and bay leaf in a large kettle. Bring to a boil. Simmer 45 minutes; add remaining ingredients. Cover and simmer 3 hours. Remove the bones. Serve piping hot. *Makes 3 quarts.*

Vegetable-Fish Chowder

¼ cup shortening
½ cup diced onion
⅓ cup diced green pepper
½ cup sliced mushrooms
1 cup diced raw potatoes
1 cup diced carrots

1 cup diced celery
1¼ teaspoons salt
¼ teaspoon black pepper
1½ quarts boiling water
1 pound haddock fillet

Melt the shortening in a heavy pot. Add the onion, peppers, and mushrooms; sauté lightly until tender. Add the potatoes, carrots, celery, salt, pepper, and water. Cook only 20 to 25 minutes. Cut the fish into bite-sized pieces. Add and cook 5 to 6 minutes longer. *Makes 6 servings.*

Main Dishes

Apple-glazed Spareribs

4 pounds spareribs, cut into 4 or 5
   rib portions
1 teaspoon salt
1 cup apple juice
½ cup dark corn syrup
2 tablespoons vinegar

2 tablespoons butter or margarine
1 teaspoon grated lemon rind
2 tablespoons lemon juice
½ teaspoon ground ginger
4 medium cooking apples, pared and
   sliced

Preheat oven to 450°. Place the ribs in a shallow baking pan. Sprinkle with the salt. Bake for 30 minutes. Drain off the excess fat. Reduce oven to 350°. Meanwhile, combine in a saucepan the apple juice, syrup, vinegar, butter or margarine, lemon rind, lemon juice, and ginger and heat. Arrange half the ribs in a 13″ x 9″ x 2″ baking dish. Top with half the apple slices. Repeat these two layers. Pour half the syrup mixture over all. Cover and bake in 350° oven for 1 hour, basting with the remaining syrup mixture every 20 minutes. Uncover. Continue baking about 30 minutes or until the ribs are tender and well browned. *Makes 4 to 6 servings.*

Chicken-stuffed Apples

6 medium-large baking apples

1 cup finely chopped cooked chicken

1 teaspoon salt
⅛ teaspoon black pepper
⅛ teaspoon ground cloves
⅓ cup soft bread crumbs

1 teaspoon sugar
2 tablespoons melted butter or
   margarine

Preheat oven to 350°. Wash the apples; peel about a quarter of the way down the apple, beginning at the stem end. Remove the cores, being careful not to cut through the bud end. Combine the chicken, salt, pepper, cloves, and bread crumbs. Spoon into the apple cavities. Place the apples in a 12″ x 1½″ x 2″ baking pan. Cover and bake 30 minutes. Mix the sugar and melted butter or margarine. Sprinkle over the apples. Bake 30 more minutes or until the apples are fork-tender — baking time depends on the size and type of apple. *Makes 6 servings.*

Dinner Artichokes

1 medium-sized onion, chopped
1 small clove garlic, minced
2 tablespoons salad oil
1 pound ground chuck
¼ cup fine dry bread crumbs
¼ cup snipped parsley

2 tablespoons ground Parmesan
   cheese
1 teaspoon salt
Dash pepper
4 medium-sized artichokes, cooked,
   with chokes removed

Preheat oven to 375°. Sauté the onion and garlic in oil in a large skillet over medium heat until tender. Crumble the meat into the skillet and cook until it browns. Mix in the bread crumbs, parsley, cheese, salt, and pepper. Fill the artichokes with the meat mixture. Stand the artichokes in a baking pan. Cover and bake about 10 minutes or until thoroughly heated. *Makes 4 servings.*

Quick Chicken-Asparagus Hollandaise

2 pounds asparagus
1 teaspoon salt
2 tablespoons lemon juice
3 chicken breasts, split, boned, and
   cooked
6 slices French bread, toasted
Slivered, toasted almonds

QUICK HOLLANDAISE
2 egg yolks
¼ teaspoon salt
¼ teaspoon Tabasco
½ cup warm melted butter
2 tablespoons lemon juice

Preheat oven to 350°. Break off the asparagus stalks as far down as they snap easily. Remove the scales and wash thoroughly. Place in a large skillet with salt and ½ inch boiling water. Bring to a boil; cook, uncovered, 5 minutes. Cover and simmer 8 to 10 minutes or until crisp-tender. While the asparagus is cooking, prepare the sauce according to package directions, substituting the lemon juice for the water, or use recipe below. Arrange the chicken on the toast in a medium-sized casserole. Pour ¾ of the sauce over the chicken. Place the asparagus spears in a layer on top. Pour the remaining sauce over the asparagus. Cover with foil and bake 10 to 15 minutes. Garnish with the slivered toasted almonds. *Makes 6 servings.*

QUICK HOLLANDAISE. With a fork or an electric beater, beat the yolks until thick and lemon-colored; add the salt and Tabasco. Add ¼ cup of the butter, one teaspoon at a time, beating constantly. Stir the lemon juice into the remaining butter; slowly add 2 teaspoons at a time to the sauce, beating constantly. *Makes about ½ cup.*

Asparagus Neptune

2½ pounds asparagus
1½ pounds flounder fillets, 4 ounces
   each
1 teaspoon salt
⅛ teaspoon ground white pepper
3 tablespoons minced shallots and
   onions
¼ cup dry white table wine

½ cup fish stock or water
2 tablespoons butter or margarine
3 tablespoons flour
½ cup Hollandaise Sauce (page 121)
½ cup heavy cream
1 tablespoon chopped parsley or
   chives

Preheat oven to 400°. Cook the asparagus until crisp-tender. Cool. Place the flounder on a wooden board, skin side up; season with the salt and pepper. Put 3 or 4 stalks of asparagus across the fish and fold over the ends of the fish to the middle. Place the fish on a buttered shallow baking pan so that the ends are on the bottom; sprinkle with the shallots or onions, white wine, and water or stock. Cover with buttered paper and bake 6 to 7 minutes. Cool. Whatever stock is on the baking pan is used in making the sauce. In a heavy pot, melt the butter, add the flour, and blend well. Whip in the hot fish stock until smooth. Cook 20 minutes. Remove the sauce from the heat. Prepare Hollandaise Sauce and whip the heavy cream. Fold together carefully. This is know as a glaçage. Place the fish in a hot casserole. Ladle ¼ cup hot sauce over the fish. Put 1 to 2 tablespoons of the glaçage on top and glaze under a slow broiler until golden brown. Garnish with the parsley or chives. *Makes 6 servings.*

Banana Omelet

6 eggs	1 tablespoon butter or margarine
4 tablespoons milk or light cream	2 medium bananas, sliced
½ tablespoon salt	2 teaspoons lemon juice
⅛ tablespoon black pepper	

Preheat oven to 350°. Beat the eggs, milk or light cream, salt, and pepper together until foamy. Pour the mixture into a hot, heavy skillet in which the butter or margarine has been melted. (The butter or margarine should foam but not brown.) As the omelet cooks, lift edges toward the center; tip pan so that the uncooked mixture flows under the cooked portion. When the bottom is brown, place the omelet under broiler, being sure to keep the broiler door open a third of the way and the thermostat set at a moderate 350° to dry the top. Make a crease through the center. Mix the bananas with the lemon juice. Arrange on half of the omelet. Fold the top half over the bananas. Slip onto a platter and serve hot, alone or with broiled ham or bacon. *Makes 4 servings.*

Broccoli-Fish Casserole

1 bunch (about 1½ pounds) broccoli	¼ teaspoon poultry seasoning
2 tablespoons lemon juice	3 tablespoons butter or margarine
1½ pounds perch or other fish fillets	3 cups seasoned, fluffy mashed
1½ teaspoons salt	potatoes
¼ teaspoon black pepper	

Preheat oven to 350°. Wash the broccoli. Cut off the tough portion of the stalks and place the tops in saucepan containing 1 inch boiling water and 1 teaspoon salt. Bring again to a boil, uncovered, and boil 5 minutes. Cover and cook until crisp-tender, 5 to 10 minutes. Place the cooked broccoli in bottom of a buttered 12″ x 7½″ x 2½″ casserole. Sprinkle with 1 tablespoon of the lemon juice. Cover with the fish. Sprinkle with the remaining lemon juice. Combine the ½ teaspoon salt, pepper, and poultry seasoning and sprinkle over the fish. Dot with the butter or margarine. Top with the mashed potatoes. Bake 1 hour or until the top is crusty and brown. *Makes 6 servings.*

Fluffy Broccoli Omelet

4 eggs, separated	1 cup finely chopped raw broccoli

½ teaspoon salt	8 strips crisp bacon
¼ teaspoon black pepper	Parsley

Preheat oven to 325°. Beat the egg whites until they stand in soft peaks. Beat the egg yolks until thick and lemon-colored. Add the broccoli, salt, and pepper to the yolks and carefully fold into the beaten egg whites. Turn the mixture into a hot, buttered 9-inch skillet. Cook over very low heat until the omelet puffs and is browned on the bottom — about 10 minutes (test by raising the edge of the omelet with a spatula). Bake until the top springs back when pressed with a finger, about 8 to 10 minutes. With a spatula, make a crease across the center of the omelet and fold over. Slip the omelet onto a warm platter and garnish with the parsley and bacon. *Makes 4 servings.*

Chicken Divan

1 large bunch broccoli	1 teaspoon salt
4 tablespoons butter or margarine	¼ teaspoon black pepper
4 tablespoons flour	½ cup heavy cream, whipped
2 cups chicken bouillon	¼ cup grated Parmesan cheese
3 tablespoons sherry	14 to 16 slices cooked chicken

Wash and drain the broccoli thoroughly. Cook in salted boiling water 10 minutes or until crisp-tender. Drain and keep hot in a covered pot. Melt the butter or margarine and blend with the flour in a saucepan. Add the chicken bouillon gradually, stirring constantly until smooth and thick. Cook the sauce over low heat for about 12 minutes, stirring often. Add the sherry, salt, and pepper and gently fold in the whipped cream. Place the cooked broccoli in a Dutch oven or heatproof platter and pour half the sauce over it. Layer the chicken slices over the sauce. Add the Parmesan cheese to the remaining sauce and pour over the chicken slices. Lightly sprinkle a little more cheese over all as a topping. Place the platter under the broiler until the sauce bubbles and is slightly browned. *Makes 6 servings.*

Broccoli and Tuna Fish au Gratin

1 small bunch fresh broccoli	1½ tablespoons butter or margarine
1 teaspoon salt	
1 can (6½ ounces) tuna fish, flaked	CHEESE SAUCE
¾ cup soft bread crumbs	¼ cup butter or margarine

¼ cup flour	1 teaspoon salt
2½ cups milk	¾ cup grated sharp Cheddar cheese
⅛ teaspoon black pepper	

Preheat oven to 350°. Wash the broccoli, cut off the tough portion of the stalk, and place in a saucepan containing 1 inch boiling water and the salt. Bring to a boil, uncovered, and boil 5 minutes. Cover and cook until tender, 5 to 10 minutes.

Place half the broccoli in a 9″ x 5″ x 3″ baking dish. Top, in alternating layers, with the tuna fish and one cup of the Cheese Sauce. Cover with the remaining broccoli and pour the remaining Cheese Sauce over all. Mix the bread crumbs with the melted butter or margarine and sprinkle over top. Bake 25 minutes or until the crumbs are brown. *Makes 6 servings.*

CHEESE SAUCE. Melt the butter or margarine in a saucepan. Blend in the flour. Gradually stir in the milk. Cook until of medium thickness, stirring constantly. Stir in the pepper, salt, and cheese. *Makes about 2 cups sauce.*

Pennsylvania Dutch Stuffed Cabbage Leaves

6 medium-tender cabbage leaves	1 teaspoon salt
1 pound lean ground chuck	¼ teaspoon black pepper
½ cup finely chopped onion	¼ cup catsup
1 tablespoon butter or margarine	¼ cup chili sauce
1½ cups soft bread crumbs	1 tablespoon cider vinegar

Cut out the coarse heavy stems of the cabbage leaves. Place in a saucepan with boiling water to cover and ½ teaspoon of salt. Cover. Boil 3 to 5 minutes or until leaves are limp. Remove the leaves from the water and drain well, reserving ½ cup liquid.

Cook the meat and onions in the butter or margarine until browned. Add the bread crumbs, salt, and pepper. Mix well. Preheat oven to 350°. Spoon ⅓ to ½ cup of the mixture onto each cabbage leaf. Roll up or fold leaves; hold in place with toothpicks. Place in a baking pan. Combine the reserved cabbage water, catsup, chili sauce, and vinegar. Pour over the cabbage. Cover and bake 30 minutes, basting with the pan liquid three times. Serve hot with some of the sauce spooned over each cabbage leaf. *Makes 6 servings.*

Chinese Celery, Mushroom, and Chicken Sauté

| ½ pound chicken breasts, boned | 2 tablespoons salad oil |

2 cups celery, sliced diagonally
¼ inch wide
1 pound mushrooms, sliced
2 tablespoons soy sauce

1 teaspoon salt
1 tablespoon cornstarch
½ teaspoon black pepper
¼ cup water

Cut the chicken into strips ¼ inch wide and 2 inches long. Sauté in hot oil 2 minutes. Add the celery, mushrooms, soy, and salt. Mix well. Cover and cook 5 minutes. Blend the cornstarch and pepper with the water. Stir into chicken and cook until the juice thickens, 1 to 2 minutes. Serve piping hot. *Makes 6 servings.*

Celery Steak, Oriental Style

1 pound round steak or boneless
chuck
1½ teaspoons salt
⅛ teaspoon black pepper
3 tablespoons flour
¼ cup shortening or salad oil
1 medium-sized green pepper, seeded,
cut in ½-inch-wide strips

1 cup onion rings
1½ cups sliced celery
¼ teaspoon ground ginger
¼ teaspoon ground mustard
1 teaspoon turmeric
1 tablespoon lemon juice
1 cup boiling water

Cut the meat into thin, narrow strips, 2 inches long, ½ inch wide, and ¼ inch thick. Rub all sides with 1 teaspoon of the salt and the pepper. Roll in the flour. Heat the shortening or salad oil. Brown the meat, adding more oil as needed. Remove the meat from the skillet and keep warm. Sauté the pepper, onion, and celery 8 minutes in the pan in which the meat was browned, adding more oil if needed. Return the meat to pan. Add the remaining ½ teaspoon salt, the spices, lemon juice, and water. Cover and simmer 10 minutes or until the meat is tender. Serve over mashed potatoes. *Makes 6 servings.*

Cantonese Celery and Beef

Deep fat for frying
1 pound sirloin or other tender,
boneless steak, thinly sliced
2 tablespoons shortening
2 cups sliced celery, cut on the
diagonal
½ cup thinly sliced onion

⅓ cup soy sauce
¼ cup red wine
2 tablespoons sugar
1 tablespoon cornstarch
2 tablespoons water
1 teaspoon salt

Preheat deep fat in skillet to 250°. Fry meat slices until browned in deep fat. Drain the meat well on paper towels. Melt the shortening in a 9- or 10-inch skillet. Add the celery and onion and sauté 3 minutes. Add the meat along with the soy sauce, wine, sugar, cornstarch, water, and salt mixed together. Mix thoroughly and cook 1 to 2 minutes. *Makes 6 servings.*

Ham and Corn–stuffed Vegetable Plate

1 package (8 ounces) herb-seasoned stuffing	1 cup cooked corn (off the cob)
1 cup diced cooked ham	2 tablespoons chopped chives

Prepare the stuffing according to package directions. Stir in the ham, corn, and chives. Place in a 1½-quart casserole and bake, covered, 30 minutes. *Makes 6 servings.*

Serve on a vegetable plate of Harvard beets, asparagus spears, and buttered cauliflower.

Meal-in-One Corn Pie

2 tablespoons butter or margarine	2 cups diced tomatoes
⅛ teaspoon minced garlic	½ teaspoon sugar
½ cup chopped onion	2 teaspoons salt
1 pound ground chuck	1¾ teaspoons chili powder
3 tablespoons flour	¼ teaspoon black pepper
2 cups fresh corn, cut off the cob	6 slices close-textured bread, buttered

Preheat oven to 350°. Melt the butter or margarine in a saucepan or skillet. Add the garlic and onion and cook 2 to 3 minutes or until limp. Add the meat and cook until the mixture is browned, stirring frequently. Blend in the flour. Add the corn, tomatoes, and seasonings. Stir and cook 5 minutes. Turn into a buttered 10″ x 6″ x 2″ baking dish. Top with the bread, buttered side up. Bake 25 minutes or until the bread is golden. Serve immediately. *Makes 4 to 6 servings.*

Dill-stuffed Sea Bass

Striped sea bass, 3 to 4 pounds	¼ cup butter or margarine
Salt and pepper	½ cup chopped onion

¼ cup chopped celery	2 cups herb-seasoned cube stuffing
1 tablespoon chopped fresh dill or	
1 teaspoon dried dill	PARSLEY SAUCE
1 tablespoon capers	¼ cup melted butter or margarine
½ teaspoon salt	2 tablespoons lemon juice
⅓ cup water	¼ cup chopped parsley

Preheat oven to 375°. Prepare the fish for stuffing by removing the head, tail, and backbone. Rub the inside with the salt and pepper. Place the butter or margarine in a saucepan and sauté the onion and celery until tender. Stir in the dill, capers, salt, water and stuffing. Place the stuffing on half of the fish, fold over the other half, and secure with a skewer and string. Grease a shallow baking pan. Place the fish in the pan and brush with soft butter. Bake 12 to 15 minutes per pound, or until the fish is easily flaked with a fork.

Golden Yellow Celery

Carefully remove to a hot platter and serve with the Parsley Sauce. *Makes 4 to 6 servings.*

PARSLEY SAUCE. Combine the butter, lemon juice, and parsley over low heat. *Makes about ⅔ cup.*

Tuna-stuffed Eggplant

2 large eggplants about 2 pounds
  each
1 small onion, chopped
¼ cup butter or margarine
1 cup soft bread crumbs
2 cans (6 to 7 ounces) tuna, drained
1 teaspoon salt

¼ teaspoon freshly ground black
  pepper
½ to 1 teaspoon ground thyme
1 cup bread cubes
2 tablespoons melted butter or
  margarine

Preheat oven to 400°. Wash the eggplants, wipe dry, and remove the green tip. Cut a lengthwise center slice from each. Scoop out inside and reserve, leaving a wall ½ inch thick. Invert the shells in a shallow baking dish; pour in 1 inch boiling water. Bake 20 minutes or until half done. Reduce oven to 350°. Chop the pulp and sauté with the onion in the butter or margarine. Add the bread crumbs, tuna, and seasonings. Spoon into the eggplant shells and put back in baking dish. Mix the bread cubes with the melted butter. Sprinkle around the edge of the tops. Bake, uncovered, 20 minutes. *Makes 4 servings.*

Ham Mediterranean (Pisto)

1 ½ cups cooked ham cut into ½-inch
  cubes
¼ cup olive oil
2 onions, sliced
1 green pepper, diced
1 small unpeeled eggplant, cut into

½-inch cubes
1 clove garlic, minced
2½ cups cooked artichoke hearts
1 teaspoon salt
2½ cups ripe tomatoes

Sauté the ham cubes in the olive oil in a large frying pan. Add the onions, peppers, eggplant, and garlic. Cook over medium heat until the onions are soft. Add the artichoke hearts, salt, and tomatoes. Cover. Cook over medium heat about 8 minutes until the mixture is heated through. *Makes 6 servings.*

Chicken Véronique

3 whole chicken breasts (about 2½
  pounds), split, boned, and skinned
4 tablespoons butter or margarine

¼ pound mushrooms, quartered
1 medium clove garlic, minced
½ teaspoon salt

⅛ teaspoon black pepper
¼ cup Sauterne or other dry white wine

1 can (10¾ ounces) chicken gravy
1 cup seedless grapes

Brown the chicken in the butter or margarine with the mushrooms and garlic. Season with the salt and pepper. Stir in the wine and gravy. Cook over low heat for 12 minutes or until tender, stirring occasionally. Add the grapes the last five minutes. *Makes 4 to 6 servings.*

Kale with Pork Hocks

6 pork hocks
Salt

2 pounds kale
1 teaspoon crumbled oregano leaves

Rinse the pork hocks in warm water. Place in a large saucepan with water to cover. Add ½ teaspoon salt per pound of the hocks. Bring to a boil. Cover and simmer 2 hours. Wash the kale and remove the outer stems. When the pork is done, remove it from pan and cook the kale in one cup of the pork liquid with ¼ teaspoon salt and the oregano for 5 minutes. Cover and continue cooking 10 minutes or until the greens are tender. *Do not overcook.* Serve with the pork hocks. *Makes 6 servings.*

Crown Lamb Roast with Mushroom Stuffing

Crown lamb roast with 12 to 15 ribs
1 teaspoon salt
⅛ teaspoon black pepper
12 to 15 small mushrooms
1 teaspoon lemon juice
2 tablespoons melted butter or margarine
Parsley

MUSHROOM STUFFING
¾ pound small mushrooms
½ cup butter or margarine
1 teaspoon lemon juice
½ cup chopped onion
½ cup chopped celery

1 quart toasted bread cubes (croutons)
½ cup chopped parsley
1 teaspoon salt
¾ teaspoon poultry seasoning
⅛ teaspoon black pepper
2 tablespoons water

LAMB GRAVY
Lamb drippings
1 tablespoon flour
1 cup cold water
¼ teaspoon salt
1/16 teaspoon black pepper
1/16 teaspoon garlic powder

The crown lamb roast is prepared by the butcher from the rack. It usually contains from 12 to 15 ribs.

Preheat oven to 325°. Wipe roast with a damp cloth and rub both sides with ¾ teaspoon of the salt and the pepper mixed together. Place on a rack in a shallow baking pan. Fill the center with the Mushroom Stuffing. Wrap the ends of the ribs separately with foil to prevent charring. Cover the top of the stuffing with foil. Bake 1 hour. Remove foil from the stuffing and continue baking 1 more hour. Remove foil from the rib ends.

Wash the small mushrooms. Boil 1 minute in ½ inch boiling water; add the lemon juice and the remaining ¼ teaspoon salt. Dip each mushroom in the butter or margarine and place one on each rib. Bake 15 minutes. Garnish with parsley just before serving. Serve with the Lamb Gravy.

MUSHROOM STUFFING. Remove the caps from the mushrooms and save enough of the smallest ones to garnish each rib of the roast. Slice the remaining mushrooms and sauté in the butter or margarine and lemon juice, along with the onion and celery. Combine with the toasted bread cubes, (measure after toasting), the parsley, salt, poultry seasoning, pepper and water. Mix lightly. Spoon into the center of the crown roast. *Makes sufficient stuffing for a 15-rib crown lamb roast.*

LAMB GRAVY. Drain the drippings from the roasting pan and blend in the flour. Stir in the water, salt, pepper, and garlic powder. Cook, stirring lightly, until slightly thickened. *Makes approximately 1 cup.*

Lemon 'n' Lime Chicken

2 broiling chickens, 2½ pounds each, quartered
2 lemons
2 limes
Salt and black pepper
1 teaspoon ground ginger
½ teaspoon garlic powder

3 tablespoons chopped parsley
1 tablespoon chopped fresh tarragon or 1 teaspoon dried tarragon
3 tablespoons snipped dill weed
Sweet paprika
¼ pound melted butter

Preheat oven to 375°. Butter a roasting pan; line it with foil, and butter again. Place the chicken quarters, skin side up, in pan. Sprinkle with the juice of half a lemon and half a lime. Sprinkle the herbs and seasonings (except the remaining lemon and lime) over the chicken in the order listed. Dribble the melted butter over all. Cover loosely with foil and bake 30 minutes. Remove the foil and bake 20 minutes longer or until done. Cool. Squeeze the juice of half a lemon and half a lime over the cooled chicken. Chill. Slice the remaining lemon and lime for garnish. *Makes 4 servings.*

Shrimp-Grapefruit Curry

3 tablespoons butter or margarine
¼ cup coarsely chopped onion
⅛ teaspoon finely chopped garlic
1 tablespoon flour
½ teaspoon curry powder
½ teaspoon salt

⅛ teaspoon black pepper
½ cup grapefruit juice
1 cup heavy cream
3 tablespoons finely chopped parsley
2 pounds cooked shrimp, hot
2 cups fresh grapefruit sections

In a saucepan, melt the butter or margarine. Add the onion and garlic and cook over low heat until the onion is transparent. Blend in the flour, curry powder, salt, and pepper. Heat together the grapefruit juice and cream and add to the onion mixture. Cook over low heat, stirring constantly, until thickened. Add the parsley, cook over low heat 5 minutes, stirring frequently. Gently stir in the hot shrimp and grapefruit sections and cook only until heated through. Serve immediately. Lobster or crab may be substituted for the shrimp. *Makes 6 servings.*

Mushroom Quiche

8 slices bacon, cut crosswise into
   1-inch bits
⅓ cup finely chopped onion
½ pound coarsely chopped
   mushrooms
1 tablespoon flour
4 large eggs, lightly beaten
1 cup heavy cream

¾ cup milk
½ teaspoon salt
⅛ teaspoon black pepper
¼ teaspoon ground mace
1 unbaked 9-inch pastry shell with a
   deep edge
¼ pound Gruyère cheese, grated

Preheat oven to 425°. Cook the bacon pieces until crisp in a large skillet. Remove the bacon and reserve. Drain all but 3 tablespoons fat from pan; reserve remainder. Add the onion to the skillet and cook over low heat until transparent. Add the chopped mushrooms; cook, tossing gently, until the mushrooms are tender. Add the remaining bacon fat if necessary. Blend in the flour. Let cool a few minutes. In a large bowl, combine the eggs, cream, milk, salt, pepper, and mace. Sprinkle the bacon over the bottom of the pie shell. Cover with the grated cheese and mushroom mixture. Pour the egg mixture over all. Bake on the lowest shelf of the oven 15 minutes. Reduce heat to 300° and bake 40 minutes longer or until custard is set. Serve hot. *Makes 1 quiche.*

Quick Orange-topped Lamb Chops

4 shoulder lamb chops (about 1 pound)
2 tablespoons shortening
1 can (10½ ounces) giblet gravy

1 medium clove garlic, minced
⅛ teaspoon crushed rosemary
4 thick orange slices
Mint jelly

Brown the chops in the shortening; pour off the fat. Add the gravy, garlic, and rosemary. Top each chop with an orange slice. Cover. Cook over low heat 45 minutes or until tender, stirring occasionally. Garnish each orange slice with a dollop of mint jelly. *Makes 4 servings.*

Orange-glazed Pork Chops

4 double-cut loin pork chops
2 tablespoons chopped onion
¼ cup butter or margarine
⅓ cup orange juice
1 teaspoon orange rind

1 tablespoon chopped pecans
¼ teaspoon salt
2 cups corn bread stuffing
Salt and pepper to taste
¼ cup corn syrup

Have the butcher make a slit or pocket in the side of each pork chop. Preheat oven to 375°. Sauté the onions in the butter until tender. Stir in half of the orange juice, the rind, pecans, salt, and stuffing. Season the pork chops with the salt and pepper and fill the pockets with the stuffing mixture. Skewer. Place in a shallow baking pan, cover with foil, and bake for 1 hour. Make the glaze by combining the corn syrup and the other ½ teaspoon of orange rind. Uncover chops and continue baking 30 minutes, brushing frequently with the orange glaze. *Makes 4 servings.*

Chicken with Almonds and Peaches

2 pounds chicken breasts, split
2 tablespoons slivered almonds
2 tablespoons butter or margarine
1 can (10½ ounces) condensed

cream of chicken soup
2 tablespoons chopped parsley
6 peach halves

Brown the chicken and almonds in the butter. Stir in the soup and parsley; cover. Cook over low heat for 45 minutes or until tender, stirring occasionally. Add the peaches for a few minutes to heat through. *Makes 4 to 6 servings.*

Sausage and Tomato-stuffed Green Peppers

4 plump, squatty green peppers
1½ teaspoons salt
1½ cups diced firm-textured bread
3 tablespoons butter or margarine

1 pound sausage meat
1 tablespoon finely chopped onion
1 large egg, lightly beaten
½ cup diced tomatoes

Wash the green peppers. Cut a thin slice from the stem ends and remove the seeds. Place the peppers in a saucepan with the boiling water to cover and 1 teaspoon of the salt. Cover. Bring to a boil and boil 5 minutes. Remove peppers from the water and invert on a tray. Set aside to drain well. Preheat oven to 350°. Sauté the bread cubes in the butter or margarine. Set aside. Crumble the sausage in a skillet and cook until brown. Discard the fat. Add the sausage to the bread cubes. Add the onion, egg, tomato, and remaining ½ teaspoon of salt. Mix well and spoon into the drained peppers. Arrange the peppers in a close-fitting casserole. Cover and bake 20 minutes. Remove cover and bake 10 minutes longer. Serve hot. *Makes 4 servings.*

Baked Stuffed Peppers

6 green peppers
2 tablespoons butter or margarine
1 onion, finely chopped
½ pound ground beef
1 tomato, peeled and chopped

1 package (8 ounces) of herb-
    seasoned stuffing
½ teaspoon salt
¼ teaspoon black pepper
1 cup canned tomato sauce

Cut a 1-inch piece from the stem end of the peppers; set aside. Carefully scoop out the seeds and fibers from each pepper. Parboil the peppers and the end pieces in boiling salted water for 5 minutes; drain and cool. Preheat oven to 375°.

Melt the butter in a skillet; sauté the onions for 5 minutes. Stir in the beef, tomatoes, and stuffing. Cook over high heat until the beef loses its redness. Add the salt and pepper; mix well. Taste for seasoning. Fill the peppers with the stuffing mixture; cover with the end pieces. Place in baking dish and pour over the tomato sauce. Bake for 45 minutes. *Makes 6 servings.*

Polynesian Pilaf

1 pineapple

¼ cup diced green pepper

1 pound cooked ham, cut into ¼-inch
  cubes
1 tablespoon butter or margarine
3 cups cooked rice

1 teaspoon chopped chives
½ teaspoon thyme leaves
4-ounce can medium-sized shrimp

Cut the pineapple in half lengthwise. With a knife, carve the fruit out of the
shell. Remove the core and cut the pineapple into chunks. Turn the pineapple
shells upside down to drain. Sauté the green pepper and ham in the butter
until lightly browned. Add to the cooked rice along with the chives, thyme,
shrimp, and pineapple chunks. Mix lightly. Heap the mixture into the pineapple shells to serve. To keep warm, wrap the shells in aluminum foil and
place in a warm oven or over outdoor grill. *Makes 6 servings.*

Plum Skillet Orientale

3 tablespoons salad oil
1 cup thinly sliced Bermuda onion
2 cups thinly sliced celery, cut on the
  diagonal
⅛ teaspoon finely chopped garlic
3 tablespoons sugar
1 tablespoon cornstarch
¼ teaspoon ground ginger
⅛ teaspoon black pepper

¾ cup chicken broth or chicken
  bouillon
2 tablespoons soy sauce
1 tablespoon lemon juice
1 tablespoon cider vinegar
1 pound raw shrimp, shelled and
  deveined
2 cups cubed cooked ham
6 plums, halved

Heat the oil in a skillet. Add the onion, celery, and garlic. Cook over low
heat, tossing gently until the vegetables are lightly glazed. In a small bowl
blend the sugar, cornstarch, ginger, pepper, broth, soy sauce, lemon juice, and
vinegar. Add to skillet along with the shrimp and ham. Cover and simmer
gently about 5 minutes or until the shrimp are pink. Toss occasionally. Add
the plums and cook 3 minutes longer. *Makes 4 servings.*

Spinach-Shrimp Omelet Ring

1 can (7 ounces) cooked and deveined shrimp
2 tablespoons butter or margarine,
  melted
¼ pound fresh spinach, washed and

  drained
4 large eggs, separated
1 teaspoon minced onion
¼ teaspoon black pepper
¼ cup milk

Preheat oven to 350°. Place the drained shrimp in a 1½-quart ring mold. Pour the butter or margarine over them. Chop the spinach very fine. Beat the egg whites until they stand in soft peaks. Beat the yolks until thick and lemon-colored, adding the onion, pepper, and milk. Combine the spinach with the yolk mixture. Gently fold into the beaten whites. Turn the omelet mixture into the ring mold. Bake for 2 0 minutes before testing. If the top springs back when pressed with finger, the ring is done. To unmold, cover the top with a platter; invert mold and platter and tap the omelet out gently. If desired, top with a cheese and lemon sauce. *Makes 4 servings.*

Spinach Steak, Chinese Style

2 packages (10 ounces each) spinach
½ pound round steak, cut ¼ inch
   thick
2 tablespoons salad oil
1 cup thinly sliced onion
1 clove garlic, minced

1 tablespoon cornstarch
½ teaspoon sugar
1 teaspoon salt
¼ teaspoon black pepper
¼ cup water

Wash the spinach and drain. Cut into ½-inch crosswise strips. Set aside. Cut the steak into ¼-inch crosswise strips.

Heat the oil in a skillet. Add the meat and sauté 10 minutes or until tender. Add the onion and garlic. Cook 1 minute. Add the spinach; stir and cook 2 minutes. Blend the cornstarch, sugar, salt, and pepper with the water. Add to the mixture. Stir and cook 1 to 2 minutes or until the juice thickens. Serve at once. *Makes 6 servings.*

Armenian Spinach and Lamb Stew

2 pounds boneless shoulder of lamb
1½ cups boiling water
5 tablespoons chopped onion
1 bay leaf
3 pounds spinach
3 cups diced tomatoes

1¾ teaspoons salt
1 teaspoon rosemary leaves
½ teaspoon black pepper
2 tablespoons flour
2 tablespoons cold water

Trim the excess fat from the lamb and reserve. Cut the lamb into 1-inch cubes. Brown on all sides in the reserved fat. Add the boiling water, onion, and bay leaf. Cover and cook 1 hour or until the meat is tender. Wash the spinach and cut it into large pieces. Add to the lamb, together with the tomatoes, salt, rosemary, and pepper. Cook 10 to 15 minutes or until the spinach is cooked through. Blend the flour with the cold water and add to the stew. Cook 1 minute or only until slightly thickened. *Makes 6 servings.*

Sausage-stuffed Acorn Squash
(or Baked Eggplant or Bermuda Onions)

2 packages (8 ounces each) corn bread stuffing
1 package (8 ounces) herb-seasoned stuffing
2 cups chicken broth or chicken bouillon
¾ pound (3 sticks) butter or margarine
½ cup chopped green pepper
½ cup chopped celery
¾ onion, chopped
1 pound sausage links cut in quarters or 1 pound sausage meat
2 eggs, beaten
¾ cup chopped pecans
1 teaspoon marjoram
¼ teaspoon black pepper
Baked acorn squash halves, baked eggplant halves, or Bermuda onion shells

Prepare the stuffings according to package directions, using the 2 cups broth and ½ pound of the butter. Meanwhile, cook the green peppers, celery, and onions in the remaining ¼ pound butter (or margarine) until tender. Remove the vegetables and brown the sausages in the same skillet. Combine all the ingredients in a large bowl. Stuff the baked acorn halves, baked eggplant, or Bermuda onion shells and serve. *Makes 12 cups stuffing.*

Hearty Tomato–Meat Ball Chowder

6 cups beef broth
6 cups peeled and diced tomatoes
2 teaspoons sugar
2¼ teaspoons salt
¼ teaspoon black pepper
1 small clove garlic, finely chopped
2 cups mashed potatoes
2 cups sliced carrots
1 cup diced potatoes
1 cup diced celery
½ cup sliced mushrooms
1 tablespoon finely chopped parsley
¼ teaspoon thyme leaves
¼ teaspoon basil leaves
½ pound ground beef
Dash black pepper
1 tablespoon butter or margarine

Place the broth, tomatoes, sugar, 2 teaspoons of the salt, the pepper, and garlic in a saucepan; cover and cook for 15 minutes. Add the mashed potatoes and continue cooking 10 minutes more until the soup is thick. Add the carrots, potatoes, celery, mushrooms, parsley, thyme, and basil and cook until the vegetables are tender. Mix the meat with the remaining ¼ teaspoon salt and a dash of pepper. Shape into ½-inch balls. Sauté in the butter until browned. Add to the chowder. Serve as main dish for luncheon or supper. *Makes 3 quarts.*

Tomato Swiss Fondue

4 eggs, separated
1 teaspoon salt
2 cups small bread cubes (about ¼-inch cubes)
4 ounces Swiss cheese, grated

1¼ cups milk
1 teaspoon minced onion
¼ teaspoon black pepper
1 pound tomatoes, cut in ½-inch slices

Preheat oven to 325°. Beat the egg whites with the salt until stiff peaks form. Beat the egg yolks until thick; mix in the bread cubes, cheese, milk, onion,

Trophy Tomato (⁷⁄₁₀ natural size)

and pepper. Fold the egg whites into the cheese mixture. Pour into a buttered 1½-quart casserole. Arrange the tomatoes on top pinwheel fashion. Bake about 1 hour or until a silver knife inserted in the center comes out clean. *Makes 6 servings.*

Zucchini Supper Casserole

3 tablespoons oil (preferably olive oil)
1 medium onion, thinly sliced
1 pound ground beef (or 2 cups ground leftover cooked beef)
3 cans (8 ounces) tomato sauce
1 cup Burgundy, claret, or other red table wine

1 teaspoon mixed Italian-style seasoning
Dash garlic powder
1 tablespoon sugar
Salt and pepper
2 pounds zucchini (6 or 7 medium-sized)
Parmesan cheese, grated

Heat the oil in a large, heavy skillet or Dutch oven; add the onion and beef. Cook, stirring frequently, until the meat is browned. Add the tomato sauce, wine, and seasonings. Cover. Simmer gently for 1 hour, stirring occasionally. While the sauce is cooking, wash the zucchini and trim ends; cook whole in boiling, salted water for about 15 minutes or just until tender; drain.

Preheat oven to 350°. When the zucchini is cool enough to handle, cut in half lengthwise and arrange, cut side up, in a single layer in a greased shallow baking dish. Pour the sauce over the zucchini; bake for 45 minutes. Serve with the grated Parmesan cheese. *Makes 5 or 6 servings.*

Fruited Loin of Pork

1 cup dried apricots
½ cup sherry
1 center-cut pork loin (3 pounds), with backbone cracked

½ cup dark corn syrup
1 tablespoon grated orange rind
¼ cup orange juice
½ teaspoon soy sauce

Preheat oven to 325°. Combine the apricots and sherry in a saucepan. Cover and cook, stirring occasionally, until the apricots are plumped with all the sherry.

Cut deep slits between the chops in the pork loin. Insert 3 or 4 apricots in each. Insert a meat thermometer, being careful not to touch the bone. Place the pork in a roasting pan. (Do not add water or cover.) Roast about 2 hours or until the pork temperature reaches 185° (allow about 40 minutes per pound). Meanwhile, combine the syrup, orange rind, orange juice, and soy sauce in a saucepan. Bring to a boil; cook 3 minutes. Brush the pork with the sauce several times during the last 30 minutes of roasting time. Do *not* baste the pork with the drippings in the pan. *Makes 6 to 8 servings.*

Chicken-Vegetable Pie

⅓ cup chicken fat, butter, or margarine
1 cup sliced mushrooms
⅓ cup chopped onion
⅓ cup flour
1½ cups chicken stock or chicken bouillon

2 cups diced tomatoes
½ cup celery
1½ cups diced chicken
½ cup chopped ripe olives
½ teaspoon salt
⅛ teaspoon black pepper
1 recipe single-crust pastry

Preheat oven to 425°. Melt the fat, butter, or margarine in a saucepan. Add the mushrooms and onion and cook until the onions are limp and transparent. Stir in the flour. Add the stock, tomatoes, and celery. Cook until slightly thickened. Add the chicken, olives, salt, and pepper. Place in a 1½-quart casserole. Cover with the pastry, rolled to ⅛ inch thickness. Trim, turn under, and flute the edges. Bake 30 minutes or until brown. *Makes 4 servings.*

Classic Spanish Omelet

2 tablespoons butter
4 tablespoons mixed, diced vegetables, using any or all of the following: eggplant, tomatoes, green and red peppers, onions, carrots, peas,

turnips, potatoes
Crushed garlic to taste
4 eggs
Salt and pepper

Heat half the butter in saucepan; add vegetables, garlic, salt, and pepper. Cover and cook slowly until the vegetables are just tender. Break the eggs into a bowl and beat lightly with a fork or wire whisk; add the salt and pepper. Heat the remaining butter in a large skillet or omelet pan; pour in the vegetables, which should be juicy. Pour in the eggs and stir gently, shaking the pan to mix well. Cook over moderate heat, lifting the edges with a spatula to allow the liquid egg to run to bottom of pan. When set on the bottom but still soft on top, fold over and serve on hot plate. *Makes 4 servings.*

Braised Beef Piquant with Vegetables

2 tablespoons shortening or salad oil
2 pounds boneless chuck, cut in 1½-inch cubes

2 tablespoons flour
1 teaspoon salt
1½ cups water

1 cup all-purpose barbecue sauce
1 cup diced celery
⅓ cup dry vermouth (optional)
5 small onions, peeled

6 small carrots, halved
1 cup dairy sour cream
Parsley sprigs

Heat the shortening in a heavy saucepan or Dutch oven. Dredge the meat in the flour and salt. Brown the meat in the shortening over medium heat. Add the water, barbecue sauce, celery, and vermouth; blend well. Bring to a boil. Reduce heat, cover, and cook slowly until the meat is almost tender, about 45 minutes, stirring occasionally. Add the onions and carrots. Continue to

Long Lemon Carrot (⅛ natural size)

cook, stirring occasionally, about 40 minutes longer or until the meat and vegetables are tender. Remove the vegetables to a heated serving dish. Stir the sour cream into the meat and sauce. Heat thoroughly, but do not boil. Garnish with the parsley. Serve with the vegetables and buttered noodles or rice. *Makes 4½ cups of meat with sauce and 3 cups of vegetables, or 5 servings.*

Note. To prepare in advance, cook as directed but do not add the sour cream. Cool, cover, and refrigerate. Just before serving, heat thoroughly, remove the vegetables, and stir in the sour cream.

Barbecue Beefburger Loaf

1½ pounds ground lean beef
½ cup sauterne or rosé
1 tablespoon minced onion
1 teaspoon salt
½ cup soft stale bread crumbs

1 long or round loaf French bread
Butter or margarine
Sliced tomatoes, as desired
Sliced avocados, as desired
Seasoned salt

Mix the beef, wine, onion, salt, and bread crumbs lightly but thoroughly. Pat to about ½ inch larger than the loaf of bread. Grill the meat to the desired degree of doneness. Meanwhile, split the loaf of bread in half horizontally. Toast over grill. Spread the cut sides of the bread with butter and place the bottom half of the bread on a hot serving platter. Top with the grilled meat; arrange the thinly sliced tomatoes and avocado slices over top; sprinkle with the seasoned salt. Cover with the top of the loaf. Cut in diagonal slices to serve. *Makes about 6 to 8 servings.*

Sirloin Steak Slices Morocco

2 pounds sirloin steak
¼ cup flour
½ teaspoon dry mustard
¼ teaspoon salt
⅛ teaspoon black pepper
Butter or margarine, melted
¼ cup orange juice

¾ cup water or beef consommé
Few grains garlic powder
½ cup sliced celery
½ cup seedless raisins
1 tablespoon cornstarch
Cold water

Trim the meat of bone and fat and cut into diagonal strips about 2 inches long by 1 inch wide. Coat with a mixture of the flour, mustard, salt and pepper. Brown in the melted butter or margarine. Add the orange juice, water or consommé, garlic powder, celery, and raisins. Simmer for 10 minutes. Thicken with the cornstarch mixed with a little cold water. *Makes 6 servings.*

Acapulco Enchiladas

2 cups diced cooked chicken
⅓ cup minced green onions
⅓ cup chopped blanched almonds
½ teaspoon salt

3 cups Chili Sauce
8 tortillas
½ cup dairy sour cream
4 ounces shredded Cheddar cheese

¼ cup pitted, sliced ripe olives

CHILI SAUCE
⅔ cup chopped onion
¼ cup chopped green pepper
1 garlic clove, minced

2 tablespoons cooking oil
1 cup tomato paste
1 cup water
¼ cup chili powder
1 teaspoon salt
½ teaspoon oregano

Combine the chicken, onions, almonds, and salt. Heat the Chili Sauce. Pre-heat oven to 350°. Dip the tortillas, one at a time, in the hot sauce until limp. Remove with tongs to a plate. Place ⅓ cup of the chicken mixture in the center of each tortilla. Top with 1 tablespoon of the sour cream. Roll up the enchiladas and place in a casserole. Sprinkle with the cheese. Garnish with the olives. Bake 15 minutes, until bubbly. Serve at once. *Makes 4 servings.*

CHILI SAUCE. Sauté the onion, green pepper, and garlic in the oil. Add the remaining ingredients. Stir until well blended. *Makes 2½ cups.*

Quick Mock Sukiyaki

1 pound round steak, cut in very thin
  strips
2 tablespoons salad oil
1 can (10¾ ounces) beef gravy
2 tablespoons soy sauce
1½ cups diagonally sliced celery

1½ cups sliced mushrooms
½ cup green onion, cut in 2-inch
  strips
½ pound spinach
Cooked rice

In a large skillet, brown the beef in the oil. Pour off excess fat. Stir in the gravy and soy sauce. Add the celery, mushrooms, and onion. Cook over low heat 15 minutes. Add the spinach; cook 5 minutes longer. Serve with the cooked rice. *Makes 4 servings.*

Side Dishes

Spring Asparagus Bouquets

2 pounds young asparagus
2 tablespoons butter
2 tablespoons flour
½ teaspoon salt
¼ teaspoon Tabasco

1 cup milk
1 cup diced sharp Cheddar cheese
6 pimiento strips
2 hard-cooked eggs, chopped

Wash and scrape the asparagus; break off the tough ends of the stalks. Place in a shallow pan of boiling, salted water and cook 25 to 30 minutes. Melt the butter in the top of a double boiler; stir in the flour, salt, and Tabasco. Blend in the milk. Add the cheese, stirring until the sauce is smooth and thickened. Cover to keep warm.

When the asparagus is tender, drain off the water immediately. Cover to keep warm. Place the asparagus in bouquets in a serving dish. Garnish each bundle with a pimiento strip. Pour the sauce over the asparagus. Sprinkle with the chopped egg. *Makes 6 servings.*

Asparagus Orientale

2 pounds asparagus
2 tablespoons salad oil

3 tablespoons water
½ teaspoon salt

1 tablespoon soy sauce   1 teaspoon cornstarch

Cut or break off asparagus stalks as far down as they snap easily. Remove the scales and wash thoroughly. Cut in very thin diagonal slices, leaving 1½-inch tips. Heat the oil in a 9-inch skillet. Add the asparagus, water, and salt. Cover and cook about 6 minutes over low heat until the asparagus is crisp-tender. Blend the soy sauce with the cornstarch and add. Stir and cook uncovered 2 minutes or until the sauce has thickened slightly. *Makes 6 servings.*

Asparagus with Guacamole Sauce

2 pounds asparagus
1 teaspoon salt
Lemon wedges
Hard-cooked eggs, sliced

GUACAMOLE SAUCE
1 cup peeled tomatoes
1 tablespoon chopped onion

½ teaspoon salt
$\frac{1}{16}$ teaspoon white pepper
2 teaspoons lemon juice
2 ripe, medium avocados, diced
1 tablespoon mayonnaise
1 teaspoon salad or olive oil
½ teaspoon Worcestershire sauce

Break off each stalk of the asparagus as far down as it snaps easily. Wash well. Place the asparagus in two layers in a large skillet; sprinkle with the salt. Pour over boiling water to a depth of 1 inch. Bring to a boil; cook, uncovered, 5 minutes. Cover and simmer 3 to 5 minutes or until the lower stalks are crisp-tender. Lift out the stalks with tongs or two forks. Chill. Serve with Guacamole Sauce. Garnish with lemon wedges and sliced hard-cooked eggs. *Makes 6 servings.*
    GUACAMOLE SAUCE. Combine all ingredients. Mix well. *Makes about 2 cups.*

Asparagus Frittata

1½ pounds asparagus
½ cup butter or margarine
¼ cup thinly sliced scallions
6 large eggs

¾ teaspoon salt
¼ teaspoon black pepper
¼ cup grated Parmesan cheese

Break off each stalk of the asparagus as far down as it snaps easily. Wash well. Cut in 1½-inch pieces. Cook, uncovered, in 1 inch boiling water 5 min-

Giant Dutch Asparagus (¼ natural size)

utes. Cover and simmer 3 to 5 minutes or until the asparagus is crisp-tender. Drain. In a 9-inch skillet, melt the butter or margarine; add the scallions and cook 3 minutes. Add the asparagus, cooking until the butter or margarine sizzles. Beat the eggs with the salt and pepper. Pour over the asparagus. Cook the eggs until almost set, lifting the edges with a spatula. Sprinkle with the Parmesan cheese. Brown slightly under broiler. Serve in wedges. *Makes 4 servings.*

French-fried Asparagus

2 pounds asparagus, cooked	1 egg, slightly beaten
½ cup fine dry bread crumbs	2 tablespoons water
1 teaspoon salt	½ cup grated Parmesan cheese
¼ teaspoon black pepper	Vegetable or salad oil
½ teaspoon paprika	

Mix the bread crumbs with the salt, pepper, paprika and Parmesan cheese. Dip the asparagus into the bread crumb mixture, then in the egg mixed with the water, and in the crumbs again. Chill 1 hour so the crumbs will cling to the asparagus while frying. Preheat deep fat to 375° on a frying thermometer. Fry asparagus until brown, 4 to 5 minutes. Drain on absorbent paper and serve at once. *Makes 6 servings.*

Sauces for Asparagus

ALMOND BUTTER SAUCE

¼ cup slivered almonds   ¼ cup butter or margarine

Sauté the almonds in the butter or margarine. *Makes about ⅓ to ½ cup.*

MUSHROOM BUTTER SAUCE

⅔ cup mushrooms, sliced   2 teaspoons lemon juice
⅓ cup butter or margarine

Sauté the mushrooms in the butter or margarine and the lemon juice. *Makes about ½ cup.*

BACON AND BREAD CRUMB SAUCE

4 strips of bacon   ¼ cup bread crumbs
3 tablespoons bacon fat

Fry the bacon until very crisp. Add the bread crumbs to the fat and heat un- til browned, stirring constantly. Crumble and add the bacon. *Makes about ½ cup.*

Bananas in Wine

3 to 4 medium-sized firm, ripe   2 tablespoons cooking sherry or
   bananas   ¼ cup sweet sherry or red wine
2 tablespoons lemon or lime juice   2 tablespoons butter or margarine
¼ cup honey

Preheat oven to 400°. Peel the bananas and cut in half lengthwise. Brush with the lemon or lime juice. Place in a buttered 12″ x 7½″ x 2″ baking dish. Mix the honey with the sherry or wine and pour over the bananas. Dot with the butter or margarine and bake 20 minutes. Baste with the pan juices and bake 10 to 15 minutes longer or until the bananas are tender. *Makes 6 to 8 servings.*
   Delicious with baked Virginia ham.

Candied Bananas

6 green-tipped bananas
¼ cup melted butter or margarine
½ cup molasses
¼ teaspoon salt

2 teaspoons grated lemon rind
¼ cup lemon juice
½ teaspoon cinnamon
½ cup grated coconut

Preheat oven to 375°. Peel the bananas and cut them in half lengthwise; place in a shallow baking dish. Combine the butter, molasses, salt, lemon rind and juice, and cinnamon. Pour over the bananas and sprinkle with the coconut. Bake 15 minutes, basting occasionally. *Makes 6 servings.*
    Excellent with ham or pork.

Swiss Green Beans

2 tablespoons butter or margarine
2 tablespoons flour
1 teaspoon salt
¼ teaspoon black pepper
1 teaspoon sugar
½ teaspoon finely chopped onion
1 cup dairy sour cream

4 cups cooked green beans, drained
    and sliced lengthwise
½ pound processed Swiss cheese,
    grated
½ cup corn flake crumbs
1 tablespoon butter or margarine,
    melted

Preheat oven to 400°. Melt butter; stir in the flour, salt, pepper, sugar, and onion. Add sour cream gradually, stirring constantly. Cook at low temperature until thickened, stirring occasionally. Fold in green beans; heat thoroughly. Pour into greased 1½-quart casserole. Sprinkle cheese over beans. Combine corn flake crumbs with butter and sprinkle over cheese. Bake about 20 minutes. *Makes 6 servings of about ¾ cup each.*

Green Lima Beans in Sour Cream Sauce

2½ cups cooked green lima beans
¾ teaspoon salt
½ cup dairy sour cream

¼ cup chopped pimiento
¼ cup rosé wine
1 tablespoon finely chopped parsley

Combine the cooked, nearly drained limas with the sour cream, pimiento, and wine. Mix lightly and heat to steaming hot. Just before serving, sprinkle with the parsley. *Makes 4 servings.*

French-fried Pole Beans

1¼ pounds pole beans
1 cup milk
1 cup flour
1½ teaspoons salt

¼ teaspoon black pepper
Oil for frying
Celery salt

Wash and trim the ends from the beans, leaving them whole. Blanch the whole beans quickly in 2 cups of boiling water. Drain and cool. Preheat the deep frying oil to 360° on a frying thermometer. Pour the milk into a mixing bowl; dip a few beans at a time into the milk. Combine the flour, salt

Geneva, or Plainpalais, White Butter Bean or Wax Bean
(¼ natural size)

and black pepper and then dip the beans into this mixture to coat them well. Fry the beans in the oil until golden brown, about 2 minutes. Drain them on absorbent paper. Sprinkle with the celery salt. *Makes 6 servings.*

Chinese-Style Pole Beans

2 tablespoons olive oil
1 pound ground beef
1 pound pole beans, cut French style
2 cups thinly sliced onion rings
2 tablespoons soy sauce
¼ teaspoon ground ginger

¼ teaspoon black pepper
1 beef bouillon cube dissolved in
   ½ cup boiling water
¼ teaspoon dry mustard
¼ teaspoon water
1 teaspoon lemon juice

In a deep, heavy skillet heat the olive oil; add the beef and cook until it loses its color. Add the beans, onion rings, soy sauce, ginger, pepper and bouillon.

Cover and simmer 10 to 15 minutes or until the beans are crisp-tender. Stir occasionally. Blend the mustard and the water. Immediately before serving, stir in the mustard and lemon juice. *Makes 4 to 6 servings.*

Pennsylvania Dutch Snap Beans

1 pound green snap beans	2 tablespoons cider vinegar
1¼ teaspoons salt	1 tablespoon sugar
2 tablespoons finely chopped onion	¼ cup cooking water
1 tablespoon bacon fat	¼ teaspoon black pepper

Wash and trim the ends from the beans. Cut into julienne strips and place in a 1½-quart saucepan with 1 teaspoon of the salt and ¼ inch boiling water. Bring to a boil and cook 5 minutes uncovered. Cover and continue cooking 8 to 10 minutes or until the beans are tender. Remove from heat. Drain and save the cooking water. Sauté the onion in the bacon fat. Add the vinegar, sugar, cooking water, the remaining ¼ teaspoon salt, and the pepper. Bring to a boil and pour over the beans. Heat and serve hot. *Makes 6 servings.*

Beets à l'Orange

8 small beets	2 tablespoons light corn syrup
Juice of 1 orange	1 teaspoon salt
1 teaspoon grated orange rind	1 tablespoon butter or margarine

Wash the beets well. Peel and grate or chop finely. (There should be about 3 cups.) Add water to the orange juice to make 1 cup liquid. Mix with the beets in a saucepan. Stir in the orange rind, syrup, salt, and margarine or butter. Cover pan tightly; bring mixture to a boil. Simmer gently 15 minutes or until the beets are tender. Serve hot. *Makes 4 servings.*

Spiced Pickled Fresh Beets

1 cup sugar	½ teaspoon whole cloves
1⅓ cups water	1½ teaspoons salt
2 cups cider vinegar	6 cups (3½ pounds) sliced cooked
2 sticks cinnamon, 2 inches long	beets
½ teaspoon whole allspice	1 cup sliced raw onion

Combine the sugar, water, vinegar, and cinnamon in a 2½-quart saucepan. Tie the allspice and the cloves in a small cloth bag and add. Bring to a boil and boil 3 minutes. Add the salt, beets, and onion. Simmer 5 minutes. Remove the spice bag and the cinnamon. Pack in hot sterilized jars. Seal at once. DO NOT USE FOR ABOUT SIX WEEKS. *Makes 8 half-pint jars.*

Beet Greens with Sour Cream and Horseradish

2 pounds beet greens
1 teaspoon salt
½ teaspoon sugar
⅛ teaspoon black pepper

¼ cup dairy sour cream
2 tablespoons horseradish
¼ teaspoon lemon juice, if desired

Wash the beet greens in five or six changes of water and cut off the coarse stems. Place in a large saucepan. Cover and cook, with only the water that clings to the leaves, 15 minutes or until the greens are tender. Drain, if necessary, and chop. Add the salt, sugar, pepper, sour cream, horseradish, and lemon juice. Mix lightly. Serve hot. *Makes 6 servings.*

Broccoli with Water Chestnuts

1 bunch broccoli
¾ teaspoon salt
1 teaspoon Accent

1 can (5 ounces) water chestnuts
4 tablespoons butter or margarine
4 bacon slices, cooked and crumbled

Choose broccoli with dark green, tightly closed buds and short, crisp stems. Remove the outer leaves and tough part of the stalks; slit the large stalks lengthwise about 1½ inches. Cook, covered, in ½ cup boiling water with the salt, 10 to 15 minutes until crisp-tender. Drain; sprinkle with the Accent. While the broccoli is cooking, drain and slice the water chestnuts. Melt the butter or margarine in a saucepan; add the chestnuts and cook until heated. Spoon the chestnuts over the broccoli; sprinkle with the bacon. *Makes 4 servings.*

Broccoli with Egg Sauce

1¼ pounds broccoli
2 tablespoons shortening or butter
¼ cup flour

3 whole cloves
1 medium onion
1 pint milk

⅓ teaspoon salt
Pinch black pepper
Pinch dry mustard

1 hard-cooked egg, chopped
1 tablespoon chopped parsley

Wash the broccoli carefully. Remove the leaves and bottom sections of the stems, cutting to serving size. Cook in boiling water until just tender, 10 to 15 minutes. Drain. Melt the shortening or butter. Add the flour and cook slowly for 5 minutes. Imbed the cloves in the onion and place in a pan with the milk; heat. When the milk is hot, remove the onion and add with the salt, pepper, and mustard to the flour mixture; stir until smooth. Cook 15 to 20 minutes over low heat. Remove from heat. Strain and add the eggs. Ladle the sauce over the stems of the broccoli. Dust with the parsley. *Makes 6 servings.*

Broccoli Sicilian

2 tablespoons olive oil
1 onion, thinly sliced
1 clove garlic, sliced
1½ tablespoons flour
1 cup chicken stock or chicken
    bouillon
4 anchovies, chopped

½ cup sliced black olives
⅛ teaspoon freshly ground black
    pepper
2 cups shredded Mozzarella or
    American cheese
1 large bunch (1¾ pounds) cooked
    broccoli

Heat the olive oil in a 1-quart saucepan. Add the onion and garlic and sauté 1 to 2 minutes or until the onion is soft. Blend in the flour. Add the stock or bouillon. Stir and cook for 5 or 6 minutes or until the mixture is of medium thickness. Add the anchovies, olives, pepper, and cheese. Mix well and serve over the broccoli. *Makes 6 servings.*

Goldenaise Broccoli

1 bunch broccoli
3 egg yolks
½ cup mayonnaise

1 tablespoon lemon juice
½ teaspoon onion salt
⅛ teaspoon thyme

Wash broccoli; remove large leaves and cut off tough ends of stalks. Cover and cook in boiling, salted water 20 minutes. Drain. Meanwhile place egg yolks in strainer and lower into simmering water to cover; simmer 5 minutes, until firm. Remove and sieve. Combine remaining ingredients in small saucepan; simmer only to heat thoroughly. Pour over broccoli in serving dish; top with sieved egg yolks. *Makes 6 servings.*

Broccoli con Prosciutto

1 bunch (1½ pounds) broccoli
1 teaspoon salt
2 tablespoons olive oil or butter or
  margarine

1 clove garlic, split
½ cup diced prosciutto or boiled ham
¼ cup grated Parmesan cheese
⅛ teaspoon black pepper

Wash the broccoli and split all the large stems to shorten cooking time. Place in a saucepan with 1 inch boiling water and the salt. Bring to a boil uncovered and boil 5 minutes. Cover and boil 3 minutes, or until about half done. Drain, reserving the liquid. Heat the oil and garlic in a 9-inch skillet. Add the broccoli and sauté 2 to 3 minutes to finish cooking it. Add a little of the broccoli water if the pan gets too dry. Add the ham and cook only until hot. Serve at once, sprinkled with the Parmesan cheese and pepper. *Makes 6 servings.*

Brussels Sprouts à la Crème

1½ pounds baby Brussels sprouts
½ cup heavy cream

1 tablespoon butter
Salt and pepper

Wash and pare the Brussels sprouts, removing the outer leaves, and cook in boiling, salted water for 7 minutes. Drain thoroughly until completely dry. While the sprouts are drying, heat the cream, reducing it to about half. Add the sprouts, butter, and seasonings. Cover pan and shake well to mix. Simmer at very low heat for a few minutes. Serve at once. *Makes 4 servings.*

French-fried Brussels Sprouts

1 quart Brussels sprouts
½ teaspoon salt
1 cup fine dry bread crumbs
½ teaspoon salt
⅛ teaspoon black pepper

1 large egg, lightly beaten
1 tablespoon milk or water
Shallow fat for frying (about ¾
  inch)
Seasoning salts (optional)

Wash and trim the sprouts. Soak in salted cold water, using 1 quart water and 1 teaspoon salt, 20 minutes. Drain. Cook, uncovered, in pan with 1 inch of boiling water and the salt 5 minutes. Drain. Combine the egg and the milk. Dip the sprouts in the bread crumbs, in the beaten egg-milk mixture, and in the bread crumbs again. Fry in hot fat, turning to cook both sides. Drain on paper towels and serve as a vegetable or sprinkle with salt and serve as an hors d'oeuvre. *Makes 4 to 5 servings.*

Pan-creamed Cabbage

½ cup butter or margarine
2 quarts shredded cabbage
1 cup light cream
1 teaspoon seasoned salt

Nutmeg
½ cup sauterne or other white dinner
   wine

Melt the butter or margarine in a large skillet or saucepan, add the cabbage. Cook over moderate heat, stirring frequently until the cabbage is wilted. Cover and cook about 5 minutes. Stir in the cream, salt, and a light sprinkling of nutmeg. Cover and cook until almost tender. Add the wine and simmer a few minutes longer or until the cabbage is tender. *Makes 5 or 6 servings.*

Cabbage Sauterne

4 cups shredded cabbage
1 package (1 ounce) white sauce mix
   (or make White Sauce, p. 72)
¾ cup cold milk

¼ cup sauterne or other white table
   wine
½ teaspoon salt
Pinch nutmeg

Cook the cabbage, covered, in 2 cups boiling, salted water just until tender-crisp. Drain. Empty white sauce mix into liquid. Slowly stir in milk, wine, salt, and nutmeg. Heat just to boiling, stirring constantly. Add drained cooked cabbage and heat gently a few minutes longer. *Makes 5 to 6 servings.*

New Cabbage with Peanut Sauce

1 head (3 pounds) new cabbage
1 teaspoon salt
⅓ cup butter or margarine

¼ cup chopped roasted peanuts
1 tablespoon lemon juice
⅛ teaspoon black pepper

Trim the cabbage; wash and cut into eight wedges. Place in a saucepan with

1 inch boiling water and the salt. Bring to a boil, uncovered, and boil 5 minutes. Cover and cook only until crisp-tender, 10 to 12 minutes. Drain. Meanwhile, melt the butter or margarine, add the peanuts, and cook until the butter or margarine is browned lightly. Add the lemon juice and pepper. Pour the peanut sauce over the cooked cabbage wedges. Serve at once. *Makes 8 servings.*

Carrots and Grapes

3 cups coarsely shredded carrots
3 tablespoons butter or margarine
¼ teaspoon anise seed
¾ teaspoon salt

½ teaspoon sugar
2 tablespoons water
1½ cups seedless grapes

Combine the carrots, butter, anise seed, salt, sugar, and water in a 1-quart saucepan. Cover and cook 5 to 10 minutes or until the carrots are tender. Stir in the grapes and serve hot. *Makes 6 servings.*

Orange-glazed Carrots

¼ cup butter or margarine
3 tablespoons orange juice
1½ tablespoons sugar
6 whole cloves

¼ teaspoon salt
10 medium carrots, sliced and cooked
   (about 5 cups)
Chopped parsley

Combine the butter or margarine, orange juice, sugar, cloves, and salt in a saucepan. Cook until the butter or margarine is melted and the sauce is hot. Remove the cloves and pour the mixture over the hot carrots, cooked only until crisp-tender. Garnish with the parsley. *Makes 6 servings.*

Cauliflower-Chestnut Casserole

1 medium head (1½ pounds) fresh
   cauliflower
1¼ teaspoons salt
1 pound chestnuts or ¾ cup sliced,

   blanched almonds
2 tablespoons butter or margarine
¼ teaspoon ground white pepper
2 tablespoons hot water

Preheat oven to 350°. Break the cauliflower into flowerets. Place them in a saucepan with 1 inch boiling water and 1 teaspoon of the salt. Bring to a boil, uncovered, and cook another 5 minutes. Cover and cook until about three-quarters done. Drain. Put a layer of cauliflower in a buttered casserole, cover with a layer of chestnuts; dot with butter or margarine and sprinkle lightly with the pepper mixed with the remaining ¼ teaspoon salt. Repeat the layers until all the ingredients are used. Add the 2 tablespoons hot water. Cover and bake 30 minutes. *Makes 6 servings.*

TO PREPARE CHESTNUTS : Prick with a fork or split the top end in a cross slit. Place them in a 350° oven or in a covered, slightly greased skillet. Cook over low heat or bake until tender. (*Note.* The brown coating around the chestnuts will come off during the boiling process.) Chop medium fine.

TO BLANCH ALMONDS : Soak the almonds in boiling water long enough to loosen the skins for easy removal.

Bacon and Cauliflower with Cheese Sauce

1 small head cauliflower
¼ cup milk
Dash nutmeg
1 can (10¾ ounces) condensed

Cheddar cheese soup
¼ cup buttered bread crumbs
4 slices bacon, cooked and crumbled

Preheat oven to 350°. Cook the cauliflower in boiling, salted water for 15 minutes or until tender; drain. Blend the milk and nutmeg into the soup. Place the cauliflower in a shallow baking dish; pour the sauce over it. Sprinkle with the bread crumbs. Bake for 15 minutes or until hot. Garnish with the bacon. *Makes 4 servings.*

Sweet and Sour Celery

2 cups diced celery
¼ cup finely diced onion
¼ cup diced green pepper
½ teaspoon salt
2 whole cloves
1 small bay leaf
1/16 teaspoon black pepper

½ cup water
1 tablespoon sugar
2 tablespoons bottled Italian salad
   dressing
1 tablespoon lemon juice
1 tablespoon cornstarch

In a medium-sized saucepan combine the celery, onion, green pepper, salt, cloves, bay leaf, black pepper, and water. Bring to a boil; lower heat and cook, covered, 15 minutes. Remove the bay leaf and the cloves. Drain and discard the liquid. Add the sugar, Italian dressing, and lemon juice. Cook over low heat for 5 minutes, stirring constantly. Add the cornstarch and stir until the celery mixture is evenly coated. Serve hot. *Makes about 2½ cups.*

Celery Fritters

¾ cup sifted all-purpose flour
1 teaspoon double-acting baking
  powder
1 teaspoon salt
¼ teaspoon white pepper
¼ teaspoon nutmeg

1/16 teaspoon cayenne
2 large eggs, well beaten
1½ cups chopped celery
2 teaspoons finely chopped onion
½ cup milk
Shortening

Sift together the flour, baking powder, salt, pepper, nutmeg, and cayenne. Stir in the eggs, celery, onion, and milk. Mix well. Melt shortening in skillet to a depth of ¼ inch. Drop the batter from a tablespoon into the hot shortening. Fry until browned, turning to cook both sides, adding shortening as needed. Drain on paper towels. *Makes 18 fritters.*

Calico Corn Bread Stuffing

1 package (8 ounces) corn bread
  stuffing
1 cup chopped celery

½ cup chopped green pepper
2 tablespoons butter or margarine
¼ cup pimiento strips

Prepare the stuffing according to package directions. Sauté the celery and green pepper in the butter or margarine 5 minutes. Stir in the pimiento strips. Combine with the stuffing. Place in 1-quart casserole and bake covered 30 minutes. *Makes 6 servings.*

Delicious with baked ham, pork chops, chicken, spareribs.

Fresh Collards, Italian Style

2 pounds collards
1 cup diced tomatoes or tomato juice
3 tablespoons olive or salad oil
1 medium onion

¾ teaspoon salt
⅛ teaspoon black pepper
¼ teaspoon ground marjoram
¼ cup grated Parmesan cheese

Wash the collards thoroughly and cut off any tough ends. Heat the tomatoes and the oil in a saucepan large enough for cooking the collards. Add the onion and collards. Cover and cook slowly 10 minutes. Remove the onion and add the salt. Cover and cook 20 minutes or until tender. Add the pepper and marjoram. Mix well and serve hot, sprinkled with the grated Parmesan cheese. *Makes 6 servings.*

Fried Corn, Tennessee Style

6 ears corn	3 eggs, beaten
1 tablespoon bacon drippings	1 teaspoon salt
3 slices cooked crisp bacon, crumbled	1/16 teaspoon black pepper

Husk the corn and remove the silks. Cut the kernels from the cobs with a sharp knife. Using the bowl of a tablespoon to prevent spattering, scrape the cobs to get out all the milk. Heat the bacon drippings in a skillet and add the

Maize or Indian Corn (1/6 natural size)

bacon. Add the corn and cook 5 minutes. Combine the eggs, salt, and pepper and pour them over the hot corn and bacon. Stir and cook until the eggs are cooked, about 5 to 10 minutes. *Makes 4 to 6 servings.*

Good also as luncheon or late supper main dish.

Quick Corn Pudding

4 eggs	1 1/3 cups milk
1 teaspoon salt	4 ears corn
1/8 teaspoon black pepper	Butter pat

Butter the top of a double boiler lightly; combine the eggs, salt, pepper, and milk and heat slightly. Slit the kernels on the corncob lengthwise and scrape out the pulp with the back of a knife. Add to the egg mixture and cook over boiling water 30 minutes or until the pudding is set. *Makes 4 to 6 servings.*

Rosy Cran-Apple Stuffing

1 cup Burgundy, claret, or other red table wine
¼ cup water
1 cup raw cranberries
1 cup chopped Washington apples
⅓ cup butter or margarine or rich drippings

1 package (8 ounces) seasoned stuffing mix
½ cup chopped walnuts
¼ cup finely chopped onion
1 teaspoon sugar
¼ teaspoon salt
½ teaspoon crushed tarragon leaves

Combine the wine, water, cranberries, apples, and butter in a saucepan. Bring to a boil, lower heat and simmer 5 minutes. Add to stuffing mix along with remaining ingredients. Mix lightly but thoroughly, adding a little more wine or water if more moist stuffing is desired. *Makes 1½ quarts.*

Serve with veal, duck, pork or turkey.

Eggplant Scallop

1 medium eggplant, cut in 1- to 1½-inch cubes
2 tablespoons butter or margarine
½ cup sliced onion
1 teaspoon crushed basil
1 medium clove garlic, minced

1 can (10¾ ounces) condensed tomato soup
½ cup water
¼ teaspoon salt
½ cup herb-seasoned stuffing mix
¼ cup grated Parmesan cheese

Preheat oven to 350°. Cook the eggplant in boiling salted water for 10 minutes; drain and place in 10″ x 6″ x 2″ baking dish. Melt butter or margarine in saucepan; add the onion, basil, and garlic and cook until the onion is tender. Add the soup, water and salt. Pour over the eggplant. Sprinkle with the stuffing and cheese. Bake 30 minutes. *Makes 4 to 6 servings.*

Fried Eggplant, Italian Style

1 large (1½ pounds) eggplant

¾ cup cooking oil

Salt and freshly ground black pepper
   to taste
2 ounces (4 tablespoons) grated

Parmesan cheese
Chopped parsley (garnish)

Peel the eggplant and cut into crosswise slices, ½ inch thick. Heat the oil in a skillet; add eggplant slices and fry until soft and brown on both sides. Sprinkle with the salt and pepper. Arrange the eggplant on a platter. Sprinkle each slice with the cheese and parsley. *Makes 4 servings.*

Stuffed Mushrooms

1½ pounds mushrooms
4 tablespoons butter or margarine
2 tablespoons salad oil
¾ cup finely diced onions
¾ teaspoon lemon juice
½ teaspoon salt

⅛ teaspoon black pepper
Pinch ground nutmeg
4 tablespoons chopped parsley
½ cup fresh bread crumbs
¼ cup grated Parmesan cheese

Remove the stems from the mushroom caps. Reserve the caps and finely dice the stems. Wash and drain the stems.

Use half the butter or margarine and ½ tablespoon of the oil to sauté the onions until they are golden brown. Add the mushroom stems and the lemon juice, salt, pepper, and nutmeg. Cook 4 or 5 minutes or until nearly dry. Add the parsley. Mix in ⅔ of the bread crumbs. Cool. Preheat oven to 350°. Wash and drain the mushroom caps. Season lightly with the salt and pepper and spread with a little oil. Fill the caps with the above mixture. Place on an oiled tray. Mix the remaining crumbs with the Parmesan cheese and sprinkle over the tops, drizzling the remaining butter or margarine over all. Bake 10 to 12 minutes. Serve immediately. *Makes 6 servings.*

Herbed Mustard Greens

2 pounds mustard greens
3 slices salt pork, 4 x ½ inch each
1½ teaspoons salt

½ teaspoon sugar
½ teaspoon marjoram leaves
⅛ teaspoon black pepper

Wash the mustard greens and cut off the root ends and coarse stems. Brown the salt pork in a heavy saucepan or Dutch oven. Add the mustard greens, salt, and sugar. Cover and cook over low heat about 5 minutes or until tender (cooking time will vary with the age of the greens). Add the marjoram and pepper and cook an additional 5 minutes. Chop very fine before serving. Serve at once on a hot platter. *Makes 6 servings.*

Long Parsnip (⅙ natural size)

Sweet Baked Parsnips

1 pound parsnips
2 tablespoons melted butter or

margarine
½ cup brown sugar

Scrape the parsnips and cook in a small amount of boiling water 30 minutes or until tender. Preheat oven to 400°. Cut in halves or quarters and place in baking dish. Brush with the melted butter and sprinkle with the brown sugar. Bake 25 minutes. *Makes 4 servings.*

Glazed Mustard Parsnips

8 boiled parsnips
2 tablespoons butter or margarine

2 tablespoons brown sugar
½ teaspoon dry mustard

Preheat oven to 400°. Cut each parsnip into eight wedges and place in a greased casserole. Dot with the butter or margarine. Mix the brown sugar and powdered mustard and sprinkle over the parsnips. Bake 20 minutes or until the vegetable is glazed and browned. *Makes 4 servings.*

Peas, French Style

2 pounds peas (2 cups shelled)	½ teaspoon sugar
6 lettuce leaves, shredded	1 teaspoon Accent
1 tablespoon finely chopped onion	2 tablespoons butter
¼ teaspoon salt	

Place all the ingredients in a saucepan; bring to a boil. Cover tightly, reduce heat, and cook 15 to 20 minutes, or until tender. *Makes 4 servings.*

Pennsylvania Dutch Potato Filling

¾ cup chopped celery	1 tablespoon parsley
½ cup chopped onion	½ tablespoon poultry seasoning
3 tablespoons butter or margarine	½ teaspoon thyme
1 package (8 ounces) cube stuffing	2 cups hot mashed potatoes, seasoned
1 egg, well beaten	to taste

Cook the celery and onion in the butter until tender. Meanwhile, prepare the cube stuffing according to package directions. Add the egg, seasonings, and mashed potatoes. Stir and place in 1½-quart casserole. Bake, covered, last 30 minutes of roasting time. *Makes 6 servings.*

Delicious and unusual stuffing for 5-pound roast chicken. Use also to stuff shoulder of veal or pork.

Barbecue Potato Casserole

1 quart cubed hot boiled potatoes	¼ teaspoon dried dill
½ cup sauterne or other white dinner wine	½ teaspoon garlic salt
	1 tablespoon wine vinegar
¼ cup salad oil	¼ cup mayonnaise
4 or 5 green onions, finely chopped	½ cup dairy sour cream

Gently combine the hot potatoes, wine, oil, onion, dill, salt and vinegar; marinate for 1 hour. Preheat oven to 350°. Add the mayonnaise and sour cream and turn into a small casserole or baking pan. Bake in the oven or on a barbecue grill until the potatoes are hot, about 20 to 30 minutes. *Makes 5 or 6 servings.*

Cottage Cheese–stuffed Potatoes

4 medium baking potatoes
¼ cup soft-type margarine
  containing liquid safflower oil
¾ cup creamed cottage cheese
¾ teaspoon salt

½ teaspoon Accent
1 teaspoon dried dill weed
1 egg
¼ teaspoon Tabasco

Preheat oven to 425°. Scrub the potatoes well; dry them. Prick the potatoes with a fork to let the steam escape during baking. Bake 1 hour or until tender when tested with a fork. Immediately cut the potatoes in half. Carefully scoop out the pulp without breaking the skin. Mash it well; add the margarine, cheese, salt, Accent, dill, egg and Tabasco. Beat until well mixed. Spoon the mixture into the potato shells. Return the potatoes to the oven and bake 20 minutes, until lightly browned. *Makes 4 to 8 servings.*

French Potato Pie

4 tablespoons soft-type margarine or
  melted butter
1 pound (3 medium) potatoes, pared
1½ teaspoons salt
1 teaspoon Accent
1 cup (4 ounces) coarsely shredded
  Swiss cheese

½ cup chopped onion
2 eggs
1 cup milk
½ teaspoon Tabasco
2 tablespoons chopped parsley
½ teaspoon paprika
¼ teaspoon dry mustard

Preheat oven to 375°. Brush 2 tablespoons of the margarine or butter over the bottom and side of a 9-inch pie plate. Grate the potatoes on coarse or medium grater; drain well. Sprinkle with 1 teaspoon of the salt and the Accent; mix well. Press the potato mixture over the bottom and side of the pie plate to form a shell. Sprinkle with the cheese. Heat the remaining butter or margarine in a small skillet. Add the onion and cook over medium heat until tender but not brown. Sprinkle over the cheese. Beat the eggs slightly. Add the remaining ½ teaspoon salt, milk, and remaining ingredients; mix well. Pour over the onion and cheese in pie plate. Bake 40 to 45 minutes, until the edge of the pie is golden brown and a knife inserted in the center comes out clean. Let stand 5 to 10 minutes before cutting. *Makes 6 to 8 servings.*

German Potato Pancakes

1½ pounds (4 medium) potatoes,
    pared
1 small onion, grated
1 egg
¼ teaspoon Tabasco
2 tablespoons all-purpose flour
½ teaspoon Accent

½ teaspoon salt
⅛ teaspoon nutmeg
3 tablespoons butter or soft-type
    margarine containing liquid
    safflower oil
Sour cream or applesauce (topping)

Grate the potatoes on medium grater; drain well. Stir in the onion. Add the egg, Tabasco, and flour. Sprinkle with the Accent, salt, and nutmeg; mix thoroughly. Heat 1 tablespoon of the butter or margarine in a skillet over medium heat. Drop the potato mixture by rounded tablespoonfuls into skillet. Spread into flat cakes. Fry until golden brown on the bottom side. Turn and brown on the other side. Add additional margarine or butter as needed. Serve with sour cream or applesauce. *Makes 12 pancakes.*

Deviled Stuffed Potatoes

6 medium baking potatoes
4 tablespoons butter or margarine
1 teaspoon Accent
½ to ¾ cup hot milk
1 can (4½ ounces) deviled ham

¾ cup shredded Cheddar cheese
6 tablespoons chopped chives
Butter or margarine bits
Paprika

Preheat oven to 450°. Select potatoes of uniform size so that they will bake evenly. Scrub the potatoes well; dry them. Bake 45 minutes to 1 hour or until tender when tested with a fork. Cut a slice from the top of each. Scoop out the centers, taking care not to break the skin. Mash the potatoes or put through a ricer. Add the butter, Accent, and enough milk to make a fluffy mixture. Add the ham, cheese, and chives and beat until light and fluffy. Season with salt to taste. Heap the mixture into the shells; dot with the additional butter. Sprinkle with paprika. Return to oven and bake 10 minutes longer. *Makes 6 servings.*

Colcannon Potatoes

1½ pounds (4 medium) potatoes,
    pared and quartered
6 tablespoons butter or margarine
    (the soft type made with liquid
    safflower oil)
2 cups shredded cabbage

6 whole scallions, sliced
⅓ cup hot milk
1 teaspoon Accent
¾ teaspoon salt
¼ teaspoon Tabasco

Cook the potatoes in unsalted boiling water until tender, 20 to 25 minutes. While the potatoes are cooking, melt 5 tablespoons of the butter or margarine in a saucepan over low heat. Add the cabbage and scallions. Cook tightly covered over low heat until tender, about 5 minutes. When the potatoes are tender, drain well. Mash until no lumps remain. Gradually add the hot milk and beat until fluffy and creamy. Sprinkle with the Accent, salt, and Tabasco; mix well. Add the cabbage and scallions; mix well and turn into a serving dish. Make a "well" in center with the back of a spoon and add the remaining tablespoon of butter or soft margarine. *Makes 6 servings.*

Colcannon Potatoes with Kale

2 pounds (5 or 6 medium) potatoes
2½ teaspoons salt
3 cups finely cut kale
3 tablespoons minced onion

3 tablespoons butter or margarine
⅛ teaspoon black pepper
1 to 2 tablespoons milk

Peel and quarter the potatoes. Place in a saucepan with 1 inch boiling water and ½ teaspoon of the salt. Cover and cook until the potatoes are tender, 15 to 20 minutes. Drain and mash until smooth. Preheat oven to 350°.

In the meantime, cook the kale in 1 inch boiling water and ½ teaspoon of the salt until tender, about 15 minutes. Sauté the onion in 1½ tablespoons of the butter or margarine. Combine with the potatoes, kale, remaining salt, pepper and milk. Beat until smooth. Turn into a shallow baking dish. Dot with the remaining butter and bake just long enough to heat thoroughly. *Makes 6 servings.*

Mushroom-stuffed Potatoes

3 large potatoes
⅔ teaspoon salt

⅛ teaspoon black pepper
½ cup hot milk

⅓ cup finely chopped mushrooms   ½ teaspoon lemon juice
1 ½ tablespoons butter or margarine   1 cup sliced mushrooms

Preheat oven to 450°. Bake the potatoes for one hour or until soft. Cut them in half and scoop out the inside, mashing the pulp thoroughly and reserving the shells. Add the salt, pepper, and milk.

Sauté the mushrooms in the butter or margarine and lemon juice. Add them to the potatoes and beat until fluffy. Pile mixture lightly into the shells. Return them to the oven and bake until lightly brown, 8 to 10 minutes. Garnish with the sliced mushrooms. *Makes 6 servings.*

Fresh Sweet Potato and Cheese Casserole

2 pounds sweet potatoes   2 tablespoons butter or margarine
2 tablespoons sugar   ½ cup milk
½ teaspoon salt   ½ cup grated sharp American cheese
⅛ teaspoon black pepper

Wash the sweet potatoes and place in a saucepan with 2 cups of boiling water. Cover and cook until tender, 30 to 40 minutes. Preheat oven to 350°.

"Rose de Malaga" Sweet Potato
(⅛ natural size)

Drain potatoes and slip off the skins. Slice and arrange them in layers in a buttered 1-quart casserole, sprinkling each layer with the sugar, salt, and pepper. Dot with the butter or margarine and pour the milk over all. Bake, uncovered, 30 minutes. Sprinkle with the cheese and bake 15 minutes more. *Makes 4 to 6 servings.*

Sweet Potato Cran-Apple Casserole

4 medium sweet potatoes
1 ½ cups cranberry relish
2 cups sliced tart apples
1 ½ teaspoons salt

⅛ teaspoon black pepper
¼ cup sugar
2 tablespoons butter or margarine

Preheat oven to 375°. Wash and peel the sweet potatoes; cut them into ¼-inch-thick slices. Reserve some relish and a few apple slices. In a 1 ½-quart casserole alternate layers of the sweet potatoes, cranberry relish, and apples, *ending with the apples.* Combine the salt, pepper, and sugar, and sprinkle it over each layer lightly. Dot with the butter or margarine. Cover. Bake 1 hour. Uncover and bake 30 minutes longer, basting frequently. Garnish with the reserved apple slices and cranberry relish. *Makes 6 servings.*

Harvest Sweet Potatoes

¼ cup butter or margarine
⅓ cup brown sugar, packed
¼ teaspoon salt
½ cup orange marmalade

¼ cup sherry
¼ cup light or dark raisins
4 to 6 cooked sweet potatoes,
   quartered

Preheat oven to 325°. Combine butter, brown sugar, salt, marmalade, and wine in a saucepan. Bring to a boil, stirring occasionally, and cook 3 minutes. Rinse and drain raisins. Add to sauce mixture. Arrange sweet potatoes in a shallow buttered casserole. Pour sauce over potatoes. Cover the casserole and bake 45 minutes. *Makes 4 to 6 servings.*

Braised Radishes

2 tablespoons butter or margarine
2 cups sliced radishes
1 bouillon cube

¼ cup hot water
⅛ teaspoon ground marjoram
¼ teaspoon salt

Melt the butter or margarine in a saucepan. Add the sliced radishes and cook for 5 minutes. Dissolve the bouillon cube in the hot water and stir into the radishes. Add the marjoram and salt and simmer for 3 to 4 minutes. *Makes 4 servings.*

French-fried Radishes

Vegetable or salad oil
½ cup cracker meal
¼ teaspoon salt

⅛ teaspoon black pepper
2 cups sliced radishes, ¼ inch thick
1 large egg, beaten

Preheat deep fat in frying pan to 375° on a frying thermometer. Wash and slice the radishes. Drain on absorbent paper. Combine the cracker meal, salt, and pepper. Dip the radish slices, a few at a time, into the seasoned cracker meal, then into the beaten egg, and again into the cracker meal. Fry in the deep fat until crisp and golden. Drain on absorbent paper and sprinkle with salt, if desired. *Makes 4 servings.*

Baked Rutabaga Cheese Chips

1 pound rutabagas
1 teaspoon salt
½ teaspoon sugar

¼ cup melted butter or margarine
1½ cups grated sharp Cheddar
   cheese

Wash and peel the rutabagas. If they are small, leave them whole; if they are large, cut them into quarters or eighths. Place them in a saucepan with 1 inch boiling water, the salt, and sugar. Cover, bring to a boil, and cook until almost tender, about 20 to 25 minutes. (Cooking time depends upon the size of the rutabagas.) Lift lid two to three times while cooking to give them a milder flavor. Preheat oven to 350°. Remove the rutabagas from the water and cool slightly. Cut them into thin slices about ⅛ inch thick. Dip them in the melted butter or margarine and then in the grated cheese. Place in a buttered baking dish. Bake 30 minutes or until browned. *Makes 6 servings.*

Rutabaga Pudding

4 cups diced potatoes
4 cups diced rutabagas
1¾ to 2 teaspoons salt
4 tablespoons butter or margarine

4 egg yolks
1 teaspoon sugar
¼ teaspoon white pepper
1 tablespoon finely chopped onion

Cook the potatoes and rutabagas in separate saucepans 20 minutes or until tender in 1 inch boiling water and almost 1 teaspoon of the salt. Drain and mash each separately. Place the rutabagas over low heat to evaporate excess moisture. Preheat oven to 400° Combine the potatoes, rutabagas, butter or margarine, egg yolks, sugar, the remaining teaspoon of salt, the pepper, and onion. Mix well. Reserve 2 cups of the mixture. Turn the remaining mixture into a buttered 1-quart casserole. Put the reserved mixture in a pastry bag or tube and make rosettes over the top, covering the entire surface. Brown 30 minutes. Serve hot. *Makes 6 servings.*

Scallions on Toast with Cheese Sauce

3 bunches scallions	2 cups White Sauce (page 72)
½ teaspoon salt	½ cup grated sharp Cheddar cheese
6 slices toast	12 strips crisp bacon

Remove the root ends of the scallions and peel the paper-thin skin covering the bulbs. Remove the green tops to within 3 inches of the bulb. Place in a saucepan with the salt and 1 inch boiling water. Cover. Boil *only* until tender, 8 or 10 minutes. Lift cover two or three times during cooking period for acids to escape so that the flavor will be milder and to help the tops retain their green color. Drain; reserve the cooking water to use as part of the liquid in making the White Sauce. Place the scallions on the toast. Stir the cheese into the White Sauce and spoon over the scallions. Top each serving with two strips of the bacon. *Makes 6 servings.*

Squash Supreme

4 cups diced yellow squash	1 cup dairy sour cream
2 tablespoons grated onion	Salt and black pepper
½ cup grated carrot	2 cups herb-seasoned stuffing
1 can (10½ ounces) cream of chicken soup	3 tablespoons butter

Preheat oven to 350°. Cook the squash in about 1½ cups of salted water until tender, about 10 minutes. Drain and mash. Add the onion, carrot, soup, and sour cream. Add salt and pepper to taste. Butter a 2-quart shallow casserole. Sprinkle half the stuffing on the bottom. Cover with the squash mixture. Top with the remaining stuffing. Dot with the butter. Bake for 30 minutes. *Makes 8 to 10 servings.*

Fresh Tomatoes and Peas

3 large ripe tomatoes
Salt and pepper to taste
¼ cup mayonnaise
3 green olives, chopped

1 tablespoon capers
1 tablespoon chopped cucumber pickle
1 cup cold cooked peas
Chopped parsley

Wash the tomatoes, cut them in half, and sprinkle with salt and pepper. Let them stand for 30 minutes to obtain the juice. Drain the juice from the tomatoes and add to the mayonnaise along with the olives, capers, cucumber pickle, and peas. Combine carefully and heap the mixture on top of the halved tomatoes. Garnish with the parsley and serve as a salad or accompaniment for fish, meat or potato dishes. *Makes 6 servings.*

Chinese Braised Turnips

6 medium (2 pounds) turnips
3 tablespoons olive or corn oil
½ teaspoon salt
½ cup water

¼ cup chopped scallions
1½ tablespoons soy sauce
¼ teaspoon black pepper
¾ teaspoon sugar

Peel the turnips and shred on a coarse shredder. Heat the oil in a skillet, add the turnips, and sauté 1 minute, stirring constantly. Add the salt and water. Cover and cook over low heat 10 minutes. Stir in the scallions, soy sauce, pepper, and sugar. *Makes 6 servings.*

Herbed Turnip Greens

¼ pound salt pork
1 cup water
2½ pounds turnip greens (in 1¼-
   pound prepacked bags)

1½ teaspoons salt
1 teaspoon sugar
½ teaspoon marjoram leaves
⅛ teaspoon black pepper

Wash the salt pork and cut into four pieces. Place in a large saucepan with the water. Cover and cook 20 minutes or until the pork is almost done. In the meantime, wash the turnip greens thoroughly and cut off the coarse stems. Add them to the pork along with the salt, sugar, marjoram, and pepper. Cover and cook 15 minutes or until the greens and the pork are tender. Serve with corn bread and roast pork or pork chops or hog jowls and black-eyed peas. *Makes 6 servings.*

Planked Vegetables

2 cups potatoes, boiled and mashed
½ cup warm milk
2 tablespoons butter
6 tablespoons grated Parmesan
  cheese
2 egg yolks, lightly beaten
½ cup melted butter or margarine
1 bunch (1½ pounds) carrots, boiled

and buttered
1½ pounds peas, boiled and buttered

GLAZED ONIONS
3 tablespoons butter
¼ cup brown sugar
1 tablespoon sauterne
1½ pounds small boiled onions

Preheat oven to 450°. Stir the warm milk, butter, 4 tablespoons of the cheese and the egg yolks into the cooked mashed potatoes until creamy. Spoon into pastry bag fitted with large star tube and pipe around the edge of a plank or heatproof platter. (Or make a border with small spoonfuls of the potato.) Drizzle with the melted butter and sprinkle with the remaining 2 tablespoons of cheese. Arrange the Glazed Onions and carrots inside the potato border. Bake about 10 to 15 minutes, until the potatoes are lightly browned and the vegetables heated. Fill in the spaces between the other vegetables with the peas, and serve at once. *Makes 8 servings as a side dish, 4 as a main dish.*

Note. If the vegetables are prepared in advance and refrigerated, baking time should be increased slightly.

GLAZED ONIONS. Melt the butter in skillet; add the brown sugar and sauterne. Add the onions and cook over low heat about 15 minutes, turning frequently.

Vegetables Plus

6 medium round potatoes, unpeeled
6 medium carrots
½ head cabbage, coarsely shredded
Salt and pepper
2 chicken bouillon cubes

1½ teaspoons butter or margarine
1½ teaspoons lemon juice
1 tablespoon chopped parsley
1 chopped green onion

Cook the potatoes and carrots in a large Dutch oven, covered, in 1 inch water for 30 minutes, or until fork-tender. Meanwhile, prepare a "steaming basket" so that the cabbage can steam without flavor transfer: Cut a piece of aluminum foil to cover the potatoes and carrots completely and make about ten slits in it. Ten minutes before the potatoes and carrots are done, place the foil tray over the vegetables in Dutch oven; add the cabbage shreds.

Cook until the cabbage is tender-crisp and the potatoes and carrots are tender.

Remove the vegetables with a slotted spoon and arrange on a serving platter. Sprinkle with the salt and pepper and cover to keep warm. To the remaining liquid in the Dutch oven, add enough water to make 1½ cups. Bring to a boil. Add the bouillon cubes, stirring to dissolve. Stir in the remaining ingredients. Pour some of the hot sauce over the vegetables before serving. Pass the remaining sauce in a gravy boat. *Makes 6 servings.*

Glazed Vegetable Medley

1 pound or 4 medium onions, carrots, parsnips, or sweet potatoes or 2 acorn squashes
2 tablespoons butter or margarine

¼ cup dark corn syrup
Salt and pepper

Preheat oven to 400°. Wash and pare the vegetables. Cut in halves, quarters, or slice as desired for serving. Cook in boiling salted water until tender. Drain. (Sweet potatoes can be cooked first, then pared, if desired.) Arrange the cooked vegetables in a greased ovenproof casserole. Dot with the butter or margarine, then add the corn syrup. Sprinkle with the salt, pepper, and other seasonings as desired. Spices and herbs add flavor interest. Bake 15 minutes or until the vegetables are well glazed. Baste often with the syrup mixture in casserole. *Makes 4 to 5 servings.*

TO PREPARE WITHOUT PRECOOKING: Arrange pieces of the pared cut-up vegetables in a greased ovenproof casserole. Dot with the butter or margarine, add the syrup and seasonings as above. Cover tightly. Bake 35 to 50 minutes or until the vegetables are tender. Uncover and bake 15 minutes more, basting often with the syrupy mixture in casserole.

Meat Substitute Dishes

Tuna Cassoulet

1 onion, chopped
1 clove garlic
2 links of sausage, chopped
3 carrots, sliced
½ teaspoon salt
¼ teaspoon Tabasco
2 cans (1 pound, 4 ounces *each*)

white beans or 2 cups (1 pound)
dry pea beans cooked according
to package directions and drained
2 cans (6½ or 7 ounces *each*) tuna
in vegetable oil
½ cup bread crumbs
Chopped parsley

Preheat oven to 400°. Into a deep, oven-proof 10-cup earthenware pot or casserole, put the onion, garlic, sausage, and carrots. Sprinkle with the salt and Tabasco; sauté about 10 minutes. Stir in the beans and tuna with its oil. Add enough water to cover the ingredients. Sprinkle with the bread crumbs. Bake about 30 minutes, until the casserole is bubbly. Sprinkle with the parsley. *Makes 6 servings.*

Southwest Chili Beans

1 pound pink or red beans
1 quart (4 cups) boiling water
1 large onion, chopped

1 clove garlic, chopped
6 slices bacon, cut fine
1 can (8 ounces) tomato sauce

1 cup claret, Burgundy, or other red table wine
2 teaspoons chili powder

½ teaspoon cumin seed
Salt to taste

Wash the beans; soak overnight in cold water. Drain. Put the beans in a heavy kettle with the boiling water, onion, garlic, bacon, tomato sauce, wine, chili powder, cumin seed, and salt. Cover; simmer very gently until the beans are tender and the sauce is rich and thick, 4 to 5 hours. Stir often, adding a little more water if needed. *Makes 6 to 8 servings.*

Mexican Tuna Chili Pot

2 cans (6½ or 7 ounces *each*) tuna in vegetable oil
2 tablespoons finely chopped onion
1 can (1 pound) tomatoes

1 can (1 pound) kidney beans
2 teaspoons chili powder
1 package (10 to 12 ounces) corn bread mix

Preheat oven to 425°. Drain 2 tablespoons of oil from the tuna into a large skillet. Add the onion and cook until tender, but not brown. Add the tomatoes, kidney beans, tuna, and chili powder; bring to a boil. Reduce heat and simmer about 10 minutes. Prepare the corn bread according to package directions. Turn the chili mixture into a 2-quart casserole. Drop the corn bread mixture by rounded tablespoonfuls in 6 mounds on top. Spoon the remaining corn bread mixture into 6 greased 2½-inch muffin cups. Place the casserole and muffin pan in the oven. Bake the muffins 10 to 15 minutes; bake the casserole 18 to 20 minutes or until the corn bread is golden brown. *Makes 6 servings.*

Tuna Orientale

2 cans (6½ or 7 ounces *each*) tuna in vegetable oil
1 cup sliced scallions
1 sliced green pepper
1 sliced red pepper

2 cups diagonally sliced celery
1 can (6 ounces) broiled mushroom slices
½ teaspoon Accent
1 tablespoon soy sauce

Drain the oil from the tuna into a large heavy skillet; reserve the tuna. Add the scallions, peppers, and celery. Cook 5 minutes. Stir while cooking. Mix in the mushroom slices, mushroom liquid, and tuna. Stir while frying about

3 minutes longer. Sprinkle with the Accent and soy sauce. Serve with hot cooked rice. *Makes 4 to 6 servings.*

Broccoli-bedded Eggs

4 medium potatoes, pared and
  quartered
2 tablespoons milk
2 cups cooked, drained broccoli
¼ cup chopped onion
¼ cup shredded Cheddar cheese
¼ teaspoon Tabasco
¾ teaspoon salt
¼ teaspoon dried leaf marjoram
4 eggs

CHEDDAR CHEESE SAUCE
2 tablespoons butter
2 tablespoons flour
2½ cups milk
¼ teaspoon dried leaf marjoram
¼ teaspoon Tabasco
¾ teaspoon salt
½ cup shredded Cheddar cheese

Preheat oven to 400°. Cook the potatoes in the water until tender, 20 to 25 minutes. Drain well and mash in a large bowl with the milk. Stir in the broccoli and the remaining ingredients except the eggs. Make nests in 4 greased individual ramekins and bake 20 minutes. Lower oven to 350°. Break an egg into each potato nest. Bake 7 minutes, or until the eggs are set. Serve with Cheddar Cheese Sauce. *Makes 4 servings.*

CHEDDAR CHEESE SAUCE. Melt the butter in medium saucepan; blend in the flour. Remove from heat and stir in the milk. Return to heat and bring to a boil over low heat, stirring constantly. Add the remaining ingredients and cook, continuing to stir until the cheese melts. *Makes about 2 cups.*

Speedy Tuna Divan

⅓ cup milk
1 can (10¾ ounces) condensed
  Cheddar cheese soup, undiluted
2 cans (6½ or 7 ounces *each*) tuna in

vegetable oil
1 tablespoon lemon juice
2½ cups cooked broccoli (or
  asparagus), drained

Gradually add the milk to the soup in a saucepan and heat, stirring frequently. Add the tuna and heat. Stir in the lemon juice. Place the broccoli or asparagus on serving platter. Top with the tuna-cheese sauce. *Makes 4 servings.*

Note. If desired, the asparagus or broccoli may be placed in a shallow baking dish or ovenproof platter. Top with the tuna-cheese sauce and place under the broiler heat for a few minutes to brown lightly.

Cabbage and Cracker Pie

1 box (3½ ounces) soda crackers, about 20	1½ teaspoon salt
1 quart finely shredded cabbage	¼ teaspoon celery seed
1⅓ cups milk	¼ teaspoon black pepper
	¼ cup butter or margarine

Preheat oven to 350°. Crumble the crackers coarsely and sprinkle half over bottom of a well-greased 10-inch pie plate. Fill pie plate with the cabbage.

Large Flat Dutch Drumhead Cabbage
(1/12 natural size)

Top with the remaining crumbs. Heat the milk with the seasonings and 3 tablespoons of the butter or margarine. Pour over the cabbage. Bake about 50 minutes. Dot top with the remaining tablespoon of butter or margarine about 10 minutes before the pie is done. *Makes 6 servings.*

Corn and Mushroom Casserole

2 tablespoons butter or margarine	2 eggs, lightly beaten
2 teaspoons lemon juice	1 teaspoon salt
1 tablespoon minced onion	⅛ teaspoon black pepper
2 cups sliced mushrooms	½ teaspoon poultry seasoning
2 cups corn cut off the cob	½ cup grated sharp American cheese

Preheat oven to 350°. Mix together the butter and lemon juice and heat in a skillet. Add the onion and mushrooms and sauté until the mushrooms are tender. Combine with the corn, eggs, salt, pepper, and poultry seasoning. Turn into a buttered 1-quart casserole placed in a pan of hot water. Bake 1 hour. Sprinkle the top of the casserole with the grated cheese about 10 minutes before baking time is up. *Makes 4 to 6 servings.*

Creamed Cauliflower Casserole

1 medium head cauliflower	⅛ teaspoon pepper
3 tablespoons butter or margarine	1 package (8 ounces) herb-seasoned
¼ cup flour	stuffing
2 cups milk	1 cup water
¾ teaspoon salt	½ cup melted butter or margarine

Preheat oven to 350°. Break the cauliflower into small pieces (flowerets) and cook until just tender in small amount of boiling salted water. Drain and place in a shallow 2-quart casserole. Melt the butter or margarine in a medium saucepan. Stir in the flour and cook a few minutes, stirring. Remove from heat and blend in the milk and seasonings. Return to heat and bring to a boil, stirring constantly, and simmer until thickened. Pour over the cauliflower. Combine the stuffing, water, and the melted butter or margarine and spoon on top, pressing down if necessary. Bake for 30 minutes. *Makes 8 to 10 servings.*

Eggplant Hungarian

2 large eggplants	PAPRIKA SAUCE
1 pint plain yoghurt or sour cream	2 tablespoons butter
½ cup olive oil	1 onion, finely chopped
1 pound ripe tomatoes	1 teaspoon paprika
1 clove garlic, crushed	1 teaspoon flour
1 bay leaf	½ pound ripe tomatoes
2 teaspoons dried thyme or basil	Salt and pepper to taste
Paprika	1 cup beef bouillon
Salt and pepper	2 tablespoons medium cream
	½ teaspoon lemon juice

Slice the eggplant. Sprinkle with salt and allow to stand for 30 minutes. Preheat the oven to 350°. Peel, seed, and mash the tomatoes and simmer with the garlic, bay leaf, and thyme to a thick pulp. Season the eggplant slices generously with salt, pepper, and paprika and place in a shallow casserole in thin layers with the tomato pulp and the yoghurt. Cover and bake 30 to 40 minutes. Serve topped with additional yoghurt or Paprika Sauce. *Makes 4 servings.*

PAPRIKA SAUCE. Melt the butter in a saucepan; add the onion, and cook, covered, until the onion is soft, about 2 or 3 minutes. Add the paprika and continue cooking another 3 minutes. Sprinkle the mixture lightly with the flour; add the tomatoes, salt and pepper, and bouillon and bring to a boil. Simmer gently about 30 minutes and strain. Reheat carefully and, stirring constantly, add the cream and lemon juice. Serve at once. *Makes about 2½ cups.*

Leek Soufflé

8 medium leeks	1 cup milk
4 tablespoons butter or margarine	½ teaspoon grated nutmeg
1 teaspoon salt	4 eggs, separated
¼ teaspoon black pepper	⅓ cup bread crumbs
½ cup sifted flour	

Wash the leeks and cut into 1-inch pieces. Cook in boiling salted water until tender, approximately 15 to 20 minutes after water returns to boil. Drain thoroughly. Chop the leeks and return to the pan with 1 tablespoon of the butter or margarine. Season lightly with the salt and pepper and cook over low heat until the butter or margarine is absorbed and the vegetables are dry. Preheat oven to 350°. Melt the remaining butter or margarine in saucepan; remove from heat. Add the flour, mix well; add the milk. Return the mixture to the heat and stir until boiling. Remove from the heat; add remaining salt, pepper, and nutmeg. Add the egg yolks and beat well. Pour the mixture over the leeks and mix gently together. Whip the egg whites in a separate bowl with a wire whisk until they peak stiffly when whisk is drawn out and gently fold into the leek mixture. Turn into soufflé dish; dust surfaces of the leek mixture with the bread crumbs and bake 20 minutes. *Makes 5 to 6 servings.*

Mushrooms and Hard-Cooked Eggs in Sour Cream

⅓ cup butter or margarine	¾ pound fresh mushrooms, sliced
½ cup finely chopped onion	(about 3¾ cups)

1 teaspoon caraway seed

2 teaspoons lemon juice

¼ cup flour

1 teaspoon salt

⅛ teaspoon black pepper

¾ cup milk

1 cup dairy sour cream

4 hard-cooked eggs, quartered

¼ cup chopped parsley

Toast or English muffin halves

Paprika (garnish)

Heat the butter or margarine in a large skillet. Add the onion, mushrooms, and caraway seed; sprinkle with the lemon juice. Sauté for 3 to 5 minutes. Combine the flour, salt, and pepper. Blend into the mushroom mixture; cook until the mixture bubbles, stirring constantly. Add the milk. Cook until thickened, stirring constantly. Mix in the sour cream. Gently add the eggs. Heat only until hot. Sprinkle with the parsley and serve immediately on the toast. Garnish with paprika. *Makes 4 to 6 servings.*

Puffy Omelet Piperade

2 tablespoons butter or margarine

2 cups pared potatoes, cut into very thin strips

¼ cup chopped onion

¼ clove garlic, minced

¼ cup chopped celery

4 eggs, separated

¼ cup water

¼ teaspoon salt

¼ teaspoon Tabasco

Preheat oven to 325°. Melt 1 tablespoon of the butter or margarine in large skillet; add the potatoes, onion, garlic, and celery. Cook over low heat until the vegetables are tender, stirring occasionally. Remove from the heat. In a small bowl beat the egg yolks until thick and lemon colored. In another bowl (with clean beaters) beat egg whites until frothy; add water, salt, and Tabasco and beat until stiff peaks form. Fold the yolks into the whites along with the potato mixture. Melt the remaining 1 tablespoon butter or margarine in the same skillet. Pour in the egg mixture. Cook over low heat 5 minutes. Bake 8 minutes until puffed and browned. *Makes 4 servings.*

Potato-Cheese Soufflé

2 cups mashed potatoes

1 cup grated sharp Cheddar cheese, about 4 ounces

1 tablespoon finely chopped onion

1 teaspoon Accent

½ teaspoon salt

½ teaspoon Tabasco

6 eggs, separated

Preheat oven to 375°. While the mashed potatoes are still warm but removed from heat, stir in the cheese. Add the onion, Accent, salt, and Tabasco. Beat the egg yolks with a fork; reserve. Beat the egg whites until stiff peaks form. Stir the egg yolks rapidly into the potato mixture. Fold in the egg whites. Turn into 2½-quart casserole and bake 35 to 40 minutes. *Makes 6 servings.*

Sweet Potatoes and Apples with Maple Syrup

2 pounds (6 medium) sweet potatoes	¾ cup maple or maple-flavored
1½ pounds (3 large) baking apples	syrup
2 tablespoons butter or margarine	1⁄16 teaspoon salt

Preheat oven to 350°. Wash the sweet potatoes and place in boiling water to cover. Cook, covered, 20 to 30 minutes, or until the potatoes are tender. Drain the potatoes and peel off the skins. Cut into crosswise slices ¼ inch thick. Wash, peel, quarter, core, and slice the apples ⅛ inch thick. Place half the sweet potatoes in a 1½-quart casserole. Top with half the apples, half the butter or margarine, and half the syrup mixed with salt. Repeat, using the remaining ingredients. Cover and bake 30 minutes. Remove cover and cook 10 more minutes. *Makes 6 to 8 servings.*

Late-seeding, or Long-stander, Spinach
(⅓ natural size)

Indian Spinach and Cottage Cheese (Sag Paneer)

¼ cup butter	2½ cups boiled spinach
½ teaspoon turmeric	⅔ cup creamy cottage cheese
1 teaspoon coriander	1 tablespoon dairy sour cream
1 teaspoon salt	

Melt the butter in a 1½-quart saucepan. Add the spices and the salt. Stir and cook over low heat about 5 minutes. Add the cooked (can be leftover) spinach; cover and cook over moderate heat until heated through. Mix the cottage cheese and sour cream. Beat to form fine curds. Add to the hot spinach and stir until thoroughly blended. Serve hot. *Makes 8 servings.*

Tuna and Pasta Florentine

2 cans (6½ or 7 ounces *each*) tuna
   in vegetable oil
1 clove garlic
1 can (6 ounces) broiled mushroom
   crowns
1 bay leaf
½ teaspoon salt

¼ teaspoon dry basil leaves
½ teaspoon Tabasco
1 can (15 ounces) tomato sauce
1 package (8 ounces) broad noodles,
   cooked
4 cups boiled spinach
½ cup grated Parmesan cheese

Preheat oven to 400°. Drain the oil from the tuna into a skillet. Add the garlic, drained mushroom crowns (reserving the liquid), bay leaf, salt, basil, and Tabasco. Sauté about 10 minutes. Add the reserved mushroom liquid, tomato sauce, and tuna liquid. In a 2-quart casserole, alternate layers of the noodles, spinach, and tuna in the sauce. Save some of the spinach and mushrooms for garnish, if desired. Sprinkle casserole with the Parmesan cheese. Bake about 20 minutes. *Makes 6 servings.*

Tomato and Brussels Sprout Casserole

2 cups soft bread crumbs
3 tablespoons melted butter or
   margarine
1 large basket Brussels sprouts

4 medium tomatoes
2 teaspoons salt
¼ teaspoon black pepper

Preheat oven to 375°. Mix the bread crumbs with the butter or margarine, reserving ⅓ cup of the bread crumbs. Soak the Brussels sprouts in cold, salted water (1 teaspoon salt to 1 quart water). Wash well and cut each in half. Slice the tomatoes ½ inch thick. Arrange alternate layers of the tomatoes and the Brussels sprouts in a greased 6-cup casserole, beginning and ending with the tomatoes. Sprinkle each layer with the salt, pepper, and bread crumbs except for the top layer. Cover. Bake 45 minutes or until tender. Remove cover. Sprinkle the remaining crumbs over the top. Bake 10 minutes or until the crumbs are brown. *Makes 6 to 8 servings.*

Tomato Quiche

2 large ripe tomatoes
¼ cup flour
½ teaspoon salt
⅛ teaspoon coarsely ground black
  pepper
2 tablespoons butter or margarine
½ cup sliced ripe olives

¾ cup minced scallions
3 slices Provolone cheese
2 eggs, slightly beaten
1 cup milk
1 cup grated Cheddar cheese
Chopped parsley

Preheat oven to 350°. Wash the tomatoes and cut them into slices ½ inch thick. Mix the flour with the salt and pepper. Coat each tomato slice with this mixture and sauté quickly in the butter or margarine. Arrange the olives and scallions in the bottom of a buttered 8-inch square casserole. Top with the Provolone cheese and tomatoes. Combine the eggs, milk, and grated cheese and pour into the casserole. Bake 1 hour or until the filling is set. Remove from oven and sprinkle with the parsley. Serve hot. *Makes 6 servings.*

Tuna Manhattan Chowder

2 cans (6½ or 7 ounces *each*) tuna
  in vegetable oil
1 small onion, sliced
1 can (1 pound) tomatoes
3 cups water

1 envelope (2 or 2½ ounces) dry
  vegetable soup mix
½ teaspoon dried leaf thyme
1 can (12 ounce) whole kernel corn

Drain 2 tablespoons of oil from the tuna into a large saucepan. Add the onion and cook until tender but not brown. Cut up the tomatoes and add to the onion with the tomato liquid, water, soup mix, and thyme. Bring to a boil, stirring occasionally; cover and cook over medium heat for 10 minutes. Stir in the tuna and cover with the liquid. Heat to serving temperature, about 5 minutes. Serve in a tureen with crusty bread. *Makes about 2 quarts or 8 servings.*

Baked Tomato Pie

9-inch pie shell
6 underripe tomatoes, sliced
1½ teaspoons salt

¼ teaspoon black pepper
¼ teaspoon garlic powder
½ cup grated Parmesan cheese

Preheat oven to 350°. Fill pie shell with the sliced tomatoes and sprinkle with the salt, pepper, and garlic. Top with the grated cheese. Bake 20 minutes or until browned. *Makes 4 servings.*

Pilaf à la Grecque

½ pound rice
3 tablespoons butter
1 large onion, sliced thin
2 cloves garlic, crushed with salt
¼ cup prunes
⅛ cup dried apricots
¼ cup seedless raisins
1½ cups ripe tomatoes, peeled,

seeded, and chopped
1 bay leaf
Juice of half a lemon
1½ cups vegetable bouillon
Pinch of saffron
Salt and pepper
Rind of one medium orange, finely
shredded and blanched

Preheat oven to 325°. Cook the rice according to package directions, but only for 12 minutes to retain firmness. Drain. While the rice is cooking, melt 1 tablespoon of the butter in stewpot; add the onion and garlic and sauté slowly for 5 minutes. Add the prunes, apricots, and raisins and simmer for 3 or 4 minutes. Add the tomatoes, bay leaf, and lemon juice and set aside. Pour ¾ cup of the hot vegetable bouillon on the saffron and let it soak. Rub the remaining butter around a deep earthenware dish or casserole. Place a third of the rice at the bottom; add the saffron and generous amounts of the seasoning to the fruit mixture, and spoon half of it over the rice. Add another third of the rice and the remaining fruit mixture; then cover with the last of the rice. Moisten with half of the bouillon; cover and bake for 1 hour. Add more bouillon if necessary to keep it moist. Stir lightly around edge with fork. Scatter the shredded orange rind on top just before serving. *Makes 4 to 5 servings.*

Note. Figs and peaches may be substituted for the prunes and apricots.

Ratatouille

⅓ cup olive oil
1 clove garlic, mashed
2 medium onions, thinly sliced
3 small zucchini, sliced
1 medium eggplant, cubed
3 ripe tomatoes, coarsely chopped

1 large green pepper, cut in strips
1 teaspoon Accent (optional)
1 teaspoon salt
¼ teaspoon black pepper
½ teaspoon dried oregano

Heat the oil in a large skillet. Add the garlic and onion and cook until the onion is tender but not brown. Place the zucchini, eggplant, tomatoes and green pepper in layers in the skillet, sprinkling each layer with Accent, salt, pepper and oregano. Cover. Cook over low heat 20 to 25 minutes or until vegetables are tender. Serve immediately, or chill and serve cold. *Makes 6 servings.*

Tuna Chow Mein

2 cans (6½ or 7 ounces *each*) tuna in vegetable oil
2 carrots, sliced
1 onion, chopped
1 green pepper, cut in rings
1 can (1 pound) mixed Chinese vegetables
1 chicken bouillon cube
2 tablespoons soy sauce
2 tablespoons molasses (optional)
2 tablespoons cornstarch

Drain the oil from the tuna into a large skillet. Add the carrots, onion, and green pepper; cook until crisp-tender, stirring occasionally. Drain the Chinese vegetables, reserving the liquid. Add water to the liquid to make 1 cup. Add to skillet with the vegetables, tuna, bouillon cube, soy sauce, and molasses. Bring to a boil, stirring occasionally. Blend the cornstarch with a little cold water and stir into the hot mixture. Cook until slightly thickened, 2 or 3 minutes. Serve with crisp noodles or rice. *Makes 4 to 6 servings.*

All-in-One Casserole

1 large onion, chopped
2 garlic cloves, minced
2 tablespoons oil
2 large carrots, diced
3 large celery stalks, sliced
2 large ripe tomatoes (or one can [1 pound] tomatoes)
1 can (6 ounces) tomato paste
1 bay leaf
½ teaspoon dried basil
½ teaspoon dried oregano
1 tablespoon salt
¼ teaspoon black pepper
2½ cups boiled spinach
1½ cups Burgundy, claret, or other red table wine
8 ounces "bow ties" or shell macaroni, cooked and drained (about 1 quart)
1½ cups grated American cheese

Cook the onion and garlic slowly in the oil until transparent. Add the carrots and celery along with the tomatoes, tomato paste, herbs, salt, and pepper. Cover and simmer 20 minutes. Preheat oven to 350°. Add the spinach and wine to the vegetables. Simmer uncovered about 20 minutes longer. Add the vegetable mixture to the macaroni and turn into a baking dish; sprinkle with the cheese. Bake about 25 to 30 minutes. *Makes 7 to 8 servings.*

Mixed Vegetable Curry

2 pounds (total) of cauliflower, Brussels sprouts, artichokes, peas, beans, celery, or your personal choice	2 apples
	2 tablespoons curry powder
	½ pound tomatoes
	2 teaspoons salt
1 tablespoon flour	1 tablespoon coriander seed
1 tablespoon turmeric	3 tablespoons chutney
¼ cup corn oil	3 tablespoons heavy cream
2 large onions	

Cut all the vegetables (except the onions) into bite-sized pieces. Mix the flour and turmeric and roll the vegetables in the mixture. Fry lightly in 1 tablespoon of the oil for a few minutes and set aside. Cut up the onions and the apples and fry in the other tablespoon of oil. Add the curry powder and continue cooking a few minutes longer. Add the tomatoes, season with the salt. Add the vegetables, coriander seed, and chutney and simmer until the vegetables are tender. Add the cream and mix gently just before serving. *Makes 4 to 5 servings.*

Vegetables in Béchamel Sauce

1 pound new potatoes, boiled with fresh mint or dried mint leaves	carrots
	½ cup bread crumbs
2 pounds fresh peas, boiled with fresh mint or dried mint leaves and 1 tablespoon sugar	2 tablespoons melted butter
	BÉCHAMEL SAUCE
½ pound fresh mushrooms sautéed in butter or margarine	2 tablespoons butter
4 ears sweet corn boiled and scraped from cob and buttered	2 tablespoons flour
	½ teaspoon salt
1½ pounds small whole glazed white onions	Dash white pepper
	½ cup milk
1½ pounds small whole glazed	½ cup chicken bouillon

Cook the six vegetables individually as directed. Preheat oven to 350°. Arrange the cooked vegetables in heaps in a shallow casserole. Lightly coat the vegetables with the Béchamel Sauce. Sprinkle with the bread crumbs, moisten with the melted butter, and bake 20 minutes. *Makes 6 servings.*

Globe Silver-skinned Onion (⅛ natural size)

BÉCHAMEL SAUCE. In a saucepan over low heat or in the top of a double boiler, over boiling water, melt the butter; add the flour, salt, and pepper. Stir until well blended. Combine the milk and bouillon and add gradually, stirring constantly. Cook until thickened. *Makes 1 cup.*

Fast Seafood Creole

3 tablespoons butter or margarine
2 onions, chopped
1 clove garlic, finely minced
½ cup chopped green pepper
½ cup chopped celery
1½ tablespoons flour
1 can (1 pound, 14 ounces) tomatoes
1 teaspoon salt
1 teaspoon sugar
1 teaspoon Accent

2 bay leaves
½ teaspoon dried thyme
¼ teaspoon allspice
1 tablespoon Worcestershire sauce
¼ teaspoon Tabasco
1 can (6½ or 7 ounces) tuna, drained
1 can (5 ounces) shrimp, drained
1 can (6 or 7 ounces) crab, drained
2 tablespoons chopped parsley

Melt the butter in a skillet; add the onion, garlic, green pepper, and celery; cook until tender but not brown. Blend in the flour. Add the tomatoes and seasonings. Simmer 15 minutes. Add the seafood and simmer 15 minutes longer. Sprinkle with the chopped parsley. Serve over hot cooked rice. *Makes 6 servings.*

Note. If desired, 1 pound fresh or frozen cleaned, deveined shrimp may be substituted for canned seafood; add the fresh or frozen shrimp to the tomato mixture during the last 5 minutes of cooking; *do not overcook.*

Cioppino

2 tablespoons salad oil	½ teaspoon Tabasco
2 carrots, grated	1 cup clam juice
2 garlic cloves, minced	1 cup water
1 large onion, chopped	1 pound shrimp, cleaned and
1 green pepper, diced	deveined
1 can (1 pound, 12 ounces) tomatoes	1 dozen oysters in the shell
1 teaspoon parsley	½ pound fillet of sole, cut into 1-inch
2 bay leaves	pieces
2 teaspoons salt	

Heat the oil in a large saucepan; add the carrots, garlic, onion, and green pepper; sauté 3 to 5 minutes. Add the tomatoes, parsley, bay leaves, salt, Tabasco, clam juice, and water. Cook and simmer 15 minutes. Add the shrimp, oysters, and sole pieces and continue cooking 15 minutes longer. Serve at once from a tureen or in large soup bowls. *Makes 6 servings.*

Clam and Cottage Cheese Mold

1 can (8 ounces) minced clams	Few drops Tabasco
1 envelope unflavored gelatin	Dash grated nutmeg
1¼ cups skim milk	⅔ cup cottage cheese
½ teaspoon Worcestershire sauce	1 tablespoon chopped green pepper
½ teaspoon salt	½ tablespoon onions flakes

Drain the clams, reserving ½ cup liquid in a saucepan. Sprinkle the gelatin on the clam liquid to soften. Place over low heat and stir until the gelatin dissolves, about 3 minutes. Remove from heat and add the milk, Worcestershire, salt, Tabasco, and nutmeg. Chill until the mixture has the consistency of unbeaten egg whites. Add the clams, cottage cheese, green pepper, and onion flakes. Turn the mixture into a 2½-cup mold or small loaf pan. Chill until firm. Unmold to serve. *Makes 3 servings.*

Salads and Salad Dressings

Chilled Vegetable-filled Artichokes

2 tablespoons lemon juice
¼ cup salad oil
1 teaspoon salt
⅛ teaspoon black pepper
2 cups cooked cubed potatoes, chilled

½ cup cooked sliced carrots, chilled
¼ cup sliced radishes
2 tablespoons snipped parsley
4 artichokes, cooked and chilled

Mix together the lemon juice, oil, salt, and pepper. Shake well. Reserve ½ of the lemon mixture. Toss the remaining lemon mixture with the potatoes, carrots, radishes, and parsley. Fill the artichokes with the vegetables. Chill at least 1 hour to blend flavors. Serve with the reserved lemon dressing. *Makes 4 servings.*

Herbed Cottage Cheese and Asparagus Salad

2 teaspoons finely chopped fresh
 basil or ½ teaspoon dried basil
 leaves
¼ cup olive or salad oil

4 teaspoons wine vinegar
¾ teaspoon salt
¼ teaspoon cracked black pepper
1½ pounds cooked asparagus

1 pound cream-style cottage cheese
1 tablespoon finely chopped chives or green onion tops

Chopped chives (garnish)
Pimiento (garnish)

Combine the basil, oil, vinegar, ½ teaspoon of the salt, and pepper. Arrange the asparagus on a large platter or plate; spoon over the dressing. Let stand at least 30 minutes at room temperature. Combine the cottage cheese, chives, and the remaining ¼ teaspoon of salt. Mix well. Place in center of platter; surround with the marinated asparagus. Garnish the cheese with additional chopped chives; garnish the asparagus with the strips of pimiento. *Makes 6 servings.*

Snap Bean Salad Italiano

2 cups cooked snap beans
2 cups diced, cooked potatoes
¼ cup chopped onion
⅛ teaspoon minced garlic
1 teaspoon salt
⅛ teaspoon black pepper
2 tablespoons salad oil

1 cup diced celery
8 diced anchovies
3 tablespoons mayonnaise
1 tablespoon cider vinegar
Head lettuce
Black olives (garnish)

Combine the beans, potatoes, onion, garlic, salt, pepper, and salad oil. Mix lightly. Cover and marinate in the refrigerator at least 1 hour. Just before serving, add the celery, anchovies, mayonnaise, and vinegar. Mix lightly. Serve on the lettuce; garnish with the olives. *Makes 8 servings.*

Snap Bean and Tuna Fish

1 pound (3½ cups) young tender snap beans
1 teaspoon salt
¼ cup olive or salad oil

2 teaspoons lemon juice
⅛ teaspoon black pepper
6 (½-ounce cans) tuna fish steaks

Wash the beans, remove tips, and cut into 1½-inch lengths. Place in a saucepan with the salt and ½ inch boiling water. Bring to a boil and cook, uncovered, 5 minutes. Cover and continue cooking until the beans are crisp-tender, about 10 minutes. Combine the oil, lemon juice, and pepper and mix well. Drain the beans and, while hot, add the oil mixture. Mix lightly and turn into a serving dish. Break the tuna fish into chunks and scatter over the top. *Makes 4 servings.*

Pickled Beet Shells

6 to 8 beets	1½ teaspoons salt
⅓ cup vinegar	1 teaspoon sugar
⅔ cup oil	1 tablespoon horseradish

Cook the beets; scoop out the centers with a spoon. Mix together the remaining ingredients. Pour the mixture over the beet shells and chill 4 to 5 hours

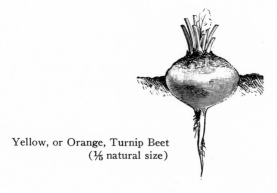

Yellow, or Orange, Turnip Beet
(⅙ natural size)

or overnight. Drain the shells and use as colorful holders for fresh vegetables, egg salad, or whatever filling you prefer. A delightfully cool, nourishing dish for summer eating. *Makes 6 shells.*

Gingered Carrot Salad

1 package (6 ounces) lemon-flavored gelatin	½ cup sherry
	2 cups grated carrots
1½ cups boiling water	3 tablespoons finely chopped candied
1 can (13½ ounces) pineapple tidbits	ginger
2 tablespoons lemon juice	Radishes and carrots (garnish)

Dissolve the gelatin in the boiling water. Drain the syrup from the pineapple into a pint measuring cup. Add cold water to make 1½ cups. Add to the dissolved gelatin along with the lemon juice and sherry. Chill until the mixture thickens. Fold in the carrots, drained pineapple, and ginger. Turn into a 5-cup mold or individual molds. Chill until firm. Unmold and serve on crisp salad greens with French dressing or mayonnaise thinned with sour cream. Garnish with the radishes and carrot curls. *Makes 6 to 8 servings.*

Cauliflowerets Vinaigrette

½ cup olive oil
⅓ cup tarragon vinegar
1 teaspoon salt
⅛ teaspoon black pepper
1 tablespoon finely chopped chives or

green onion tops
1 tablespoon finely chopped parsley
2 teaspoons finely chopped capers
1 tablespoon pickle relish
1 medium head cauliflower

Combine all the ingredients except for the cauliflower. Beat with a rotary beater. Break cauliflower into flowerets and cook only until just barely tender. Pour dressing over flowerets. Let stand overnight or at least 4 to 5 hours. Serve chilled. *Makes 1 cup sauce; serves 6 to 8.*

Cucumber Lime Salad

1 package (3 ounces) lime-flavored
  gelatin
1½ cups boiling water
2 tablespoons cider vinegar
1 teaspoon grated onion
¾ teaspoon salt

½ teaspoon prepared horseradish
¼ teaspoon mustard
1 large cucumber, grated
Lettuce
Mayonnaise
Paprika

Dissolve the gelatin in the boiling water; add the vinegar, onion, salt, horse-radish, and mustard. Chill until slightly thickened. Whip the gelatin with the rotary beater until fluffy. Fold in the cucumber. Pour into 6 individual molds; chill until firm. Unmold on the lettuce; garnish with the mayonnaise and paprika. *Makes 6 servings.*

Dutch Pepper Salad

1 medium head cabbage (about 2
  pounds)

1 medium carrot
1 small onion

1 medium green pepper, chopped
½ cup light cream
⅓ cup apple cider vinegar

¼ cup granulated sugar
1 teaspoon salt

Finely grate the cabbage, carrot and onion; add the green pepper. Blend the cream and apple cider vinegar, sugar, and salt. Pour over the cabbage, mix well, and cover. Chill several hours to blend the flavors. *Makes 8 to 10 servings, about 15 cups.*

Panama Radish Salad

4 bunches (1 quart) radishes
⅓ cup thin onion slices, separated into rings
1 cup finely diced tomato
1¼ teaspoons salt
⅛ teaspoon finely chopped garlic

⅛ teaspoon black pepper
1 teaspoon finely chopped mint
2 tablespoons lemon juice
2 tablespoons salad or olive oil
Parsley sprigs

Wash the radishes and slice. Add the onion and tomatoes. Combine the seasonings, lemon juice, and oil. Mix well and pour over the salad. Toss lightly. Garnish with the parsley. *Makes 6 servings.*

Potato Sour Cream Salad

1 teaspoon salt
⅛ teaspoon white pepper
2 tablespoons finely minced onion
1 tablespoon chopped parsley
2 tablespoons chopped chives

2 tablespoons lemon juice
¾ cup dairy sour cream
¾ teaspoon prepared mustard
5 cups cooked, sliced potatoes
1 hard-cooked egg, chopped

Combine the salt, pepper, onion, parsley, chives, lemon juice, sour cream, and mustard in a large bowl. Add the potatoes and eggs gently and let stand 1 hour before serving. *Makes 6 servings.*

Tongue 'n' Chicken–stuffed Tomato

½ head lettuce
6 tomatoes
6 ounces cooked tongue, diced

6 ounces cooked chicken, diced
1 tablespoon lemon juice
½ cup mayonnaise

¾ teaspoon salt
¹⁄₁₆ teaspoon black pepper
2 cups diced celery

Green pepper, carrot, radish,
   cucumber, parsley (garnish)

Wash the lettuce thoroughly. Separate the leaves from the core. Chill. Cut the tomatoes in four equal slices from top to bottom — but not completely through the tomato. Spread the slices slightly. Combine the tongue, chicken, lemon juice, mayonnaise, salt, pepper, and celery. To serve, line a cold plate with the lettuce. Spread open the tomatoes and fill with the tongue and chicken mixture. Garnish as desired with pepper rings, carrot curls, celery hearts, radish roses, cucumber slices and a sprig of parsley. Serve with French dressing or vinaigrette sauce. *Makes 6 servings.*

Perfection Salad

1 package (3 ounces) lemon-flavored
   gelatin
1 cup boiling water
½ cup cold water
2 tablespoons apple cider vinegar
1 teaspoon salt
1 cup grated cabbage

½ cup finely grated carrots
½ cup chopped celery
¼ cup chopped sweet pickles
2 tablespoons chopped pimiento
Lettuce
Parsley or carrot curls (garnish)

Dissolve the gelatin in the boiling water; add the cold water, vinegar, and salt. Chill until partially set. Fold in the cabbage, carrots, celery, pickles, and pimiento. Pour into individual molds; chill until firm. Unmold on lettuce cup. Garnish with parsley or carrot curls. *Makes 5 to 6 servings.*

Salad Salerno

½ cup red wine vinegar
¼ cup salad oil
¾ teaspoon salt
½ teaspoon crushed oregano leaves
⅛ teaspoon black pepper
2 tomatoes, peeled and cut in chunks
1 cucumber, peeled and thinly sliced

1 cup sliced celery
1 onion, sliced and separated into
   rings
¼ cup sliced, pitted ripe olives
¼ cup broken walnuts
Shredded lettuce (1 small head)

Combine the vinegar, oil, salt, oregano, and pepper in a covered jar; shake vigorously. Pour over the tomatoes, cucumber, celery, onion rings, olives, and walnuts in a bowl. Toss well. Cover; chill at least 1½ hours, tossing occasionally. Serve on shredded lettuce. *Makes 4 to 6 servings, about 5 cups.*

Mixed Fresh Vegetable Salad

3 cups green beans, boiled
2 tablespoons minced onion
⅓ cup salad oil
2 tablespoons lemon juice
⅛ teaspoon dry mustard
1 teaspoon salt

⅛ teaspoon black pepper
6 ounces cooked ham, diced
2 tablespoons chopped parsley
2 cups cooked, sliced potatoes
3 cups diced tomatoes
⅓ head Romaine lettuce

Cut cooked green beans in 1-inch pieces. Combine the onion, oil, lemon juice, mustard, salt, pepper, ham, and parsley thoroughly in a large mixing bowl, adding the beans, potatoes, and tomatoes carefully; marinate for at least ½ hour, turning the mixture occasionally. Serve on a bed of Romaine lettuce. *Makes 6 servings.*

Watercress (⅓ natural size)

Mixed or Latticed Green Salad

2 heads Romaine lettuce
2 heads iceberg lettuce
1 head chicory
2 bunches watercress
1 head escarole
1 pound endive
2 pounds cucumbers, diced
1 bunch celery, diced
½ pound radishes, diced

1½ pounds cooked ham, julienne
2 pounds American cheese, julienne
2 bunches scallions

TOMATO–SESAME SEED DRESSING
½ cup toasted sesame seeds
½ cup tomato purée
1½ quarts French dressing

Tear the Romaine, iceberg, chicory, watercress, and escarole into bite-sized pieces. Mix thoroughly. Remove the leaves from the endive. When ready to serve, combine the mixed greens with the cucumbers, celery and radishes. Place the endive around the edge of a large salad bowl and heap the salad mixture in the center. Garnish with a lattice of the ham and cheese and scallions. Serve with Tomato–Sesame Seed Dressing. *Makes 6 servings.*

DRESSING. Mix all ingredients thoroughly.

FRUIT SALADS

Molded Cottage Cheese and Apple Salad

2 packages unflavored gelatin	1½ cups hot water
½ cup cold water	⅓ cup lemon juice
8 ounces cottage cheese, sieved	⅔ cup sugar
½ teaspoon salt	1½ cups diced, unpeeled apples
⅛ teaspoon white pepper	Extra diced apples, unpeeled, for
½ cup milk	center of ring
⅓ cup mayonnaise	Apple slices
1 teaspoon grated lemon rind	

Soften one package of the gelatin in ¼ cup of the cold water. Dissolve in top of double boiler over hot water. Combine with the next 6 ingredients. Mix well. Turn into a 5-cup ring mold that has been rinsed in cold water. Chill. In the meantime, soften the remaining package of gelatin in the remaining ¼ cup cold water. Add the hot water, lemon juice, and sugar and stir until dissolved. Chill until about as thick as unbeaten egg whites. Fold in the diced apples. Pour into mold over the cottage cheese layer. Chill until ready to serve. Unmold and fill the center with the extra diced apples and arrange the apple slices around the outside. *Makes 6 to 8 servings.*

Ensalada Guacamole (Pineapple Avocado Salad)

3 medium avocados	1 teaspoon sugar
1½ cups diced pineapple	½ teaspoon salt
1 tablespoon lemon juice	$\frac{1}{16}$ teaspoon black pepper
3 tablespoons salad or olive oil	

Cut the unpeeled avocados in half lengthwise. Remove the pits. Spoon out enough avocado in the center to make room for the filling. Dice the scooped-out avocado and mix with the pineapple. Combine the lemon juice, oil, sugar, salt, and pepper. Beat with a rotary beater. Pour over the fruit and mix lightly. Pile in the cavities of each avocado. Chill. Serve in individual glass bowls surrounded by crushed ice. *Makes 6 servings.*

Fruited Rhubarb and Banana Mold

1¾ pounds rhubarb	1 cup orange juice
1¼ cups sugar	1¼ cups sliced bananas
⅛ teaspoon salt	2 medium oranges, sliced
2 envelopes unflavored gelatin	2 medium bananas, sliced

Preheat oven to 350°. Cut the rhubarb into 1-inch pieces. Place in an oven-proof saucepan with the sugar and the salt. Cover. Bake 1 hour. Remove from oven and drain off the juice. (There should be 2 cups; if not, add hot water to juice.) Soften the gelatin in the orange juice and add to the hot rhubarb juice. Chill until the mixture begins to thicken. Carefully fold in the drained rhubarb and the 1¼ cups sliced bananas. Turn into a rinsed 5-cup ring mold. Chill until firm and ready to serve. Turn out onto a serving plate. Fill the center with the sliced oranges mixed with the remaining 2 sliced bananas. *Makes 6 to 8 servings.*

This may be served as a salad with mayonnaise or as a dessert with whipped cream or soft custard.

Blueberry-Nectarine Iceberg

1 head iceberg lettuce	¼ teaspoon ground ginger
3 nectarines	⅛ teaspoon ground cloves
1 basket blueberries	½ cup honey
	1 cup orange juice
SPICY ORANGE DRESSING	2 to 3 tablespoons lemon juice
1 tablespoon cornstarch	¼ cup corn oil
½ teaspoon salt	Dairy sour cream

Core, rinse, and thoroughly drain the lettuce; chill in film bag or vegetable crisper in refrigerator. Wash, drain, and chill the nectarines and blueberries.

DRESSING. In a small saucepan, combine the cornstarch, salt, ginger, and cloves; blend in the honey, then the orange juice. Cook, stirring, until the mixture thickens; remove from heat. Stir in the lemon juice. Pour into a small bowl and cool. When cold, gradually beat in the oil and chill.

To serve, cut the lettuce crosswise into 1-inch-thick slices. Slice the nectarines, removing the pits. Arrange the nectarine slices on the lettuce, spoon on the blueberries and pour the Spicy Orange Dressing over all. Top with the sour cream. *Makes 6 salads.*

Lime Cantaloupe and Grape Mold

1 envelope unflavored gelatin	2 cups diced cantaloupe or
¼ cup water	cantaloupe balls
½ cup hot water	1 cup Thompson seedless grapes
2 tablespoons lime juice	Cantaloupe balls
¼ cup sugar	Clusters of Thompson seedless
1 cup ginger ale	grapes

Soften the gelatin in the cold water. Add the hot water and stir until the gelatin has dissolved. Add the lime juice, sugar and ginger ale. Chill over ice water until the mixture begins to thicken. Fold in the cantaloupe and grapes. Turn into a lightly oiled 1½-quart mold. Chill until firm and ready to serve. Just before serving unmold onto a serving plate. Garnish with the cantaloupe balls and clusters of grapes. *Makes 6 servings.*

Molded Cherry Cream Cheese Salad

4 envelopes unflavored gelatin	½ cup lemon juice
1 cup cold water	Extra cherry halves
2 cups hot water	1 package (4 ounces) cream cheese,
¾ cup sugar	softened
2 cups pitted sweet cherries	1 cup grapes
¼ teaspoon salt	Salad greens

Soften the gelatin in cold water. Stir in the hot water, sugar, cherries, and salt. Add the lemon juice. Arrange a pattern of cherry halves in the bottom of a lightly oiled 2-quart mold and cover with a little of the gelatin mixture. Chill until firm. Chill the remaining mixture until it begins to thicken. Beat the cream cheese with a little of the gelatin mixture and fold into the gelatin along with the grapes. Turn into the mold. Chill until firm and ready to serve. Turn out onto a serving plate and garnish with the salad greens and additional cherries. *Makes 12 servings.*

Pineapple Slaw with Sour Cream Dressing

3 cups shredded green cabbage
½ cup diced pineapple
½ cup diced apples
1 ½ teaspoons minced onions
¾ teaspoon chopped parsley
¾ teaspoon salt

⅛ teaspoon white pepper
1 tablespoon oil
1 tablespoon lemon juice
2 tablespoons mayonnaise
2 tablespoons dairy sour cream
6 sprigs parsley

Combine the cabbage, pineapple, apples, onions, and parsley in a large bowl and mix well. Blend together the salt, pepper, oil, lemon juice, mayonnaise, and sour cream. Lightly mix together the fruit and vegetable mixture and the sauce. Refrigerate for ½ hour before serving. Garnish with the parsley sprigs. *Makes 6 servings.*

Molded Tangerine Salad

2 envelopes unflavored gelatin
½ cup cold water
1 cup hot water
⅔ cup sugar
1 cup grapefruit juice
¼ cup lemon juice

1 cup tagerine sections
1 cup diced pears
1 cup creamy cottage cheese
Salad greens
Mayonnaise

Soften the gelatin in the cold water. Stir in the hot water and sugar. Add the grapefruit and lemon juice. Chill half the mixture until it is as thick as fresh egg whites. Set the remaining half aside at room temperature. Fold the tangerines and pears into the chilled mixture. Pour the gelatin fruit mixture into a 6-cup mold that has been rinsed in cold water. Chill until almost firm. Meantime, chill the remaining gelatin until it is as thick as fresh egg whites. Beat the cottage cheese until creamy and mix with the remaining gelatin. Beat until smooth and pour over the fruit layer. Chill until firm and ready to serve. Unmold on the salad greens. Serve with mayonnaise, if desired. *Makes 8 servings.*

Zesty Citrus Salad

3 cups grapefruit sections
3 cups orange sections
Juice from citrus sections

1 ½ cups thinly sliced onion rings
½ head iceberg lettuce
6 sprigs parsley

Combine the grapefruit and orange sections. Place the onion rings in the citrus juices and refrigerate to crisp the rings. When ready to serve, line a cold plate with lettuce. Place the mixed fruit on the lettuce and top with the drained onion rings. Garnish with the parsley sprigs. *Makes 6 servings.*

Serve with a citrus French dressing and egg-stuffed celery.

Fresh Fruit Kebab Salad

1½ large avocados
⅔ fresh pineapple
3 large oranges
3 large bananas

6 tablespoons Lime French dressing
   for marinade (see page 204)
½ head Boston lettuce
2½ cups raspberry sherbet

Peel the avocados, pineapple, oranges, and bananas. Cut into cubes, placing each fruit in a separate bowl. Pour Lime French dressing into each bowl. Marinate for 10 minutes, stirring twice. Place the cubes on 4-inch skewers. On a chilled plate, arrange a bed of lettuce. Put three kebabs around the edge of the plate and a scoop of raspberry sherbet in the center. Serve with additional Lime French dressing, if desired. *Makes 6 servings.*

SALADS WITH MEAT OR FISH

Asparagus and Ham Salad

¾ teaspoon dry mustard
1 teaspoon water
½ cup salad oil
1 teaspoon salt
⅛ teaspoon black pepper
¼ teaspoon chopped garlic
1 teaspoon grated onion

2 tablespoons lemon juice
2 tablespoons cider vinegar
18 stalks asparagus, cooked
6 slices boiled ham
Head lettuce
Tomato wedges

Combine the mustard and water; let stand 10 minutes for flavor to develop. Add the oil, salt, pepper, garlic, onion, lemon juice, and vinegar. Add the cooked asparagus and chill at least 1 hour. To serve, wrap 3 stalks of asparagus in a slice of ham. Serve on the lettuce; garnish with the tomato wedges. *Makes 6 servings.*

Avocado, Crabmeat, and Grapefruit Salad

3 medium-sized avocados
3 teaspoons lime or lemon juice
1 medium pink-fleshed grapefruit
1 cup crab meat
1 teaspoon salt

⅛ teaspoon freshly ground black
 pepper
2 tablespoons mayonnaise
Parsley sprigs

Cut the unpeeled avocados in half lengthwise. Remove the pits. Brush the edges and the cavity of the avocado with 1 teaspoon lemon or lime juice to prevent discoloration. Peel the grapefruit, being sure to remove all the white

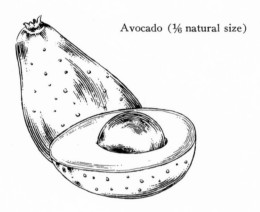

Avocado (⅛ natural size)

membrane. Cut into sections. Blend with the crabmeat, salt, and pepper. Combine the remaining lime or lemon juice and the mayonnaise and add to the salad mixture. Toss lightly and pile into the cavities of the avocados. Chill. Garnish with the parsley. *Makes 6 servings.*

Chicken Avocado Salad

1½ cups diced cooked chicken
1 cup thinly sliced celery
1 tablespoon lemon juice
½ teaspoon grated lemon rind
2 green onions, finely chopped
½ teaspoon salt
⅛ teaspoon paprika

¼ cup Chablis or other white table
 wine
1 medium-sized ripe avocado
½ cup coarsely chopped salted
 cashew nuts
½ cup mayonnaise
Crisp lettuce

Combine the chicken, celery, lemon juice and rind, onions, salt, paprika, and wine. Let stand in refrigerator several hours to blend the flavors. When ready to serve, cut the avocado in half; remove the pit and skin. Cut into small chunks or balls. Add this with the nuts and mayonnaise to the chicken mixture. Toss lightly to blend the ingredients. Serve in crisp lettuce cups. *Makes 3 or 4 servings.*

Deviled Lobster–stuffed Tomato

2 cups diced, cooked lobster
½ cup diced celery
1½ tablespoons minced green
  peppers
1 tablespoon minced onion
2 tablespoons chopped green olives
3 tablespoons mayonnaise
3 tablespoons finely chopped tomato

2 teaspoons lime juice
1½ teaspoons salt
1 teaspoon crumbled marjoram
  leaves
⅛ teaspoon black pepper
⅛ teaspoon cayenne
6 tomatoes
Bibb lettuce

Combine the lobster, celery, peppers, onion, and olives and mix well. Blend together the mayonnaise, tomato, lime juice, salt, marjoram, pepper, and cayenne. Stir this dressing into the lobster mixture, mixing until lightly blended. Quarter the tomatoes but do not cut all the way through; spread each section by filling with some of the lobster mixture, mounding it in the center. Serve on the Bibb lettuce, topping each with a 1¼-inch slice of the tomato cut from the bud end. *Makes 6 servings.*

Molded Shrimp Ring with Grapefruit and Avocado Salad

2 envelopes unflavored gelatin
½ cup cold water
1 cup boiling water
2 tablespoons sugar
1 tablespoon paprika
¼ teaspoon salt
¾ cup grapefruit juice
4 tablespoons lemon juice

½ cup mayonnaise
2 cups peeled, deveined, and diced
  shrimp
½ cup diced celery
Sections from two grapefruit
1 medium avocado, peeled and sliced
Salad greens

Soften the gelatin in the cold water. Add the hot water and stir until the gelatin is dissolved. Stir in the sugar, paprika, salt, grapefruit and lemon juices. Chill until the mixture begins to thicken. Fold in the mayonnaise, shrimp, and celery. Turn into an oiled 5-cup ring mold. Chill until the salad is firm and ready to serve. Turn out onto a serving plate. Fill the center with the grapefruit sections and avocado slices. Garnish with the salad greens and additional grapefruit sections. Serve with additional mayonnaise. *Makes 6 to 8 servings.*

Turkey and Tangelo Salad

2 cups diced cooked turkey
1 cup diced celery
1 teaspoon finely chopped onion
1 ¼ teaspoons salt
¼ teaspoon white pepper
2 cups diced tangelo sections, well

drained (about 2 tangelos)
3 tablespoons mayonnaise
1 tablespoon lemon juice
Lettuce
Tangelo sections (garnish)

Combine the turkey, celery, onion, salt, pepper, and diced tangelos. Blend the mayonnaise and lemon juice and add to the turkey mixture, stirring lightly. Serve on the lettuce leaves. Garnish with the tangelo sections. *Makes 5 servings.*

Turkey Patio Salad

2 cups diced cooked turkey
1 ½ cups tangerine sections or 1 can
   (11 ounces) mandarin orange
   segments, drained
1 cup cubed pineapple

1 cup diced celery
½ teaspoon seasoned salt
¼ cup chopped roasted pecans
¼ cup mayonnaise
Lettuce

Combine the turkey, tangerine or mandarin orange sections, the pineapple, celery, seasoned salt, and pecans. Moisten with the mayonnaise. Serve on a bed of lettuce. *Makes 6 to 8 servings.*

Tropical Ham Salad

1 cup orange sections, chilled
1 cup grapefruit sections, chilled
3 cups ham cut into ½-inch cubes
1 avocado, peeled and cut into
   wedges
¼ cup flaked coconut
Lettuce leaves

TROPICAL DRESSING
½ cup dairy sour cream
1 tablespoon orange and grapefruit
   juice
1 ½ teaspoons sugar
½ teaspoon horseradish
½ teaspoon salt
Dash dry mustard

Drain the orange and grapefruit sections, reserving 1 tablespoon juice. Gently combine the fruit with the ham, avocado, and coconut in a large bowl. Spoon the mixture onto the lettuce leaves. Top with the Tropical Dressing. *Makes 4 servings.*

DRESSING. Whip the sour cream until fluffy, about 1 minute. Fold in the orange and grapefruit liquid and then the remaining ingredients. *Makes 4 servings* (about ¾ cup).

SALAD DRESSINGS

Blue Cheese Dressing

½ cup crumbled blue cheese
½ cup cream-style cottage cheese
¼ cup dairy sour cream

¼ teaspoon Tabasco
2 tablespoons milk

Combine all the ingredients. Blend well. Serve with tossed greens, such as lettuce, escarole, chicory, watercress, Romaine, and/or spinach. *Makes 1 cup.*

Chiffonnade Dressing

½ cup salad oil
¼ cup tarragon or salad vinegar
1 teaspoon sugar
½ teaspoon salt
¼ teaspoon paprika

¼ cup minced cooked beets
1 hard-cooked egg, minced
2 tablespoons minced parsley
2 teaspoons minced onion

Combine the oil, vinegar, sugar, salt, and paprika in a small bowl. Beat with a rotary beater until thoroughly blended. Add the remaining ingredients. Cover and chill. Stir well before serving. Serve over tossed salad or lettuce wedges. *Makes about 1¼ cups.*

Cucumber Sauce

1 cup finely chopped, peeled
   cucumbers

½ cup heavy cream
2 tablespoons cider vinegar

¼ teaspoon salt   ½ teaspoon paprika
¹⁄₁₆ teaspoon white pepper

Drain the cucumber well. Beat the cream until thick but not stiff. Gradually beat in the vinegar until the cream stands in soft peaks. Fold in the drained cucumber, salt, pepper, and paprika. Serve over molded fish or egg salads. *Makes approximately 1 pint.*

Basic French Dressing

½ teaspoon salt   ⅓ cup wine vinegar
½ teaspoon sugar   ¼ teaspoon Tabasco
½ teaspoon dry mustard   ⅔ cup salad oil
½ teaspoon paprika

Combine all the ingredients. Shake or beat well. Serve with tossed greens or fruit salads, or as a marinade for sliced vegetables, such as tomatoes, celery, carrots, and peppers. *Makes about 1 cup.*

Onion French Dressing

1 large (2 inch) onion, peeled and   1 teaspoon dry mustard
  shredded   1 teaspoon paprika
1 cup olive or salad oil   2 tablespoons wine vinegar
1 clove garlic, peeled and split   2 tablespoons lemon juice
1¼ teaspoons salt

Peel and shred the onion on a fine shredder. Add to the olive or salad oil. Peel and split the garlic and add to the oil. Add the salt, powdered mustard and paprika. Let the mixture stand 1 hour. Remove the garlic and add the wine vinegar and lemon juice. Beat with a rotary beater. Serve over vegetable or meat salads. *Makes 1⅓ cups.*

Especially good over salad of escarole and Belgian endive.

Lime French Dressing

1 cup salad oil   ¹⁄₁₆ teaspoon white pepper
¼ teaspoon salt or salt to taste   1 clove garlic, peeled
½ teaspoon dry mustard   2 teaspoons finely chopped onion

⅓ cup lime juice   1 egg white

Combine the first six ingredients and let stand 1 hour. Remove the garlic.

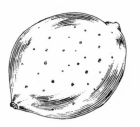

Lime (⅘ natural size)

Add the lime juice and egg white and beat with a rotary beater. Chill and serve over vegetable or fruit salads. *Makes 1¼ cups.*

Louisiana Mayonnaise

1 cup mayonnaise   ¼ cup lemon juice
¼ teaspoon Tabasco

Blend all the ingredients until smooth. Chill. Serve with hot vegetables or salads. *Makes about 1 cup.*
   VARIATIONS: *Curry.* Add 1 tablespoon curry powder to basic recipe. *Orange.* Substitute 2 tablespoons orange juice for the lemon juice. *To-mato.* Add 2 to 3 tablespoons tomato catsup to the basic recipe.

Sandwiches

Avocado and Crab Sandwich

1 cup mashed avocado
1 cup flaked crab meat
Lemon juice

Tabasco
Mayonnaise or cream cheese

Combine the avocado and crab meat. Season with the lemon juice and Tabasco to taste. Mix together with the mayonnaise or cream cheese. Spread on sandwich bread.

Beet and Cream Cheese Sandwich

3-ounce package cream cheese,
   softened
1 tablespoon mayonnaise
6 slices sandwich bread
1 cup finely chopped, cooked beets

1 ½ tablespoons French dressing
   (see page 204)
12 slices tomato
Salt and pepper
Parsley

Soften the cream cheese and blend with the mayonnaise. Spread over one side of the bread slices. Combine the beets with the dressing and spread over the cream cheese. Top each with two slices of the tomato and sprinkle lightly

Large Early Red, or Powell's Early, Tomato
(½12 natural size)

with salt and pepper. Serve as an open-faced sandwich. Garnish with parsley. *Makes 6 servings.*

Carrot, Egg, and Liverwurst Sandwich

Liverwurst, sliced
Hard-cooked eggs, sliced

Raw carrot, shredded
Salt and pepper to taste

Layer ingredients on rye toast and season to taste.

Celery Sandwich with Chicken or Turkey

1 cup chopped celery
1 cup chopped cooked chicken or
   turkey

½ cup mayonnaise or whipped cream
   cheese
½ cup fennel (optional)

Mix together and spread on whole wheat toast.

Celery and Lobster Sandwich

1 cup lobster, diced
1 cup celery, diced
2 tablespoons tomato catsup

½ cup mayonnaise
Thin white bread

Combine the lobster, celery, tomato catsup, and mayonnaise. Spread on the white bread.

Shrimp and Chutney Sandwich

1 cup shrimp, diced
¼ cup chopped chutney

¼ cup tomato catsup
Cracked wheat bread

Combine the shrimp, chutney, and tomato catsup. Spread on the cracked wheat bread.

Chutney and Lamb Sandwich

¼ cup chopped chutney
1 cup chopped cooked lamb

3 tablespoons mayonnaise or
   whipped cream cheese

Mix the ingredients together and spread on sandwich bread.

Cucumber and Salmon Sandwich

½ cup diced cucumber, seeded
1 cup flaked salmon

¼ cup mayonnaise or salad dressing

Combine all ingredients and spread on cracked wheat bread.

Cucumber Tea Sandwiches

White bread, thinly sliced
Butter

Cucumbers, finely sliced
Salt and pepper

Trim the crust from very thinly sliced white bread; spread with butter and finely sliced cucumbers seasoned to taste with salt and pepper.

Lemon and Sardine Sandwich

1 can sardines

Juice of a lemon

⅛ pound (½ stick) butter or
  margarine, softened

Whole wheat bread

Combine the sardines, lemon juice, and the butter or margarine. Spread on the whole wheat bread.

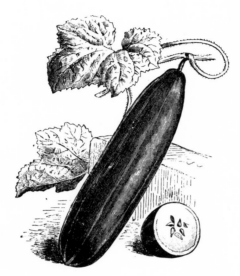

Greek, or Athenian, Cucumber (⅕ natural size)

Toasted Mushroom Sandwiches

2 tablespoons butter or margarine
½ pound mushrooms, chopped
  (about 1¼ cups)
¼ pound sharp Cheddar cheese,
  grated

1 egg, lightly beaten
½ teaspoon salt
12 thin slices white bread
12 slices tomato, ½ inch thick
6 strips bacon

Rinse, pat dry and chop mushrooms. Heat butter or margarine in a skillet. Add mushrooms and sauté until golden, 3 to 5 minutes. Remove the pan from the heat. Stir in the cheese, egg, and salt; set aside. Using a 2-inch round cookie cutter, cut bread into circles. Preheat broiler. Place a tomato slice on each bread circle. Spread mushroom-cheese mixture over tomatoes. Top each circle with a bacon strip. Arrange sandwiches on broiler tray. Place under the broiler until the bacon is crisp and the cheese is bubbly. *Makes 6 servings.*

Green Pepper, Egg, and Bacon Sandwich

Hard boiled eggs, chopped
Crisp bacon, chopped
Green pepper, chopped

Mayonnaise
Oatmeal bread

Combine the eggs with the bacon, green pepper, and mayonnaise to moisten thoroughly. Spread on oatmeal bread.

Radish and Anchovy Sandwich

1 small can anchovy fillets, chopped
Stuffed olives, chopped
1 cup cream cheese, softened

2 tablespoons radish, chopped
Thin rye bread

Combine the anchovy fillets with an equal amount of the olives, cream cheese, and the chopped radish. Spread on the rye bread.

Tomato, Tuna, and Nut Sandwich

1 cup flaked tuna
½ cup chopped celery

¼ cup chopped walnuts or pecans
½ cup mayonnaise or salad dressing

Combine all the ingredients. Spread, with sliced tomatoes, on thin-sliced pumpernickel. *Makes about 2 cups spread.*

Sardine Salad Sandwich

½ cup sliced celery
1 cup quartered cherry tomatoes
½ cup sliced green onions
½ cup diced green pepper

1 can (3¾ ounces) sardines, drained
Oil and vinegar dressing
Chopped parsley
French bread

Combine the vegetables in a salad bowl. Break the sardines into bite-sized pieces over them. Toss the salad lightly with oil and vinegar dressing (bottled or homemade). Garnish with the chopped parsley. Serve with, or between, crusty French bread. *Makes 4 servings.*

Watercress and Cream Cheese Sandwich

Watercress, chopped   Orange bread
Cream cheese

Combine the watercress and the cream cheese; mix well and spread on the orange bread.

Sauces, Relishes, Preserves, and Garnishes

Cranberry-Horseradish Sauce

1 pound fresh cranberries
2 cups sugar

1 cup water
4 teaspoons horseradish

Wash the cranberries and place in a saucepan with the sugar and water. Cover, bring to a boil and cook 8 to 10 minutes or until all the skins burst. Remove from heat and stir in the horseradish. Cool. Serve over turkey, pork, or ham. This is an especially tasty spread for cold pork or turkey sandwiches. *Makes approximately 4 cups.*

Ruby Cranberry Sauce

1 cup Burgundy, claret, or other red
  dinner wine
1 cup water
¼ teaspoon salt

1½ teaspoons grated orange peel
2 cups sugar
1 quart raw cranberries

Stir the wine, water, salt, orange peel, and sugar together in a large saucepan. Bring to a boil. Add the cranberries; boil gently until the berries begin to pop their skins, about 15 minutes. Remove from heat and cool. *Makes 1 quart.*

Serve with poultry or pork.

Tangy Cream Sauce

2 tablespoons butter or margarine   1 cup milk or light cream
¼ teaspoon Tabasco
2 tablespoons flour   VARIATION
¼ teaspoon salt   ¼ to ½ cup grated American cheese

Melt the butter or margarine in a saucepan; stir in the Tabasco. Add the flour and salt; stir to a smooth paste. Add the milk or cream and cook over low heat, stirring constantly, until the mixture thickens and comes to a boil. *Makes 1½ cups.*
    Serve with cooked onions, potatoes, spinach, or broccoli.
    VARIATION: Add cheese when the above mixture comes to a boil. Stir until cheese melts.

Quick Hollandaise

2 egg yolks   ½ cup warm melted butter
¼ teaspoon salt   2 tablespoons lemon juice
¼ teaspoon Tabasco

With a fork or an electric beater, beat the yolks until thick and lemon-colored; add the salt and Tabasco. Add ¼ cup of the butter or margarine, one teaspoon at a time, beating constantly. Stir the lemon juice into the remaining butter or margarine; slowly add 2 teaspoons at a time to the sauce, beating constantly. *Makes about ½ cup.*
    Serve with cooked asparagus, broccoli, or artichoke.

Parsley–Browned Butter Sauce

3 tablespoons butter or margarine   1 tablespoon chopped parsley
¹⁄₁₆ teaspoon black pepper

Melt the butter or margarine in a saucepan. Cook until lightly browned. Remove from the heat and stir in the pepper and parsley. *Makes ¼ cup.*
    Delicious over braised celery.

Tabasco Butter

½ cup butter or margarine   ¼ teaspoon Tabasco

Melt the butter. Stir in the Tabasco. *Makes ½ cup.*
    Serve with cooked vegetables.

Nectarine-Orange Sauce

1 cup (3 to 4) crushed nectarines   ½ cup fresh orange juice
1 tablespoon sugar   1½ teaspoons cornstarch

Combine the nectarines and sugar in a saucepan. Bring to a boil. Simmer
5 minutes. Blend the orange juice with cornstarch until smooth and add to
the cooked mixture. Cook, stirring constantly, until thickened, 2 to 3 minutes. *Makes 1½ cups.*

Strawberry-Banana Sauce

1 pint strawberries   1/16 teaspoon salt
⅓ cup sugar   1 medium-sized banana, sliced
1 teaspoon lemon juice

Hull the strawberries; wash and mash. Add the sugar, lemon juice, salt, and
banana. Mix well. *Makes 2 cups.*
    Serve over ice cream, pudding, or cake.

Apple and Pear Catsup

4 cups diced tart apples   ¼ cup cider vinegar
4 cups diced firm ripe pears   2 sticks cinnamon, each 2 inches long
½ cup water   1 teaspoon whole allspice
1½ cups light brown sugar   ½ teaspoon whole cloves

Place the apples, pears, and water in a 3-quart saucepan. Cover and cook over
medium-low heat until the apples fall apart and the pears are soft, 10 to 15
minutes. Stir in the sugar, vinegar, and cinnamon. Tie the allspice and
cloves in a cheesecloth bag and add. Cook 10 to 15 minutes or until as thick
as catsup. Remove the spices. Turn into hot sterilized jars and seal airtight

at once. Or cool, refrigerate, and use as needed. Serve as a meat accompaniment. *Makes 4 half-pint jars.*

Blueberry Jam

4 cups sugar
1½ quarts blueberries
2 tablespoons lemon juice

1 package (¾ ounce) powdered
   pectin

Measure the sugar into a bowl and set aside. Wash the blueberries and turn into a 6- or 8-quart saucepan. Crush the berries and add the lemon juice.

Blueberries (⅔ natural size)

Add the pectin and mix well. Place over high heat; stir and cook until the mixture comes to a hard boil. Boil 1 minute. Stir in the sugar at once. Bring to a full rolling boil and boil hard 1 minute, stirring constantly. (A full rolling boil cannot be stirred down.) Remove from heat. Stir and skim off the foam with a metal spoon. Stir and cool about 5 minutes. Pour into hot sterilized jars. Seal at once. *Makes 7 half-pint jars.*

Spiced Cantaloupe

4 medium cantaloupes
   (approximately 9 to 10 pounds)
2 teaspoons alum
4 cups granulated sugar

2 cups white vinegar
4 cinnamon sticks, 3 inches long
1 tablespoon whole allspice
1 tablespoon whole cloves

Cut the melons in half lengthwise; remove the seeds and rind. Cut each half into quarters, then each quarter crosswise into ¼-inch pieces. Combine the alum with 3 quarts water; pour over the melons. Cover; let stand overnight. Drain and rinse. Combine the sugar, vinegar, 1 cup water, and the spices (tied in a cheesecloth bag) in a large kettle; boil 5 minutes. Add the melon;

simmer uncovered 20 minutes, stirring gently occasionally. Remove the spice bag. Pack the melon into hot sterilized jars. Pour the boiling syrup over the melon to within ⅛ inch of the top, making sure the melon is covered. Seal each jar at once. *Makes 6 to 7 pints.*

California Chutney

2 cups light raisins
2 cups dark raisins
3 medium oranges
1 lemon
2¼ cups walnuts (two 4¾-ounce
   packages)
3 cups sugar
½ cup chopped candied ginger

½ cup instant minced onion
2½ cups muscatel or port
¼ teaspoon garlic powder
½ teaspoon cinnamon
¼ teaspoon ginger
½ teaspoon salt
½ cup wine vinegar

Put the raisins, oranges, lemon, and walnuts through the coarse blade of a food chopper, or chop them very fine. Combine all the ingredients in a large kettle. Simmer slowly about ¾ hour until the mixture thickens to chutney consistency; stir occasionally. Seal in sterilized jars, if desired. Or cover and store in refrigerator or freezer. *Makes 1¾ quarts.*

Corn Relish

16 to 20 ears young tender corn
1¼ cups chopped (4 medium)
   onions
1 cup chopped (2 medium) green
   peppers
1 cup chopped (2 medium) sweet
   red peppers
1 cup chopped celery

2⅔ cups white vinegar
2 cups water
1½ cups granulated sugar
1½ tablespoons mustard seed
1 tablespoon salt
1 teaspoon celery seed
½ teaspoon turmeric

Peel the husks and silks from the corn; trim the blemishes. Boil the corn 5 minutes, then quickly dip in cold water. Cut the kernels from the cob; measure 2½ cups of cut corn. Combine the corn with the remaining ingredients in a large kettle; simmer, uncovered, 20 minutes. Pack into clean, hot jars, leaving head space as jar manufacturer directs. Make sure the vinegar solution covers the vegetables. Adjust the covers; process in boiling water bath 15 minutes. *Makes 7 pints.*

Bread and Butter Pickles

8 cups thinly sliced cucumbers
2 cups thinly sliced small onions
¼ cup salt
2 cups cider vinegar

1 cup sugar
2 teaspoons whole mustard seed
½ teaspoon whole celery seed
½ teaspoon turmeric

Arrange alternate layers of the cucumbers, onions, and salt in a large bowl. Let stand overnight or 6 to 8 hours. Drain. Mix the remaining ingredients in a 4-quart preserving kettle. Bring to a boil. Add the cucumbers and onions. Cook until clear, 5 to 10 minutes. Pack in hot sterilized jars. Seal airtight. *Makes 3 pints.*

Cranberry and Orange Jelly

4 cups raw cranberries
½ cup orange juice

1½ cups sugar

Wash the cranberries and place in a saucepan with the orange juice. Cover and cook 10 minutes or until the skins pop. Remove from heat and put through a sieve, pushing as much of the pulp through as possible. Stir in the sugar and cook 2 to 3 minutes. Cool and chill. If desired, mold in a 1-quart gelatin mold. Chill until serving time. Unmold onto a serving dish. *Makes 2 cups.*
 Serve with meat or poultry.

Peach-Pineapple Conserve

1 medium pineapple
4 pounds peaches
1 whole orange, grated and seeded
1 whole lemon, grated and seeded

½ pound blanched almonds, chopped
½ pound seedless raisins
6 cups sugar

Wash pare, core, and slice the pineapple. Wash, pare, and cut the peaches into small pieces. Combine the pineapple, peaches, grated lemon and orange, almonds, and raisins. Bring to a boil in 1 inch water and cook over medium heat until the fruit is pulpy and soft. Add the sugar. Continue to cook, stirring frequently to prevent burning, until the mixture is thick. Cool slightly. Pour into sterilized glasses and seal immediately. *Makes about 8 half-pint jars.*

Pepper Relish

4 pounds (18 medium) green peppers
1 pound (3 to 4 large) onions
1¼ cups granulated sugar
2 cups white vinegar
2 tablespoons salt

1 teaspoon mustard seed
1 teaspoon ground cinnamon
½ teaspoon allspice
½ teaspoon ginger
½ teaspoon ground cloves

Clean and quarter the peppers and onions. Put them through the coarse blade of a food grinder; drain, discarding the liquid. Combine the remaining ingredients; bring to a boil. Add the vegetables; simmer, uncovered, 5 minutes. Continue simmering while quickly packing one hot sterilized jar at a time. Fill to within ⅛ inch of the top, making sure the vinegar solution covers the vegetables. Seal each jar at once. *Makes 4 pints.*

Note. Use this relish within six months. When made from tender young peppers, the relish will retain a fresh flavor longer.

Spiced Pumpkin

12 cups cubed (1 inch), pared,
    seeded pumpkin, about 3½ pounds
4½ cups granulated sugar

2 cups white vinegar
2 tablespoons whole allspice
2 tablespoons whole cloves

Cover the pumpkin with water. Cook about 10 minutes or until tender; drain. Combine the sugar and vinegar in a large kettle; heat to boiling. Add the spices tied in a cheesecloth bag. Add the pumpkin. Simmer, uncovered, 30 minutes, stirring occasionally. Remove the spice bag. Continue simmering while quickly packing one hot sterilized jar at a time. Fill to within ⅛ inch of the top, making sure the vinegar solution covers the pumpkin. Seal each jar at once. *Makes 4 to 5 pints.*

Rhubarb-Lemon Marmalade

2½ quarts diced (about 3 pounds)
    rhubarb
5 cups sugar
5 tablespoons lemon juice
4 sticks cinnamon, each 2 inches long

1 cup raisins
1 cup chopped nuts
2 tablespoons grated lemon peel
1 teaspoon pure vanilla extract

Place the rhubarb, sugar, lemon juice, and cinnamon in a 4-quart saucepan.

Mix well. Cook over medium heat 1 hour or until the mixture has thickened, stirring frequently to prevent scorching. Skim off all rising surface skin. Stir in the raisins, nuts, lemon peel, and vanilla extract. Heat thoroughly. Remove and discard the cinnamon. Ladle the marmalade into hot sterilized jars. Seal airtight at once. *Makes six ½-pint jars.*

Serve as a spread on bread or as a relish for meats, as it is not too sweet.

Pickled Watermelon Rind

2 pounds watermelon rind	6 cinnamon sticks, each 3 inches long
4 cups granulated sugar	2 tablespoons whole allspice
2 cups white vinegar	2 tablespoons whole cloves

Cut the rind into 1-inch cubes; trim the outer green skin and pink flesh (about 9 cups). Soak overnight in salted water (3 tablespoons salt to a quart of water); drain. Cover with fresh water and cook until tender; drain.

Red-seeded Watermelon (⅛ natural size)

Combine the sugar and vinegar in a large kettle; heat to boiling. Add the spices tied in a cheesecloth bag; then add the rind. Simmer, uncovered, until transparent, about 45 minutes, stirring occasionally. Remove the spice bag. Pack the rind tightly into hot sterilized jars. Pour the boiling syrup over the rind to within ⅛ inch of the top, making sure the vinegar solution covers the rind. Seal each jar at once. *Makes 3 pints.*

Note. For crisper, more attractive rind, soak overnight in limewater instead of salted water. Limewater powder may be purchased in drugstores; follow manufacturer's directions.

Zucchini Pickles

4 pounds zucchini, sliced (4 quarts)
1 pound small onions, sliced
  (3½ cups)
½ cup salt
1 quart wine vinegar

2 cups sugar
2 teaspoons celery seed
2 teaspoons turmeric
1 teaspoon dry mustard
2 teaspoons mustard seed

Cut the unpeeled zucchini into very thin slices. Peel the onions and slice thinly. Cover with water and add the salt. Let stand 1 hour; drain. Combine the vinegar, sugar, celery seed, turmeric, dry mustard, and mustard seed. Bring to a boil and pour over the vegetables. Let stand 1 hour. Bring to a boil and cook 3 minutes. Place in jars and seal at once. *Makes about 6 pints.*

Vegetable Garnishes

FLUTED CUCUMBERS OR BANANAS. Score a whole peeled or unpeeled cucumber (or peeled banana) lengthwise with the tines of a fork. Cut crosswise into thin slices.

CARROT CURLS. Pare a large, crisp carrot with a vegetable peeler. Using the peeler, cut lengthwise, paper-thin strips. Roll each strip tightly; fasten with a toothpick. Chill on ice or in ice water for an hour or more. Remove picks before serving.

CELERY CURLS. Slash small stalks or short pieces of celery lengthwise, cutting to within ½ inch of the leaves or the end of a piece. Or slash both ends, allowing ½ inch in the center to hold the piece together. Chill on ice or in ice water. If desired, dip the slashed ends in paprika before serving.

Early White-tipped Scarlet Turnip Radish
(⅓ natural size)

RADISH ROSES. With a small, sharp paring knife, cut the tail from each radish. Make six to eight deep cuts into each radish from the top to the stem end. Place on ice or in ice water for an hour or more to open the rose petals.

GREEN ONION FLOWERS. Cut the green onions into 3- or 4-inch lengths. Trim the base slightly and, with a sharp knife, slit the onions vertically about four times, leaving a 1-inch base. Drop them into ice water and they will curl.

ADDITIONAL GARNISHES. Green or red pepper rings, parsley sprigs, watercress, cherry tomatoes, olives, pimiento, pomegranate seeds, coconut, and raisins.

Vegetable Relish

2½ pounds (10 medium) green peppers, quartered
1 pound (½ medium head) cabbage, quartered
1 pound (7 medium) carrots, halved
1 pound (4 large) onions, quartered

2¾ cups white vinegar
¾ cup water
1½ cups granulated sugar
3 tablespoons salt
1 tablespoon mustard seed
1 tablespoon celery seed

Grind the prepared vegetables in food chopper, using a coarse blade. Drain, discarding liquid. Combine the remaining ingredients in a large kettle; bring to a boil. Add the vegetables; simmer, uncovered, for 5 minutes. Continue simmering while quickly packing one hot sterilized jar at a time. Fill to within ⅛ inch of top, making sure the vinegar solution covers the vegetables. Seal each jar at once. *Makes 5 to 6 pints.*

Breads

Apple Pancakes

1 cup sifted all-purpose flour
½ teaspoon salt
1½ teaspoons double-acting baking powder
1 cup apple sauce
¼ teaspoon grated lemon rind

¼ teaspoon ground cinnamon
1 tablespoon sugar
¾ teaspoon pure vanilla extract
2 eggs, separated
1½ teaspoons melted butter or margarine

Sift the flour, salt, and baking powder into a mixing bowl. Blend in the apple sauce, lemon rind, cinnamon, sugar, and vanilla extract. Beat egg yolks slightly and add along with the melted butter or margarine. Beat the egg whites until they form soft peaks. Fold them into the batter. Pour ¼ cup batter for each pancake onto a hot, greased griddle. Cook to brown both sides. *Makes 18 pancakes of 4-inch diameter.*

Serve for breakfast or brunch with maple syrup and bacon or sausage.

Banana-Orange Bread

¾ cup sugar
½ cup shortening
1 tablespoon grated orange rind

2 eggs
1 cup mashed bananas
1¾ cups unsifted flour

2 teaspoons baking powder   ½ teaspoon salt
½ teaspoon baking soda

Preheat oven to 350°. Grease a 5″ x 9″ loaf pan. Cream the sugar and short-ening together; blend in the orange rind. Beat in the eggs until the mixture is light and fluffy. Blend in the bananas. Combine the flour, baking powder, soda, and salt thoroughly. Add to the batter and stir just until smooth. Pour into the prepared pan and bake until firmly set when lightly touched on center top, 50 to 60 minutes (bread may crack across the top). Cool on rack for 10 minutes, then remove from pan. *Makes 1 loaf*, about 145 calories per half-inch slice.

Blueberry–Sour Cream Pancakes

1⅓ cups flour (unsifted)   1 cup whole or skim milk
½ teaspoon baking soda   1 cup blueberries
1 teaspoon salt
1 tablespoon sugar   BLUEBERRY SYRUP
¼ teaspoon nutmeg   1 cup blueberries
1 egg, beaten   ¼ cup water
1 cup dairy sour cream   ¼ cup sugar

Stir the flour, soda, salt, sugar, and nutmeg together thoroughly. Combine the egg, sour cream, and milk, and add to the dry ingredients, stirring just enough to combine them well. Add the blueberries carefully, blending them just enough to mix in the berries. Drop the batter by quarter-cupfuls onto a hot, greased griddle. Cook until the surface is covered with bubbles; turn and cook until the other side is well browned. Serve with the hot Blueberry Syrup. *Makes 18 pancakes about 3 inches in diameter.*
   Note. The batter should be thick and the pancakes light and puffy.
   SYRUP. Combine the ingredients and bring to a boil. Crush the berries with the back of a spoon. Simmer 2 to 3 minutes. Serve hot. *Makes about 1 cup;* contains about 20 calories per tablespoon.

Cranberry Nut Bread

1½ cups cranberries   1 teaspoon salt
1 cup sugar   ⅔ cup corn flake crumbs
2½ cups sifted flour   ½ cup chopped walnuts
4 teaspoons baking powder   1 cup milk

1 egg, slightly beaten   2 tablespoons shortening, melted
1 tablespoon grated orange rind

Preheat oven to 375°. Put the cranberries through a food chopper; mix with ¼ cup of the sugar. Sift together the flour, baking powder, salt, and the remaining ¾ cup sugar; combine with the corn flake crumbs and nutmeats. Combine the milk, egg, orange rind, shortening, and cranberries; mix well. Add the dry ingredients, stirring *only until combined*. Spread evenly in greased 5¼″ x 9¼″ loaf pan. Bake about 1 hour. Let stand until cold before cutting into thin slices. Serve with whipped cream cheese. *Makes 1 loaf.*

Sugarplum Coffee Cake

1 cake yeast   5 cups flour
2 tablespoons warm water   1 teaspoon salt
½ cup shortening   ½ cup seedless raisins
½ cup sugar   ½ cup chopped walnuts
2 eggs   ½ cup chopped citron
¾ cup milk   ½ cup candied cherries

Dissolve the yeast in the water. Cream the shortening and sugar. Beat the eggs and add to the creamed mixture. Add the milk and yeast. Add 1 cup of the flour and mix well. Cover. Let rise in a warm place 1 hour. Grease an 8-inch round cake pan. Add the salt, fruits, nuts, and the remaining 4 cups flour. Knead thoroughly and put into cake pan. Cover and let rise in a warm place about 2 hours or until doubled in bulk. Preheat oven to 350°. Bake for 1¼ hours. Remove from pan and cool slightly. Frost with plain icing, if desired. *Makes 1 cake.*

Fruit Muffins

1¾ cups unsifted flour   1 cup milk
2 teaspoons baking powder   ¼ cup salad oil or corn oil
½ teaspoon salt   1 cup whole cranberry sauce, or 1 cup
¼ cup sugar   blueberries, or 1 cup finely chopped
1 egg, beaten   dried apricots

Preheat oven to 400°. Grease muffin pans. Mix the flour, baking powder, salt, and sugar thoroughly in a large bowl. Combine the egg, milk, and oil separately. Add to the dry ingredients and stir about twenty strokes, just until the flour is moistened (batter will be lumpy). Fold the fruit gently into the batter; do *not* beat. Fill the muffin pans two-thirds full. Bake about 20 minutes. *Makes 12 medium-sized muffins;* about 180 calories per muffin with cranberry sauce; 145 calories per muffin with blueberries; or 155 calories per muffin with dried apricots.

Maple-glazed Coconut Buns

¾ cup maple-blended syrup
6 tablespoons melted butter
½ cup chopped pecans

⅔ cup flaked coconut
1 dozen (1 package) brown-and-
  serve soft rolls

Preheat oven to 400°. Combine ½ cup of the syrup and 2 tablespoons of the butter in an 8- or 9-inch-square pan. Bake 5 to 8 minutes, or until bubbly. Sprinkle the pecans and coconut over the syrup mixture. Meanwhile, combine the remaining ¼ cup syrup and 4 tablespoons of butter; dip the rolls, coating all sides. Arrange the rolls on top of the coconut mixture and bake 20 to 25 minutes, or until browned. Invert the pan of rolls onto a serving platter. *Makes 12 rolls.*

Sherry Fruit Bread

¼ cup sherry
2 cups coarsely grated, peeled
  Washington apples
¼ cup soft shortening
⅔ cup sugar
2 beaten eggs

2 cups sifted all-purpose flour
1 teaspoon baking powder
1 teaspoon baking soda
1 teaspoon salt
½ cup grated American cheese
½ cup chopped filberts or walnuts

Preheat oven to 325°. Pour the sherry over the apple. Cream the shortening and sugar until fluffy; beat in the eggs. Sift the flour, baking powder, soda, and salt together; add to the creamed mixture alternately with the apple. Stir in the cheese and nuts. Turn into a greased and floured loaf pan (8½″ x 4½″ x 3″). Bake 50 to 60 minutes. Cool thoroughly before storing or slicing. *Makes 1 loaf.*

Fruited Oatmeal Bread

2 cups boiling water

1 cup oatmeal

1 yeast cake
½ cup warm water
½ cup sugar
5–5½ cups flour

1 tablespoon salt
2 tablespoons melted shortening or
  salad oil
1 cup dates and nuts, mixed

Pour boiling water over the oatmeal and stir; cool. Crumble the yeast into a bowl, add warm water, half the sugar, and ½ cup of the flour. When the mixture is light and bubbly, stir in the oatmeal. Add the remaining ¼ cup sugar, salt, and shortening. Combine the dates and nuts and the remaining 5 cups flour and add to the oatmeal. Cover and let rise until light. Preheat oven to 375°. Knead, shape into two loaves, let rise, and bake 50 to 60 minutes. *Makes 2 loaves.*

Desserts

Almond-baked Apples

6 medium baking apples, peeled and
    cored
¼ cup (4 tablespoons) butter or
    margarine, melted
¼ cup fine dry bread crumbs
4 tablespoons sugar
½ teaspoon vanilla extract
¼ cup very finely chopped blanched
    almonds
1 tablespoon sugar

6 teaspoons butter or margarine

VANILLA SAUCE
¼ cup sugar
1 teaspoon cornstarch
¹⁄₁₆ teaspoon salt
2 large egg yolks
1 cup milk
½ cup heavy cream, whipped
1 teaspoon vanilla extract

Preheat oven to 350°. Peel the apples and remove the cores. Roll the apples
in the butter or margarine and then in the bread crumbs mixed with 2 tablespoons of the sugar. Mix 1 tablespoon of the sugar, vanilla extract, and
almonds to a paste, adding a little water at a time until well blended. Spoon
into the cavities of the apples. Place in a baking pan. Sprinkle the remaining
1 tablespoon sugar over the apples and dot each with 1 teaspoon of butter
or margarine. Cover with foil and bake 40 minutes. Remove the cover and
bake 45 minutes or until the apples are tender (baking time will depend on
the size and type of apple). Serve cold with the Vanilla Sauce.

    VANILLA SAUCE. Combine the sugar, cornstarch, and salt in the top of a double boiler. Blend in the egg yolks and ¼ cup of the milk. Add the remaining milk. Stir and cook over hot (not boiling) water until the custard coats a metal spoon and has thickened. Remove from the hot water and cool. Fold in the whipped cream and vanilla extract. Serve over the Almond-baked Apples. *Makes 6 servings.*

Charlotte de Pommes (*Apple Charlotte*)

2 pounds cooking apples	1 teaspoon grated lemon peel
¼ cup water	¾ cup light brown sugar, firmly
1 cup fine dry bread crumbs	packed
½ teaspoon ground nutmeg	3 tablespoons butter or margarine

Preheat oven to 375°. Wash and pare the apples. Slice and place in a saucepan with the water. Cover and cook over low heat until the apples are tender. Place a ¼-inch layer of fine bread crumbs in a buttered 9-inch pie plate. Top with a layer of the cooked apples. Mix the nutmeg, lemon peel and sugar and sprinkle ¼ cup over the apples. Repeat using the remaining ingredients, having a ¼-inch layer of bread crumbs over the top. Dot with the butter or margarine. Bake until the top has browned slightly, about 25 minutes. Serve warm. *Makes 6 servings.*

Porcupine Meringue Apples

6 baking apples	6 teaspoons butter
6 tablespoons seedless raisins	3 egg whites (at room temperature)
¾ cup brown sugar	Dash salt
½ teaspoon cinnamon	6 tablespoons white sugar
½ teaspoon nutmeg	¼ cup blanched almonds
2 tablespoons lemon juice	

Preheat oven to 375°. Wash and core apples, remove about 1 inch of peel from stem end. Place in a baking dish; put 1 tablespoon of the raisins and 2 tablespoons brown sugar mixed with cinnamon and nutmeg in each cavity; sprinkle with lemon juice and dot with butter. Add boiling water to cover bottom of baking dish. Bake about 40 to 45 minutes or until tender, basting three or four times with water in baking dish. Meanwhile, beat the egg whites with a dash of salt until stiff but not dry. Gradually beat in white sugar, sprinkling a little at a time over the surface. Continue beating until very smooth and glossy. Pile meringue on apples; stud with almonds. Return to oven and bake about 5 to 8 minutes or until delicately brown. *Makes 6 servings.*

Vineyard Apple Crisp

5 apples, peeled, cored, and thinly
   sliced
1 teaspoon cinnamon
⅓ cup sherry
1 cup sifted all-purpose flour

½ cup brown sugar
½ cup butter or margarine
Dash salt
Light cream

Preheat oven to 375°. Arrange the apples in the bottom of a greased baking dish. Sprinkle with the cinnamon and sherry. Mix the flour, brown sugar, butter, and salt together with a pastry blender or fingers to make a crumbly mixture; sprinkle evenly over the apples. Bake, uncovered, for about 45 minutes, or until the apples are tender and the crust is slightly brown. Serve warm with cream. *Makes 5 or 6 servings.*

Minted Apricots

¼ cup sugar
¼ cup lime juice
2 tablespoons chopped mint

2 cups sliced apricots
Mint leaves (garnish)

Combine the sugar, lime juice, and mint. Bring to a boil; strain and cool. Add the apricots. Chill 2 to 3 hours. Serve in sherbet glasses garnished with the mint. *Makes 3 to 4 servings.*

Bananas in Sour Cream

2 large bananas, sliced
½ pint (1 cup) dairy sour cream
¼ cup diced oranges

2½ tablespoons light brown sugar
¼ teaspoon vanilla extract
Grated orange peel (garnish)

Place all the ingredients except the orange peel in a mixing bowl. Toss lightly. Serve in sherbet glasses. Garnish with the orange peel. *Makes 4 servings.*

Banana Soufflé

3 firm ripe bananas
1½ tablespoons lemon juice
⅓ cup sugar
1 tablespoon cornstarch
⅛ teaspoon salt
½ teaspoon nutmeg
¼ teaspoon grated lemon rind

¾ cup milk
3 egg yolks, beaten
3 egg whites
2 tablespoons butter or margarine
1½ teaspoons vanilla extract
Whipped cream
Sugar

Preheat oven to 350°. Peel and slice the bananas and dip in the lemon juice. Set aside. In a saucepan, combine the sugar, cornstarch, salt, nutmeg, and lemon rind. Add the milk and mix well. Stir and cook over medium heat until thickened. Add a little of the hot mixture to the beaten egg yolks. Then mix it with the remaining hot mixture. Stir in the butter or margarine and sliced bananas. Beat the egg whites until they stand in soft stiff peaks. Fold into the mixture along with the vanilla extract. Turn into a 1½-quart soufflé dish. Place in a pan of hot water. Bake about 1 hour or until firm. Serve with the whipped cream sweetened to taste with the sugar. *Makes 6 servings.*

Bananes au Rhum

6 large ripe bananas
¼ cup hot olive oil, melted butter, or
   margarine
½ teaspoon vanilla extract

3 tablespoons rum or sherry
2 tablespoons confectioner's sugar
Vanilla ice cream (optional)

Peel the bananas and cut each into four lengthwise slices. Sauté in the hot oil. Drain on paper towels; cool. Place in a serving dish. Blend the vanilla with the rum or sherry and pour over the bananas. Sprinkle with the confectioner's sugar. Chill. If desired, top with vanilla ice cream. *Makes 6 servings.*

Vanilla Banana Pudding

¼ cup sugar
2 tablespoons cornstarch
¼ teaspoon salt
2 large egg yolks

1½ cups milk
1½ teaspoons vanilla extract
1 package (4 ounces) vanilla wafers
1 pound bananas, sliced

VANILLA MERINGUE
1/16 teaspoon salt
1/2 teaspoon vanilla extract

2 egg whites
4 tablespoons sugar

Preheat oven to 325°. Combine the sugar, cornstarch, and salt. Add the egg yolks and 1/4 cup of the milk. Heat the remaining milk and gradually stir into the egg and sugar mixture. Cook over low heat or hot water until the mixture coats a metal spoon, stirring constantly. Add the vanilla extract. Arrange the wafers and the bananas in alternate layers in a 1-quart casserole, having the wafers as the bottom layer and the bananas on top. Pour the custard over all. Top with the Vanilla Meringue. Bake 15 minutes or until brown. This is best served warm.

VANILLA MERINGUE. Add the salt and vanilla to the egg whites and beat until they stand in soft peaks. Gradually beat in the sugar. *Makes 6 to 8 servings.*

Fast Banana Cream Crunch Pudding

1/3 cup butter or margarine
1 package (9 or 9 1/2 ounces) yellow
    cake mix
1 package (3 1/4 ounces) *instant*
    vanilla pudding mix

1 1/2 cups milk
1/4 cup sherry
1/2 cup whipping cream
2 small bananas
Nutmeg

Preheat oven to 350°. Cut the butter into the cake mix until the particles are very fine. Press the mixture against the bottom and sides of a rectangular baking dish (about 6" x 10" x 2"). Bake about 20 minutes or until very lightly browned; cool. Combine the pudding mix and milk and beat slowly with rotary beater about 1 minute, until the mixture thickens. Stir in the sherry; let stand a few minutes until set. Whip the cream until stiff and fold into the pudding. Turn part of the pudding into the baked crust. Top with the sliced bananas. Cover with the remaining pudding and sprinkle with the nutmeg. Chill 4 or 5 hours or overnight to allow the crust to soften slightly. *Makes 6 to 8 servings.*

Banana Muscatel

4 bananas, peeled
2 tablespoons melted butter or
    margarine

1/3 cup muscatel or other dessert
    wine
2 tablespoons brown sugar

⅛ teaspoon ground cloves   1 tablespoon lemon juice
Pinch salt

Arrange the bananas in a shallow pan. Combine the butter, wine, sugar, cloves, salt, and lemon juice; pour over the bananas. Place under broiler until the fruit is a delicate brown, basting frequently. Serve hot. *Makes 4 servings.*

Blueberry Chiffon Pudding

1 envelope unflavored gelatin   ¼ teaspoon salt
¼ cup water   1 teaspoon grated lemon rind
⅓ cup sugar   1 teaspoon vanilla extract
2 eggs, separated   1 cup blueberries
1 cup skim milk   2 tablespoons sugar

Soften the gelatin in the water and set aside. Combine the sugar, egg yolks, milk, and salt in a saucepan. Stir and cook over very low heat 3 minutes. Add the gelatin, lemon rind, and vanilla. Cool and chill until the custard begins to thicken. Fold in the blueberries. Beat the egg whites until they stand in soft, stiff peaks; then gradually beat the remaining sugar into them. Fold into the mixture. Chill. Serve in sherbet glasses. *Makes 1 quart or 6 servings.*

Blueberry Custard Parfait

¼ cup sugar   ½ teaspoon grated lemon peel
¼ teaspoon salt   ¼ teaspoon ground nutmeg
2 large eggs, lightly beaten   ⅓ cup heavy cream
1½ cups milk   1 tablespoon superfine sugar
1 teaspoon vanilla extract   2 cups blueberries
1 teaspoon grated orange peel

Combine the sugar and salt in the top part of a double boiler or in a 1-quart saucepan. Blend in the eggs and milk. Stir and cook over hot (not boiling) water or very low heat until the custard coats a wooden spoon. Remove from heat; cool and chill. Stir in the vanilla extract, orange and lemon peels, and nutmeg. Beat the heavy cream and sugar until it holds its shape. Fold into the custard mixture. Arrange alternate layers of the blueberries and custard in parfait glasses. Chill. *Makes 6 servings.*

Blueberry Cream

1 pint (2 cups) blueberries
⅛ teaspoon salt
1 large egg white
1 cup diced large marshmallows

1 cup heavy cream, whipped
½ teaspoon vanilla extract
3 tablespoons sugar

Wash and drain the blueberries. Add the salt to the egg white and beat until stiff. Fold in the marshmallows, 1½ cups of the blueberries, the whipped cream, and vanilla. Chill until ready to serve. Just before serving, crush the remaining ½ cup of blueberries and fold into the mixture. *Makes 4 cups.*

Cantaloupe Surprise

Cantaloupe, halved
Blueberries

Strawberries
Sugar

Fill the cantaloupe halves with sugared blueberries and strawberries. Chill and serve.

Cantaloupe Snow Pudding

1 envelope unflavored gelatin
¼ cup cold water
1 cup hot water
¾ cup sugar
¼ cup lemon juice
1 large egg white
1⁄16 teaspoon salt
½ teaspoon vanilla extract
2 cups finely diced ripe cantaloupe

Whipped cream (optional)

CUSTARD SAUCE
¼ cup sugar
⅛ teaspoon salt
2 large eggs
2 cups milk
½ teaspoon vanilla extract
¼ teaspoon grated lemon peel

Soften the gelatin in the cold water. Add the hot water and stir until the gelatin has dissolved. Add the sugar and lemon juice and chill over ice water until the mixture begins to thicken. Add the egg white, salt and vanilla. Beat with an electric or rotary beater until the mixture is fluffy. Fold in the cantaloupe. Chill until ready to serve. Serve in tall sherbet glasses with or without Custard Sauce and whipped cream. *Makes 8 servings.*

CUSTARD SAUCE. Combine the sugar and salt in a 1-quart saucepan or in the top of a double boiler. Beat in the eggs and ¼ cup of the milk. Heat the remaining milk and add to the mixture. Stir and cook over low heat or hot water until the custard coats a metal spoon. Remove from heat and stir in the vanilla and lemon peel. Cool and chill. *Makes 1½ to 2 cups or 8 servings.*

Cantaloupe Coupe

1 ripe cantaloupe   1 pint vanilla ice cream
2 tablespoons kirsch

Cut the cantaloupe in half; drain and remove the seeds. Cut into balls with a French melon ball cutter or a half-teaspoon measurer or dice. Add the

Saint-Laud Market-Garden Melon
(⅛ natural size)

kirsch and steep 3 to 4 hours. Fill sherbet glasses with alternating layers of the cantaloupe and ice cream, with cantaloupe as the bottom and top layers. *Makes 6 servings.*

Frosted Cherries

Cherries   Sugar
Egg white, slightly beaten

Dip the cherries into slightly beaten egg white; sprinkle with the sugar and place them on waxed paper until the sugar dries. Serve alone or over custard, or with vanilla or lemon fondue.

Stewed Cherries

1 quart sweet cherries	½ cup water
½ cup sugar	⅛ teaspoon salt

Wash the cherries; remove the stems and pits. Place in a saucepan with the water, sugar, and salt. Cover and simmer until almost tender, 4 to 6 minutes. *Makes 3½ cups.*

Serve as a dessert or a delicious meat relish.

Coconut Bread Pudding

1 cup soft bread crumbs	2 large egg yolks
4 cups hot milk	½ cup sugar
2 tablespoons butter or margarine	1 cup flaked coconut
¼ teaspoon salt	½ teaspoon grated lemon rind
2½ teaspoons vanilla extract	Vanilla Meringue (page 231)
1 large whole egg	

Preheat oven to 325°. Soften the crumbs in 1 cup of the hot milk. Mash well. Add the remaining hot milk and the butter or margarine, salt, and vanilla. Beat the whole egg and egg yolks together slightly. Blend in the sugar and add to the bread crumb mixture along with the coconut and lemon rind. Turn into a buttered 1½-quart casserole. Set in a pan of hot water and bake 1½ hours. Top with the Vanilla Meringue. Bake 15 minutes. Serve warm. *Makes 6 to 8 servings.*

Brownie Coconut-Pecan Pie

⅔ cup sugar	3 eggs, slightly beaten
⅛ teaspoon salt	1 teaspoon vanilla
1 cup light corn syrup	1⅓ cups flaked coconut
1 package (4 ounces) sweet cooking chocolate, broken into squares	½ cup coarsely chopped pecans
3 tablespoons butter	1 unbaked 9-inch pie shell
	Whipped cream (optional)

Preheat oven to 375°. Combine the sugar, salt, and syrup in a saucepan. Bring to a boil over high heat, stirring until the sugar is dissolved. Boil 2 minutes. Remove from the heat; add the chocolate and butter, stirring until the chocolate is melted and the mixture is smooth and blended. Gradually pour over the eggs, stirring constantly. Add the vanilla, 1 cup of the coconut, and the nuts; mix well. Pour into the pie shell. Bake 40 to 45 minutes, or until the filling is puffed in the center and the outside edge is set. Cool. Garnish with the whipped cream and remaining coconut. *Makes 1 (9-inch) pie.*

Brown Betty Cranberry-Apple Pie

Pastry for single-crust 9-inch pie
3 large tart apples
2 cups cranberries
1 cup sugar
2 tablespoons cornstarch
½ teaspoon salt

½ teaspoon ground cinnamon
½ teaspoon ground nutmeg
1 cup soft bread crumbs
¼ cup (½ stick) butter or
   margarine

Preheat oven to 450°. Line a 9-inch pie plate with pastry rolled ⅛ inch thick. Trim, turn under, and flute the edge. Peel and slice the apples; there should be 5 cups. Wash the cranberries and mix with the apples. Turn into the pastry-lined pie plate. Combine the sugar, cornstarch, salt, spices, and bread crumbs. Mix well. Add the butter or margarine and mix until well blended. Sprinkle over the fruit. Bake 10 minutes. Reduce the heat to a moderate 350° and bake 45 to 50 minutes or until the fruit is tender. Cool before serving. *Makes 1 pie.*

Cranberry Tapioca Parfait

1 egg, separated
2 cups milk
3 tablespoons quick-cooking tapioca
5 tablespoons sugar
½ teaspoon salt
¼ teaspoon ground mace
½ teaspoon vanilla extract
2 teaspoons lemon juice

1 teaspoon grated lemon rind
1 cup heavy cream, whipped

CRANBERRY-ORANGE SAUCE
1 pound cranberries
2 cups water
2 cups sugar
1 teaspoon grated orange peel

Beat the egg yolk and ¼ cup of the milk in a saucepan. Add the remaining milk, tapioca, 3 tablespoons of the sugar, the salt, mace and vanilla. Stir and cook over medium heat until the mixture has thickened, 6 to 7 minutes. Beat the egg white until it stands in soft, stiff peaks. Gradually beat in the remaining 2 tablespoons sugar, 1 tablespoon at a time. Fold in the tapioca along with the lemon juice and rind. Cool. Fold in the whipped cream. Fill parfait glasses with alternating layers of pudding and Cranberry-Orange Sauce. Top with the additional whipped cream, if desired. *Makes 8 to 10 servings.*

CRANBERRY-ORANGE SAUCE. Wash and sort the berries. Combine the water and sugar and bring to a boil. Add the cranberries and grated orange peel to the boiling syrup. Cook over low heat until the berries pop. Put the sauce through a strainer or food mill, or leave the berries whole, as desired. *Makes 4 cups.*

Black-Bottom Lime Parfait

1 cup chocolate pudding	¼ teaspoon grated lime peel
1 envelope unflavored gelatin	6 drops green food coloring
¼ cup cold water	¼ teaspoon salt
4 large eggs, separated	½ teaspoon vanilla extract
1 cup sugar	½ cup heavy cream, whipped
⅓ cup lime juice	3 tablespoons chopped pistachio nuts
½ teaspoon mace	(garnish)

Prepare your favorite chocolate pudding and distribute 1 cup of it among eight parfait glasses. Refrigerate. Soften the gelatin in the cold water and set aside. Beat the egg yolks until thick and lemon-colored. Gradually beat in ½ cup of the sugar, the lime juice, and mace. Stir and cook over low heat or hot (*not* boiling) water until the mixture coats a metal spoon. Remove from heat and stir in the softened gelatin, lime peel, and food coloring; mix well until the gelatin dissolves. Chill until the mixture begins to thicken. Add the salt to the egg whites and beat until they stand in *stiff* peaks. Beat in the remaining ½ cup of sugar. Fold the beaten whites into the gelatin mixture along with the vanilla extract and whipped cream. Pour over the chocolate layer in the parfait glasses and return to refrigerator to set. Immediately before serving, garnish with the nuts. *Makes 8 servings.*

Lemon-Banana Freeze

1½ cups sugar	1 teaspoon vanilla extract
¾ cup light corn syrup	1 teaspoon grated lemon peel
1¾ cups water	⅛ teaspoon salt
½ cup lemon juice	1 large egg white
1 cup mashed bananas	

Combine the sugar, corn syrup, and 1 cup of the water. Mix well. Cook to soft ball stage (238°). Remove from the heat. Add the remaining water and lemon juice. Cool. Add the bananas, vanilla, and lemon peel. Mix well. Pour into an ice cube tray. Freeze to a mush. Turn into a bowl and beat with a rotary or electric beater until fluffy. Add the salt to the egg white and beat until soft peaks are formed. Fold into the frozen mixture. Pour into the ice cube tray. Freeze until firm and ready to serve. *Makes 1 quart.*

Ginger-sauced Melon

½ cup Chablis or other white table wine
½ cup sugar
1 teaspoon whole cloves
2 tablespoons lime or lemon juice

1 tablespoon finely chopped candied ginger
2 cups watermelon and cantaloupe balls or cubes
Mint sprigs (garnish)

Combine the wine, sugar, and cloves in a small saucepan. Simmer about 5 minutes. Strain out the cloves; add the lemon juice and ginger; chill. Arrange melon balls in sherbet glasses. Spoon over chilled wine syrup; garnish with a sprig of mint and serve at once. *Makes 4 servings.*

Melon Delight

Watermelon balls
Cantaloupe balls
Honeydew balls

Confectioner's sugar
Port, muscatel, or sweet sauterne

Mix the melon balls together. Sprinkle with the confectioner's sugar and add enough of the wine to half cover the balls. Chill thoroughly and stir once or twice before serving.

Nectarine Delight

1½ pounds peeled nectarines, sliced into eighths
1½ cups orange juice
2 tablespoons cornstarch
¼ cup flour
1 cup light brown sugar

¼ teaspoon salt
2 cups milk
6 large egg yolks, beaten
2 tablespoons butter or margarine
1 teaspoon ground nutmeg
1 teaspoon vanilla extract

2 packages ladyfingers   1 tablespoon grated orange peel

Place the nectarines in a bowl with the orange juice; set aside. In the top of a double boiler, combine the cornstarch, flour, brown sugar, and salt. Add the milk and cook over boiling water, stirring constantly until thick. Cover and cook about 10 minutes. Blend a little of the hot mixture into the egg yolks; then stir the egg yolks back into the hot mixture. Cook 3 minutes longer. Stir the butter or margarine, nutmeg, and vanilla extract into the custard. Cover, remove the top part of the double boiler and cook directly over the heat. Arrange the ladyfingers along the side of a 1½-quart bowl; arrange a layer of nectarine slices between, next to the ladyfingers, reserving some for garnish. Blend the orange peel and juice into the custard. Ladle into bowl. Garnish the top with the extra nectarine slices. Chill until served. *Makes 8 servings.*

Hot Nectarine Sundae

2 cups crushed nectarines   2 teaspoons lemon juice
½ cup sugar   1 quart vanilla ice cream
½ cup orange juice   Chopped pecan nuts (garnish)
¹⁄₁₆ teaspoon salt

Combine the nectarines, sugar, orange juice, and salt in a saucepan; bring to a rapid boil. Reduce heat and simmer, uncovered, about 15 minutes, or until the sauce is medium thick. Remove from heat and stir in the lemon juice. Spoon over the 6 individual servings of ice cream. Sprinkle with the chopped nuts. *Makes 6 servings.*

Orange Rum Spanish Cream

2 tablespoons unflavored gelatin   2¼ teaspoons orange rind
2 cups milk   1 tablespoon lemon juice
½ cup sugar   ⅛ teaspoon salt
2 eggs, separated   ¾ teaspoon rum
1¼ cups orange juice   Fresh orange sections (garnish)

Soften the gelatin in ½ cup of the milk for 5 minutes. Heat the balance of the milk in a double boiler. Dissolve the gelatin in the hot milk. Add the sugar and mix well. Pour the hot mixture into the well-beaten egg yolks, beating constantly. Cook in double boiler, stirring continually until the mixture thickens and coats the spoon. Remove from heat and add the orange juice, rind, and lemon juice. Beat the egg whites with the salt and rum until stiff. Fold into the warm mixture. Pour into hot 4-ounce glasses; chill. Garnish with the orange sections. *Makes 6 servings.*

Note. The Orange Rum Spanish Cream will form a layer of custard and one of jelly if the egg whites are added while the mixture is hot. If a custard consistency throughout is desired, cool the mixture. When it starts to set, fold in the stiffly beaten whites and flavoring. This dessert can be made into an Orange Bavarian by folding in 1 quart of heavy whipped cream.

Sliced Peach and Blueberry Cup

Peaches, sliced

Blueberries

Raspberry sherbet

Cinnamon cookies

Serve the sliced peaches, blueberries, and a scoop of raspberry sherbet with cinnamon cookies.

Peach Bavarian

1 tablespoon unflavored gelatin

¼ cup cold water

½ cup boiling water

¼ cup lemon juice

⅓ cup sugar

1 cup crushed peaches

¼ teaspoon salt

1 egg white

2 tablespoons sugar

¾ cup heavy cream

Soften the gelatin in the cold water, then dissolve it in the boiling water. Add the lemon juice and sugar. Cool. Add the peaches. Chill until thick but not set. Add the salt to the egg white and beat until soft peaks form. Add the sugar, beating constantly until stiff. Whip the cream. Fold the beaten egg white and whipped cream into the gelatin mixture. Pour into a 1½-quart mold or six individual molds. Chill until set. *Makes 6 servings.*

Note. Use only clean eggs in this recipe, with *no cracks* in the shells.

Chantilly Cream with Peaches

1 cup coarsely crushed peaches

1 cup sifted confectioner's sugar

⅛ teaspoon salt

1 cup heavy cream

1 teaspoon vanilla extract

Whipped cream

Sliced peaches   Ladyfingers or strips of sponge cake

Combine the peaches, ¼ cup of the sugar, and the salt and set aside. Whip the cream until almost stiff. Gradually beat in the remaining ¾ cup sugar and the vanilla. Fold in the peaches. Turn the mixture into a serving bowl. Garnish with the whipped cream, put through a decorator's tube, if desired, and the sliced peaches. Serve with the ladyfingers or strips of sponge cake. *Makes 4 servings.*

Pear Crumble

6 fresh pears   ½ teaspoon cinnamon
⅓ cup port   ½ teaspoon nutmeg
1 tablespoon lemon juice   ⅓ cup butter or margarine
¾ cup flour   Light cream
1 cup brown sugar

Preheat oven to 375°. Pare, core, and slice the pears. Arrange in a greased baking dish (8″ x 8″ x 2″) and sprinkle with the wine and lemon juice. Mix the flour, sugar, and spices. Blend with the butter or margarine, using pastry blender or fingers; pat firmly over the pears. Bake until the pears are tender and the crust is brown, 30 to 40 minutes. Serve warm with cream. *Makes 6 to 8 servings.*

Persimmon Topping

The crimson pulp of a ripe fresh persimmon, mashed slightly, makes an attractive and delicious topping for vanilla ice cream or pudding.

Pineapple and Strawberry Cup

2 cups pineapple wedges   ½ teaspoon vanilla extract
3 tablespoons sugar   2 cups sliced strawberries
1 tablespoon lemon juice   Mint leaves (garnish)
⅛ teaspoon salt

Combine the pineapple, sugar, lemon juice, salt, and vanilla. Let stand at least 3 hours in refrigerator. Just before serving, add the strawberries. Serve in sherbet glasses. Garnish with the fresh mint leaves. *Makes 6 servings.*

Stewed Prune Pudding

1 pound prunes
2 cups sifted all-purpose flour
1 teaspoon baking soda
¼ teaspoon salt
½ teaspoon cloves
½ teaspoon nutmeg
½ teaspoon cinnamon
½ cup butter or margarine
½ cup sugar
½ cup light corn syrup

2 eggs, slightly beaten
¼ cup milk
⅓ cup sweet sherry or muscatel
½ cup chopped walnuts

SHERRY SAUCE
½ cup butter or margarine
⅛ teaspoon cinnamon
2½ cups sifted powdered sugar
¼ cup sherry

Wash the prunes. Place in a colander over boiling water; cover and steam 20 minutes. Remove the pits; cut the prunes into fine slices with scissors. Mix and sift the flour, soda, salt, and spices. Cream the butter or margarine and sugar until light and fluffy; beat in the corn syrup and eggs. Combine the sifted dry ingredients alternately with the milk and wine, mixing well after each addition. Add the prunes and nuts. Turn into a well-greased 2-quart mold; cover tightly. Place the mold on a rack in a kettle, pour in boiling water to half the depth of the mold. Cover the kettle and steam for 3 hours, adding more water as necessary. Serve hot with Sherry Sauce. *Makes 10 to 12 servings.*

SHERRY SAUCE. Beat the butter or margarine until creamy. Mix the cinnamon with the powdered sugar and add to the butter or margarine alternately with the sherry. Beat until the mixture forms stiff creamy peaks. Serve over steamed pudding. *Makes about 2 cups.*

Raspberry Whip

3 cups raspberries
1 egg white, unbeaten
⅓ cup sugar
1⁄16 teaspoon salt

½ cup cold water
1 envelope unflavored gelatin
½ cup heavy cream, whipped

Combine 2 cups of the raspberries, the egg white, sugar, and salt in a mixing bowl. Add ¼ cup of the cold water. Soften the gelatin in the remaining ¼ cup cold water in the top of a double boiler. Dissolve over hot water and add to the berry mixture. Chill until the mixture begins to thicken. Beat 1 minute with an electric beater. Fold in the whipped cream and the remaining cup of berries. Serve in sherbet glasses. *Makes 6 servings.*

Strawberry Mousse

2½ cups sliced strawberries
16 marshmallows
⅓ cup port wine

1 cup dairy sour cream
⅛ teaspoon salt

Crush the strawberries thoroughly. Quarter the marshmallows; combine with the wine and stir over very low heat until they are completely melted.

British Queen Strawberry (⅝ natural size)

Cool. Stir in the strawberries, sour cream, and salt. Turn into a refrigerator tray and place in the freezing compartment with the control set at the lowest temperature. Freeze until barely firm. (Reset temperature control to normal.) *Makes 5 servings.*

Watermelon Bowl

1 watermelon
1 honeydew melon
1 cantaloupe

Other seasonal fruits
Port, sherry, or sauterne

Cut a watermelon in half lengthwise; scoop out the meat from both halves with a rounded spoon or a melon ball cutter. Prepare honeydew and cantaloupe balls in the same way. Mix the melon balls with any other desired fruits — pineapple, grapes, sliced peaches, figs. Pour enough port, sherry, or sauterne over the fruit to cover. Chill for several hours. Just before serving, drain the fruit thoroughly and heap into one half of the scooped-out watermelon shell. Set the filled shell on a platter for serving.

Desserts 243

Wine-filled Watermelon

1 watermelon

White wine (sauterne) or
champagne

Cut a deep wedge (about 4 inches square) in the center of a whole water-melon. Pour in white dinner wine (e.g., a sweet sauterne is especially good,

Green Climbing Melon (⅕ natural size)

or champagne). As the wine is absorbed, add more from time to time until about 2 cups have soaked into the melon. Replace the wedge and chill thoroughly for at least 4 to 5 hours before serving.

Fruit Ambrosia

2 tablespoons sugar
2 tablespoons water
2 tablespoons orange juice
1 ½ teaspoons lemon juice
2 tablespoons kirsch
½ diced medium pineapple

1 medium grapefruit
1 ½ large oranges, diced
2 medium pears, diced
2 medium apples, diced
½ pound bananas, sliced
½ cup shredded coconut

Prepare the syrup by combining the sugar, water, orange juice, lemon juice, and kirsch. Stir until the sugar is dissolved. Blend the syrup with the fruits. Mound the fruit in dessert or sherbet glasses and sprinkle well with the shredded coconut. Serve very cold. *Makes 6 servings.*

Simple Harvestime Dessert

Fruit: Apples, pears, grapes, or others of the season
Nuts: Unshelled walnuts, pecans, or filberts

Cheese: Gouda, Cheddar, or anything you like
Wine: Port, muscatel, or other dessert wine

Place fruit, nuts, cheese, and possibly some crackers on a large platter. Provide nutcrackers and fruit or cheese knives. Serve with glasses of dessert wine.

Dessert Kebabs

2 golden Delicious apples, cored
2 red Delicious apples, cored
2 cups pineapple chunks, pared
Mint leaves
Crushed ice

Baked 9-inch pie shell
1 glass (10 ounces) apple jelly
1¼ cups sherry
1 teaspoon finely cut mint
1 teaspoon grated lemon peel
3 crushed coriander seeds

Wash and cut cored apples and pared pineapples into chunks. Toss together in a large bowl. Thread apples and pineapple alternately on skewers and place on crushed ice in a large bowl. Serve with Dessert Kebab Dip. *Makes about 8 skewers.*

DESSERT KEBAB DIP. Turn jelly into a small saucepan; break with fork and melt over low heat. Add remaining ingredients and simmer gently 5 minutes. Strain through cheesecloth. Chill. Surround with crushed ice. *Makes 2 cups.*

Honey-Wine Fruit Compote

¾ cup honey
½ cup port
2 tablespoons lemon juice

1 teaspoon grated lemon rind
2 cups diced fruit (e.g., apples, pears, whatever is in season)

Mix the honey, port, lemon juice, and lemon rind in a saucepan; bring to a boil and simmer 15 minutes. Drain the fruit thoroughly and place in a bowl. Pour the honey sauce over the fruit. Chill. *Makes 4 servings.*

Fresh Fruit Compote

2 cups diced cantaloupe
½ cup blueberries
2 cups sliced strawberries
¼ cup sugar
⅛ teaspoon salt

½ cup water
1 tablespoon lemon juice
2 teaspoons vanilla extract
Mint leaves (garnish)

Combine the fruit and set aside. Combine the sugar, salt, water, and lemon juice in a saucepan. Bring to a boil and boil 1 minute. Add the vanilla and pour over the fruit. (If desired, replace the above fruit with other fruit in season.) Cool and chill in refrigerator. Serve in sherbet glasses garnished with the mint. *Makes 8 servings.*

Cakes and Pies

Deep Dish Apple Cake

2 ¼ cups sifted all-purpose flour
1 ¼ cups sugar
3 teaspoons baking powder
½ teaspoon salt
1 cup shortening
2 eggs, slightly beaten

2 teaspoons vanilla extract
¼ cup water
1 teaspoon cinnamon
¼ teaspoon allspice
1/16 teaspoon mace
8 cups sliced apples

Sift the flour with 1 cup of the sugar, the baking powder, and salt. Add the shortening, mixing with a pastry blender or fork until the mixture is the size of peas. Add the eggs and vanilla; mix until well blended. Roll half of the dough between waxed paper. Place in greased 11" x 7" x 1½" casserole; set aside. Preheat oven to 350°. In a medium saucepan, bring the water and the remaining ¼ cup sugar to a boil. Add the cinnamon, allspice, and mace. Stir in the apples; cook 5 minutes. Add to the dough-lined casserole. Roll the remaining half of the dough. Cut into strips and lattice over the apple filling. Bake 35 to 40 minutes, until browned. *Makes 10 servings.*

Quick Gingerbread Upside-Down Apple Cake

1 pound gingerbread mix

1 apple

⅓ cup sugar
1 teaspoon lemon juice
½ teaspoon allspice

½ cup heavy cream
1 tablespoon confectioner's sugar

Preheat oven to 350°. Prepare the mix according to package directions. Peel, core, and slice the apple. Spread over the bottom of a well-greased, lightly

McIntosh Apple (⅓ natural size)

floured pan. Sprinkle with the sugar, lemon juice, and allspice. Pour the mix over the apple. Bake 25 to 30 minutes. Invert. Cut into 2½-inch squares and top with the sweetened whipped cream. *Makes 6 servings.*

Blackberry Dumplings

1½ cups flour
¼ cup shortening
½ teaspoon salt
Cold water
1 pint blackberries

SUGAR SAUCE

2 cups sugar
1 cup water
Pinch cream of tartar
1 tablespoon butter
¼ teaspoon nutmeg

Mix the first four ingredients as for a pie crust, then divide into four equal parts. Flour hands and then thin each portion of dough with fingers to a circle of about 5 inches in diameter. Fill with the washed blackberries. Press the edges of the dough together until you have a rounded dumpling. Drop into a kettle of boiling water and boil 45 minutes. Serve hot with Sugar Sauce. *Makes 4 dumplings.*

SUGAR SAUCE. Combine all the ingredients and boil at medium heat until the mixture thickens. *Makes about 1½ cups.*

Spiced Carrot Loaf Cake

½ cup dark brown sugar
½ cup sugar
½ teaspoon cinnamon
¼ teaspoon nutmeg
⅛ teaspoon cloves
¾ cup salad oil
1 teaspoon vanilla extract
2 cups sifted all-purpose flour

1 teaspoon double-acting baking
  powder
¼ teaspoon salt
2 large eggs, well-beaten
1 cup grated carrots
½ teaspoon grated lemon peel
½ cup coarsely chopped walnuts

Preheat oven to 350°. In a mixing bowl, combine the brown sugar, white sugar, cinnamon, nutmeg and cloves. Add the oil and vanilla; mix well. Sift together the flour, baking powder, and salt. Add it to the batter, alternating with the beaten eggs, starting and ending with the flour mixture. Blend well after each addition. Stir in the carrots, lemon peel, and nuts. Turn into a greased 9″ x 5″ x 3″ loaf pan and bake 1 hour 5 minutes, or until a cake tester inserted in the center comes out clean. Remove to rack and let stand 10 minutes. Turn out of pan and cool thoroughly before slicing. *Makes 1 loaf cake.*

Cranberry–Cream Cheese Pie

½ cup sugar
4 packages (3 ounces *each*) cream
  cheese
3 eggs, separated
1 teaspoon vanilla extract
½ teaspoon grated lemon rind
Jellied whole cranberries

Whipped cream (optional)

GRAHAM CRACKER CRUST
1¼ cups graham cracker crumbs
¼ cup sugar
⅓ cup softened butter or margarine

Preheat oven to 325°. Gradually blend the sugar with the cream cheese. Mix well with a spoon or an electric mixer. Beat the egg yolks until thick and lemon-colored. Add to the cheese mixture. Stir in the vanilla and lemon rind. Beat the egg whites until they stand in soft, stiff peaks. Fold into the cheese mixture. Pour into a chilled 9-inch unbaked pie shell or a graham cracker crumb crust. Bake 40 minutes or until the filling is puffed in the center. Remove from the oven and cool. Beat the cranberry jelly with a fork to break it up. Spread on the surface of the pie. Top with the whipped cream, sweetened to taste, if desired. *Makes 1 pie.*
  GRAHAM CRACKER CRUST. Blend the sugar with the butter or margarine.

Gradually blend in the crumbs and turn into a buttered 9-inch pie pan. (Be sure the pan measures 9 inches in diameter across the top.) Press uniformly over the bottom and sides of pie pan. Chill 2 hours. (Do not bake before adding the filling.) *Makes 1 9-inch pie crust.*

Cranberry-Orange Cheese Pie

FILLING
1½ teaspoons unflavored gelatin
2 tablespoons cold water
2 packages (3 ounces *each*) cream
  cheese, softened
1 egg, separated
½ cup sweetened condensed milk
¼ teaspoon salt
1 teaspoon grated orange rind
½ teaspoon vanilla extract
1 cup shredded coconut (garnish)

CRUMB CRUST
30 thin lemon wafer cookies
  (1½ cups crumbs)
¼ cup butter or margarine, melted

TOPPING
1½ teaspoons unflavored gelatin
2 tablespoons cold water
1½ cups cranberry-orange relish

CRANBERRY-ORANGE RELISH
4 cups (1 pound) cranberries
2 oranges
2 cups sugar

FILLING. Soften the gelatin in the cold water, then dissolve over hot water. Beat the cream cheese until fluffy. Add the egg yolk, milk, salt, orange rind, and vanilla. Beat well. Stir in the dissolved gelatin. Beat the egg white until stiff but not dry. Gently fold into the cheese mixture. Pour into the crumb crust. Chill until firm.

CRUMB CRUST. Finely crush or put through a food chopper (fine blade) the cookies. Blend with the melted butter or margarine. Press into the bottom and sides of an 8-inch pie plate. Chill.

TOPPING. Soften the gelatin in the cold water; dissolve over hot water. Stir into the cranberry-orange relish. Spread on top of the cheese mixture. Garnish with coconut.

CRANBERRY-ORANGE RELISH. Put the cranberries and oranges (quartered, with seeds removed) through a food chopper (coarse blade). Stir in the sugar and chill. Use 1½ cups of relish for the pie. Save the remaining 2½ cups to serve with a main course — chicken, turkey, pork, or ham.

Lemon-Lime Sky High Pie

1 envelope unflavored gelatin
1¼ cups sugar
¼ teaspoon salt
6 eggs, separated
⅓ cup water
⅓ cup lemon juice

⅓ cup lime juice
1 teaspoon grated lemon rind
1 teaspoon grated lime rind
½ teaspoon cream of tartar
1 9-inch baked pastry shell or crumb
  crust

Mix together the gelatin, ½ cup of the sugar, and the salt in the top of a double boiler. Beat the egg yolks with the water and lemon and lime juices; stir into the gelatin mixture. Place over boiling water and cook, stirring constantly, until the gelatin dissolves and the mixture thickens slightly, about 6 minutes. Add the lemon and lime rinds. Chill, stirring occasionally, until the mixture mounds slightly when dropped from a spoon. Beat the egg whites with the cream of tartar until stiff but not dry; gradually add the remaining ¾ cup of sugar and beat until very stiff. Fold in the gelatin mixture. If necessary, chill until the mixture will pile firmly. Turn into the pastry shell, piling high in the center. Chill until firm, several hours or overnight. Garnish with whipped cream and a lime twist. *Makes 1 pie; 8 servings.*

Lemon Meringue Pie

1½ cups sugar
¼ cup plus 2 teaspoons cornstarch
¼ teaspoon salt
½ cup plus 1 tablespoon lemon juice
½ cup cold water
5 egg yolks, well beaten
2 tablespoons butter or margarine
1¼ cups boiling water

1 to 3 teaspoons grated lemon peel
Few drops yellow food coloring
1 baked 9-inch pastry shell

MERINGUE
5 egg whites
½ teaspoon cream of tartar
½ cup plus 2 teaspoons sugar

Preheat oven to 350°. In a saucepan, thoroughly combine the sugar, cornstarch, and salt. Blend in the lemon juice, then the cold water and egg yolks until very smooth. Add the butter or margarine and gradually stir in the boiling water. Bring to a boil over medium heat, stirring constantly; boil 2 to 3 minutes. Stir in the grated peel and food coloring. Partially cool while preparing the meringue. Pour the hot filling into a baked 9-inch pastry shell; top with the meringue, sealing well at the edges. Bake 12 to 15 minutes until golden brown. Cool on wire rack. *Makes 1 pie.*

MERINGUE. Have the egg whites at room temperature. Place in large mixer bowl. Beat until frothy; add the cream of tartar and beat at high speed until the whites hold soft peaks and have just lost their frothy appearance. Add the sugar very gradually and continue beating until all the sugar is used and the whites are stiff, but not dry. *Makes meringue for 1 9-inch pie.*

Note. If you wish, you can substitute 1 teaspoon lemon juice for the cream of tartar in the recipe; it also acts as a stabilizer when making a meringue. Recent tests show that salt should not be used, as it actually weakens the meringue.

Lime Chiffon Pie

1 envelope unflavored gelatin
½ cup muscatel wine
4 eggs, separated
1 cup sugar
½ teaspoon salt

½ cup lime juice
½ teaspoon grated lime peel
Green coloring (optional)
Baked 9-inch pie shell
Whipped cream (garnish)

Soften the gelatin in the wine. Beat the egg yolks; add ½ cup of the sugar, the salt, and lime juice; cook, stirring, in the top of a double boiler until thick. Stir in the gelatin, lime peel, and a little green coloring. Cool. When it begins to thicken, fold in the egg whites beaten stiff with the remaining ½ cup of sugar. Pour into the baked pie shell; chill until firm. Top with the whipped cream. *Makes 1 pie.*

Orange Coconut Cake

2 cups sifted all-purpose flour
2 teaspoons baking powder
½ teaspoon salt
⅔ cup shortening
1⅓ cups sugar
2 teaspoons grated orange rind
½ teaspoon grated lemon rind
1 egg yolk
2 whole eggs
⅔ cup orange juice

SEVEN-MINUTE COCONUT FROSTING
2 egg whites
1½ cups sugar
5 tablespoons cold water
¼ teaspoon cream of tartar
1½ teaspoons light corn syrup
1 teaspoon vanilla extract
1 cup shredded coconut
Orange slices

Preheat oven to 375°. Sift together the flour, baking powder and salt; set aside. Cream the shortening with the sugar and the orange and lemon rinds. Beat in the egg yolk and whole eggs, one at a time. Add the flour mixture alternately with the orange juice, mixing well after each addition and beginning and ending with the flour. Pour the batter into two well-greased and lightly floured 8-inch layer cake pans. Bake 25 minutes or until a cake tester inserted into the center comes out clean. Cool in the pans 10 minutes. Turn out on wire racks to finish cooling. Frost with Seven-Minute Coconut Frosting. *Makes 8 servings.*

SEVEN-MINUTE COCONUT FROSTING. Place the egg whites, sugar, water, cream of tartar, and corn syrup in the top of a double boiler and beat until thoroughly blended. Place over rapidly boiling water and beat constantly with an electric mixer or a rotary beater for 7 minutes until stiff peaks form. Remove from heat. Stir in the vanilla. Continue beating 1 minute longer. Fill and frost the cake. While the icing is still soft, hold the cake firmly in one hand and fill the palm of the other hand with grated coconut. Cup the hand with the coconut to fit the curve of the cake and press lightly against the side of the cake. Sprinkle the coconut over the top of the cake. Garnish with the orange slices.

Note. To shred fresh coconut, remove the outer shell. *To grate in blender,* remove all the skin, cut the meat into small chunks, and proceed on low or chop, turning the blender on and off until the pieces are the desired size. *To shred by hand,* leave an inner coating ·to protect fingers and grate on coarse grater.

Peach Upside-Down Cake

¼ cup butter or margarine	powder
6 tablespoons brown sugar	½ teaspoon salt
6 peaches	⅔ cup shortening
2 cups sugar	3 eggs
1 cup water	1½ teaspoons vanilla extract
2½ cups sifted all-purpose flour	1 cup milk
4 teaspoons double-acting baking	Whipped cream or ice cream

Preheat oven to 375°. Melt the butter or margarine in the bottom of a 9" x 9" x 2" baking pan. Blend in the brown sugar, spreading it evenly over the bottom. Peel the peaches and slice into eighths. Boil 1 cup of the sugar with the water for 5 minutes. Add the peaches and cook, covered, 3 to 5 minutes, or until almost tender. Drain and arrange in rows over the brown sugar mixture. Sift together the flour, baking powder, and salt. Set aside. Cream the shortening with the remaining cup of sugar until fluffy. Beat in the eggs, one at a time. Add the vanilla extract. Stir in the flour mixture alternately with the milk, heating well after each addition. Pour the batter over the peaches. Bake 45 to 55 minutes or until done. Cool in pan 15 minutes on wire rack. Invert on wire rack, peach side up. Serve topped with whipped cream or ice cream, if desired. *Makes 1 cake.*

Summer Raspberry Tarts

1 basket raspberries (about
  1½ cups)
4 teaspoons cornstarch
¼ cup sugar
Few grains salt
½ teaspoon grated orange rind

⅓ cup orange juice
½ cup port
1 teaspoon lemon juice
6 baked 3-inch tart shells
Whipped cream

Rinse berries. Blend cornstarch, sugar, and salt. Add orange rind, juice, and port; cook and stir over moderate heat. Stir in lemon juice. Fill tart shells with berries; spoon sauce over them. Top with whipped cream. *Makes 6 tarts.*

Uncooked Fruit Cake

1 cup pitted prunes
1 cup seedless raisins
1 cup dried apricots
1 cup mixed candied peels and citron
1 cup pitted dates

1 cup candied cherries
1½ cups roasted unblanched almonds
¼ teaspoon salt
1 cup sweet sherry, port, tokay, or
  other dessert wine

Rinse the dried fruits and drain. *Pack* them into cup to measure. Cut the peels to measure. Put the fruits and almonds through a food chopper using a medium blade. Sprinkle the salt over the mixture. Add the wine and mix thoroughly. Pack into glass loaf pan (about 7½″ x 3½″ x 2½″). Cover with waxed paper. Store in refrigerator 2 to 3 days before serving. *Makes 3½-pound cake.*

Vanilla Fruit Tarts

1½ cups plus 3 tablespoons water
¾ cup sugar
1½ teaspoons lemon juice

2½ cups sliced fresh apples
4 baked tart shells, 4 inches in
  diameter

⅔ cup strawberries

1½ tablespoons cornstarch

1 teaspoon vanilla extract

Combine 1½ cups of the water, the sugar, and lemon juice in a saucepan. Boil 3 minutes. Add the apples; cover. Cook until tender, about 5 minutes. Remove the apples and divide equally among the baked tart shells. Arrange the strawberries over the tops. Blend the cornstarch with the remaining 3 tablespoons of water. Add to the syrup. Cook until clear and medium thick, stirring constantly. Add the vanilla and pour over the tarts. *Makes 4 servings.*

Beverages

Wine and Apple Starter

1 bottle (⅘ quart) red or rosé table
   wine
2 cups apple juice
3 sticks cinnamon

Ice cubes
Lime slices (garnish)
Orange wedges (garnish)

Have all ingredients well chilled. Combine the wine and apple juice. Pour over the ice cubes and garnish with the fruit. *Makes 1¼ quarts.*

Banana Eggnog

2 ripe bananas
2 eggs
½ teaspoon sugar

2 cups chilled skim milk
2 teaspoons vanilla extract
Nutmeg

Peel and mash the bananas. Add the eggs and sugar; beat until smooth and well mixed. Add the milk and vanilla; continue to beat until just combined. To serve, pour into chilled glasses and sprinkle the top with nutmeg. *Makes 4 servings.*

Cranberry Port Sodas

2 cups cranberries
1 cup port
Few grains salt

1 cup sugar
1 pint vanilla ice cream
Sparkling water

Rinse the cranberries and remove any stems. Combine with the port, salt, and sugar. Bring to a boil; lower heat and simmer until the berries are tender, about 5 minutes. Remove from heat and cool. When ready to make the sodas, spoon the ice cream into serving glasses. Add 2 or 3 tablespoons of the cranberry syrup and fill the glass with the sparkling water. A little extra port may be floated on top of each serving, if desired. *Makes 6 to 8 servings.*

Cucumber Lemon Limeade

1½ cups lemon juice
Peels from the juiced lemons
2 cups sugar
2 quarts water

1 cup fresh lime juice
1 cup thinly sliced cucumbers
Mint leaves

Squeeze the lemons and reserve the peels. Combine the sugar and 1 quart water in a saucepan. Bring to a boil and boil 1 minute. Remove from heat. Add all the lemon peels and steep 5 minutes. (Do not add the lime peels.) Remove and discard the peels, draining well to remove all the syrup that the peels have absorbed. Add the remaining water, lemon and lime juices, and cucumber. When ready to serve, place ice in a large punch bowl and pour in the punch. Garnish with the mint. *Makes 3 quarts.*

Fresh Nectarine Nectar

1 cup (3 to 4) peeled, sliced
   nectarines
½ cup orange juice

1 tablespoon lemon juice
1 tablespoon sugar
1 cup finely cracked ice

Place all the ingredients in an electric blender; cover. Mix until the ingredients are thoroughly blended, about 1 minute. Serve at once. *Makes 2½ cups.*

Lime Froth

⅔ cup lime juice
¼ cup sugar
2 unbeaten egg whites

Few drops green food coloring
  (optional)
1 cup finely crushed ice

Place all the ingredients in a shaker or 1-quart fruit jar. Shake well until the ingredients are well blended and the mixture is frothy. Serve in fruit juice glasses or in tall-stemmed cocktail glasses. If desired, mix the ingredients in an electric blender. *Makes approximately 1 cup.*

Party Eggnog Punch

6 eggs, well beaten
½ cup light corn syrup
¼ teaspoon ginger
¼ teaspoon cloves
¼ teaspoon cinnamon
¼ teaspoon nutmeg

2 quarts orange juice, chilled
½ cup lemon juice, chilled
1 quart vanilla ice cream
1 quart ginger ale, chilled
Nutmeg

Combine the eggs, corn syrup, ginger, cloves, cinnamon and nutmeg. Stir in the orange and lemon juices. Cut the ice cream into chunks the size of small eggs; put into large punch bowl. Pour the ginger ale over the ice cream. Stir in the egg mixture. Sprinkle with the nutmeg. *Makes 6 quarts.*

Ginger Mint

Squeeze the juice of 1 fresh lime into an 8-ounce glass; fill with chilled ginger ale and garnish with a maraschina cherry and a sprig of fresh mint.

Orange Blossom Champagne Punch

4 bottles (⅘ quart *each*) sauterne
  or other white table wine, chilled
8 cups orange juice
1⅓ cups lemon juice
2 cups Cointreau

4 cups sugar
6 strips lemon peel
4 bottles (⅘ quart *each*) champagne,
  chilled

Combine the sauterne, orange juice, lemon juice, Cointreau, and sugar in a punch bowl; stir to dissolve the sugar. Give each strip of lemon peel a twist; drop them into the punch bowl. Just before serving, pour in the champagne and add a block of ice or tray of ice cubes. For a wedding punch garnish with floating orange blossoms, real or artificial.

Orange Velvet

¾ cup orange juice
¼ cup lime juice
1 cup sweet sherry

Powdered sugar to taste
1 unbeaten egg white

Combine all the ingredients in a blender. Add cracked ice or ice cubes and mix vigorously.

Raspberry and Lime Swizzle

1½ cups sugar
2 quarts cold water
1⅔ cup lime juice

1⅔ cups raspberry puree
Lime slices (garnish)

Combine the sugar, 2 cups of the water and ⅓ cup of the lime juice. Stir until the sugar is dissolved. Bring to a boil and boil 5 minutes. Cool slightly. Add the raspberry puree and remaining 1½ quarts water and 1⅓ cups lime juice. Chill thoroughly. Garnish with the lime slices. *Makes approximately 2½ quarts.*

Low-Cal Rosé Shake

2 cups strawberries
½ cup rosé wine
1 pint low-calorie ice cream

½ cup skim milk
Mint leaves (garnish)

Wash and hull the berries. Put all the ingredients into a blender and whiz about 30 seconds. Or mash the berries and beat all the ingredients together with a rotary beater. If a thinner shake is desired, add a little more skim milk. Garnish with the sprigs of fresh mint. *Makes 4 to 6 servings of 3 ounces each.*

Fruited Burgundy Cooler

1 bottle (⅘ quart) Burgundy or
   other red table wine
¼ cup lemon juice
1 cup sugar

1 orange, very thinly sliced
1 lemon, very thinly sliced
2 cups chilled sparkling water

Combine the wine, lemon juice, and sugar in the pitcher; stir to dissolve the sugar. Add the orange and lemon slices. Chill in the refrigerator for 3 or 4 hours. Just before serving, add the sparkling water; stir well. Pour over ice cubes in tall glasses. *Makes 8 tall servings.*

Holiday Spiced Wine

1 quart water
3 cups sugar
12 whole cloves
4 inches stick cinnamon
6 whole allspice
½ teaspoon powdered ginger

Rind of 1 orange
Rind of 1 lemon
2 cups orange juice
1 cup lemon juice
1 (⅘ quart) bottle Burgundy or
   claret

Combine the water, sugar, spices, and orange and lemon rinds in a saucepan. Bring to a boil, stirring until the sugar is dissolved; simmer 10 minutes. Remove from heat and let stand 1 hour. Strain. Add the orange juice, lemon juice, and wine; heat gently. *Do not boil.* Serve hot in mugs. *Makes 20 (3-ounce) servings.*

Hot Spiced Cider Punch

4 cups water
4 cups apple juice
⅔ cup orange juice
¼ teaspoon cinnamon

⅛ teaspoon nutmeg
1 orange, quartered
8 whole cloves

Combine the first five ingredients in a saucepan; blend well. Heat just to boiling. Stick 1 or 2 whole cloves into each orange quarter. Float the orange quarters on the hot punch. Serve hot in punch cups or mugs. *Makes about 2 quarts or 16 servings using punch cups, or 8 servings using mugs.*

Fruit Pitcher Punch

Cracked or crushed ice
Fruit garnish: cherries, apricot and
   peach halves, melon strips or
   cubes, strawberries, pineapple
   slices, lemon and orange slices

2 cups fruit juice: pineapple,
   pineapple-grapefruit, orange, or
   any desired combination
¼ cup lemon juice
1 bottle (⅘ quart) sherry

Pack a pitcher (2½- to 3-quart size) a half to two-thirds full of cracked ice. Arrange the fruits of your choice in a decorative pattern in the ice. Pour in the fruit juice. Set the pitcher in the freezer for ½ hour or longer until fruit juice and ice are frozen. When ready to serve, bring the pitcher and glasses to the serving area. Pour in the sherry. Stir to blend as the ice melts. Garnish each serving with sprigs of mint, if desired. *Makes about 8 to 10 servings.*

Sangría

1 bottle (⅘ quart) Burgundy or
   other red dinner wine
1 orange
1 lemon or 2 limes, sliced
Variety of fresh fruit (such as 1 or 2

   sliced fresh peaches, 1 or 2 sliced
   plums, and ½ cup fresh berries)
1 jigger (3 tablespoons) brandy
Sugar (optional)
1 bottle (7 ounces) sparkling water

Pour the wine into a glass pitcher. Peel the orange in one long spiral strip. Put the peel in the wine, with one end of the spiral curled over the spout of the pitcher. Squeeze the orange; add the juice to the wine along with the lemon or lime slices and the brandy. For best flavor, allow to stand several hours. About 1 hour before serving, add the remaining fresh fruit. Taste; add sugar, if desired. (The traditional Spanish Sangría is refreshingly fruity but not too sweet.) Just before serving, add the sparkling water. Pour the Sangría into tall glasses or large wine glasses, half filled with ice cubes. Pieces of fruit may be added to each glass. *Makes about 10 (3-ounce) servings.*

Fresh Fruit Punch

¾ cup sugar
1 pint water
½ cup grapefruit juice

½ cup lemon juice
1½ cups orange juice
1 cup finely minced pineapple

1½ teaspoons lemon rind
1½ teaspoons orange rind
¾ teaspoon whole cloves
2 2-inch pieces stick cinnamon

¾ teaspoon whole allspice
¼ cup strong tea
1¼ pounds cracked ice

Combine the sugar and water and cook for 5 minutes, stirring occasionally. Combine with the fruit juices and pineapple, which has been put through a blender or fine strainer. Add the lemon and orange rind. Steep the spices in the tea for 15 minutes and strain into the fruit juices. Cool and serve over the cracked ice. *Makes 6 servings.*

To serve 50:

3 pounds sugar
1 gallon water
1 quart grapefruit juice
1 quart lemon juice
3 quarts orange juice
2 quarts finely minced pineapple
¼ cup lemon rind

¼ cup orange rind
2 tablespoons whole cloves
12 2-inch pieces stick cinnamon
2 tablespoons whole allspice
1 pint strong tea
10 pounds cracked ice

Holiday Specials

Hollyberry Dip

1 package (8 ounces) cream cheese
½ cup light corn syrup
½ cup dairy sour cream

1 cup chopped cranberries
3 tablespoons grated orange rind

Place the cream cheese in a small mixing bowl. Add the syrup; beat until fluffy. Fold in the sour cream, cranberries, and orange rind in the order listed. Serve with crackers. *Makes about 2 cups.*

Christmas Sandwich Wreath

DEVILED SPREAD
1 can (4½ ounces) deviled ham
¼ cup chopped celery
½ teaspoon Worcestershire sauce
20 party pumpernickel slices
Softened butter
CHICKEN APPLE SPREAD
1 can (4¾ ounces) chicken spread
¼ cup chopped apple

1 tablespoon dairy sour cream
20 party rye slices
Softened butter

NIPPY PÂTÉ SPREAD
1 can (4¾ ounces) liverwurst spread
¼ cup chopped green pepper
1 tablespoon mayonnaise
20 party cheese bread slices
Softened butter

Combine the first 3 ingredients of each recipe. Spread the bread with the softened butter. Spread half of the bread slices with the meat spread mixture; close sandwiches with remaining slices. Each recipe makes 10 sandwiches. On a serving tray, place the sandwiches upright in a circle, alternating the brown pumpernickel with the golden cheese bread and the light brown rye. They'll stand together easily. Decorate the wreath with a bright satin or paper bow and serve with a cheery punch. *Wreath contains 30 small sandwiches.*

Holiday Stuffing

1 package (7 ounces) cube stuffing	¼ cup butter or margarine
1 cup chopped onions	1 cup cranberries, cut in half
1 cup sliced mushrooms	3 tablespoons sugar
½ cup chopped pecans	½ cup chopped parsley

Prepare the stuffing according to package directions. Sauté the onions, mushrooms, and pecans in the butter or margarine 5 minutes. Combine the cranberries and sugar. Add all the ingredients to the stuffing, stirring only to blend. Place in 1½-quart casserole and bake at 350°, covered, for the last 30 minutes of roasting time. *Makes 6 servings.*

VARIATIONS: Try any of the following suggestions with your favorite basic turkey stuffing.

APPLE-RAISIN STUFFING. Use 1 chicken bouillon cube dissolved in water to make stuffing. Add 1½ cups unpeeled, diced apple, ½ cup seedless raisins and ½ teaspoon poultry seasoning.

APRICOT-SESAME STUFFING. Rinse 1 cup diced apricots in hot water; drain; cut with scissors into thirds. Add to stuffing with 2 tablespoons sesame seeds, ¼ cup snipped parsley and ¼ tablespoon *each* of thyme, nutmeg and cloves.

MUSHROOM STUFFING. Cook 1 cup sliced mushrooms with the onion and celery. Add to stuffing.

PARSLEY STUFFING. Add ½ cup chopped parsley to stuffing.

RAISIN STUFFING. Soak 1 cup seedless raisins in hot water 10 minutes. Drain; add to stuffing.

GIBLET STUFFING. Simmer the turkey giblets with onion slices, a celery stalk, a parsley sprig, and seasoning 3½ to 4 hours. Drain; chop coarsely. Add to the stuffing. Use broth in the gravy or to replace the water in stuffing.

NUT STUFFING. Toast 1 to 1½ cups chopped nuts in butter before adding to the stuffing. Almonds, Brazil nuts, chestnuts, filberts, macadamia nuts, or walnuts may be used.

WATER CHESTNUT STUFFING. Add 1 cup thinly sliced water chestnuts to the stuffing.

OYSTER STUFFING. Cook oysters, celery, and onions in butter 5 minutes. Use the oyster liquor to replace the water in the stuffing. Combine the oyster mixture and stuffing with ½ teaspoon salt, ¼ teaspoon pepper, and ½ teaspoon poultry seasoning.

Stuffed Mushrooms

1 pound large mushrooms	¼ cup water, white wine, or sherry
4 tablespoons butter or margarine	1 cup herb-seasoned stuffing
¼ cup finely chopped green onions	

Preheat oven to 350°. Remove the stems of the mushrooms and trim so that the brown feathery part shows. Sauté the caps in about 2 tablespoons of the butter or margarine until golden. Remove to a baking dish. Finally chop ¼ cup of the mushroom stems. Sauté with the onions, including some green tops for color, in about 2 more tablespoons of the butter or margarine. Add the water or wine. Lightly stir in the stuffing. Spoon into the mushroom caps. Bake until piping hot, about 10 minutes. Arrange as garnish on the meat platter.

Christmas Lemon-Coconut Pie

2 egg yolks	1 teaspoon grated lemon rind
½ cup water	2 egg whites
1 envelope unflavored gelatin	½ cup heavy cream
⅓ cup lemon juice	¼ cup grated coconut
⅔ cup sugar	1 9-inch pastry shell, baked
⅛ teaspoon salt	

Beat the egg yolks in the top of a double boiler; mix in the water, gelatin, lemon juice, ⅓ cup of the sugar, and the salt. Cook over hot water, stirring constantly, until the mixture thickens. Remove from heat. Stir in the lemon rind. Chill until the mixture mounds when dropped from a spoon. Whip the egg whites stiff; gradually beat in the remaining ⅓ cup of sugar. Whip the cream stiff. Fold the whipped egg whites and cream into the lemon mixture.

Fold in the coconut. Pile in the pastry shell. Chill about 3 hours, or until firm. Before serving, decorate with a wreath of whipped cream and holly sprigs, if desired. *Makes 1 pie.*

Champagne and Strawberry Mold

CLEAR LAYER
2 envelopes unflavored gelatin
2 cups cold water
¼ cup sugar
1 can (6 ounces) frozen lemonade
   concentrate (kept frozen)
½ cup champagne

CREAM LAYER
3 envelopes unflavored gelatin

1¾ cups cold water
½ cup sugar
2 cans (6 ounces *each*) frozen
   lemonade concentrate (kept
   frozen)
1 cup champagne
2 cups heavy cream, whipped
1 quart strawberries, sliced and
   sweetened

CLEAR LAYER. Sprinkle the gelatin over 1 cup of the cold water in a medium saucepan. Place over low heat; stir constantly until the gelatin dissolves, about 3 minutes. Remove from heat; add the sugar and stir until dissolved. Add the frozen lemonade concentrate; stir until melted. Add the remaining 1 cup of water and the champagne. Pour into a 12-cup mold and chill until almost firm. Begin preparing the cream layer.

    CREAM LAYER. Sprinkle the gelatin over the cold water in a medium saucepan. Place over low heat; stir constantly until the gelatin dissolves, about 3 minutes. Remove from heat; add the sugar and stir until dissolved. Add the frozen lemonade concentrate; stir until melted. Add the champagne. Chill, stirring occasionally, until mixture is the consistency of unbeaten egg white. Fold in the whipped cream. Turn into the mold with the almost-firm clear gelatin mixture. Chill until firm. Unmold onto the serving platter; serve with heaping portions of sweetened sliced strawberries. *Makes 12 servings.*

Christmas Pie

1 envelope unflavored gelatin
½ cup sugar
⅛ teaspoon salt
3 eggs, separated

½ cup cold water
¼ cup green crème de menthe
¼ cup white crème de cacao
1 cup heavy cream

Extra whipped cream (garnish)
Chopped pistachio nuts
Chopped cherries
Very thin orange slices

CHOCOLATE CRUMB SHELL
1¼ cup chocolate wafer crumbs
¼ cup sugar
⅓ cup butter or margarine, melted

Combine the gelatin, ¼ cup of the sugar, and the salt in a medium saucepan. Beat the egg yolks and water together; stir into the gelatin mixture. Place over low heat, stir constantly until the gelatin dissolves and the mixture thickens slightly, about 5 minutes. Remove from heat; stir in the liqueurs. Chill, stirring constantly, until the mixture is the consistency of unbeaten egg white. Beat the egg whites until stiff but not dry. Gradually add the remaining ¼ cup of sugar; beat until very stiff. Fold into the gelatin mixture. Whip the cream; fold in. Turn into a Chocolate Crumb Shell. Chill until firm. Garnish with wreath of whipped cream; sprinkle with the pistachio nuts and top with the cherries and orange slices. *Makes 1 pie.*

CHOCOLATE CRUMB SHELL. Preheat oven to 400°. Combine all the ingredients. Press over the bottom and side of a 9-inch pie plate. Bake 5 minutes. Cool.

Holiday Fruit and Nut Balls

1 cup chopped, pitted prunes
1½ cups seedless raisins
½ cup dried apricots
1 cup walnut meats
1 package (6 ounces) graham
  crackers
½ cup sweet sherry, muscatel, or

  other dessert wine
¼ cup honey
1 teaspoon grated orange or lemon
  peel
Dash of salt
Shredded coconut

Put the fruits, nuts, and crackers through a food chopper, using the finest blade. Add the wine, honey, orange or lemon peel, and salt; mix well (it's best to use your hands). Shape into marble-sized balls and roll them in the coconut. Store in a tightly covered tin or jar. These keep for ages. *Makes about 100 balls.*

Hot Yule Punch

2 quarts cider
2 cinnamon sticks
1 can (12 ounces) pineapple juice

1 cup light corn syrup
½ cup lemon juice
½ teaspoon nutmeg

BAKED ORANGES

3 small, perfect oranges (preferably
    navel)
Whole cloves

Preheat oven to 300°. Combine the cider and cinnamon in large saucepan.
Cover. Bring to a boil; simmer 5 minutes. Add the pineapple juice, syrup,
lemon juice, and nutmeg. Heat well. Remove the cinnamon sticks. Pour over
the Baked Oranges in the punch bowl. Serve hot. *Makes about 2 to 3 quarts.*

BAKED ORANGES. Preheat oven to 300°. Stud the oranges with the cloves
about ½ inch apart. Place in a baking pan with water covering bottom.
Bake about 30 minutes.

Menus for Meatless Meals

Common White Kohlrabi
(⅕ natural size)

A word about the extensive use of eggs and tuna in the economy meat-substitute dishes that follow. Eggs and tuna are obvious choices simply from the standpoint of food value in relation to cost. However, there are a few facts about the inclusion of eggs in the diet that should be brought to the attention of the reader.

There is no dispute as to the nutritional content of the egg, but relatively recent cholesterol studies have shown it to be of questionable merit in our regular everyday diets. Dr. Jean Mayer, professor of nutrition in the Harvard School of Public Health and past chairman of the White House Conference on Food, Nutrition and Health, has said it very well. "Eggs are an excellent food — for some people. Eggs are an inexpensive source of good quality protein, Vitamin A, iron, and other vitamins and trace minerals. They are a valuable part of the diet of children and young women. But the yolk of an egg contains huge amounts of cholesterol. And that is not good for middle-aged men and women, whose cholesterol average is already too high and for whom any further increase presents a clear and present danger. In the carefully reached opinion of the vast majority of health specialists, eating more than *2 or 3 eggs a week* contributes to the increased risk of heart disease in [these] middle-aged people."

Consequently, the menus that follow and that include eggs are to be considered usable according to the above guidelines — for most people a safe and sensible choice once a week.

Starred recipes may be found in this book.

Stuffed Celery Roquefort
* Pilaf à la Grecque
Fried Zucchini
Bread Twists and Butter
Chilled Watermelon Topped with
　　Blueberries
Cinnamon Cookies

* Hungarian Mushroom Soup
* Broccoli-Fish Casserole
* Orange-glazed Carrots
Bread Sticks
* Bananes au Rhum

Cranberry Juice
* Apple Pancakes
* Rhubarb-Lemon Marmalade
* Broiled Apple Rings
Café au Lait

* Cream of Parsley Soup
* Tuna-stuffed Eggplant
* Carrots and Grapes
Sesame Seed Rolls
* Brownie-Coconut Pecan Pie

* Chinese Cabbage Soup
Broiled Fish
Spring Green Peas and Scallions
* Fruit Muffins
* Strawberry Mousse

* Cream of Broccoli Soup
* Shrimp-Grapefruit Curry with
　　California Chutney
Escarole and Endive Salad
Parker House Rolls
* Blueberry Cream

* Roquefort-stuffed Mushrooms
Broiled Fish
* Cooked Asparagus with Guacamole
　　Sauce
* Fruited Rhubarb and Banana Mold
* Uncooked Fruit Cake

* Cream of Cauliflower Soup
* Chinese Celery, Mushroom, and
　　Chicken Sauté
* Banana-Orange Bread
Green Bean Salad
* Cantaloupe Snow Pudding

* Corn and Cheese Soup
* Turkey and Tangelo Salad
* Spiced Pickled Fresh Beets
Melba Toast
* Black-Bottom Lime Parfait

* Gazpacho
* Tuna Loaf
* Zucchini Pickles
Club Rolls
* Blueberry Custard Parfait

* Vegetable Fish Chowder
* Omelet Piperade
* Sugarplum Coffee Cake

* Cantaloupe Supreme
* Cioppino
* Salad Salerno
Italian Bread Loaf
* Lemon-Banana Freeze

* Asparagus Vinaigrette
* French Potato Pie
* Gingered Carrot Salad
* Charlotte de Pommes

* Senegalese Celery Soup
* Acapulco Enchiladas
Spinach Salad
* Raspberry Whip

* Artichoke-Crab California
* Baked Tomato Pie
* Cabbage with Peanut Sauce
* Perfection Salad
* Fast Banana Cream Crunch
　　Pudding

* Pickled Fish Fillets with Mushrooms
* Fresh Asparagus Frittata
* Dutch Pepper Salad
* Lemon-Lime Sky High Pie

Stuffed Artichokes
* Sweet Potato Cran-Apple Casserole
* Sherry Fruit Bread
* Mixed or Latticed Green Salad
* Orange Coconut Cake

* Scandinavian Fruit Soup
* Lemon-Lime Chicken
* Cauliflower-Chestnut Casserole
* Cranberry–Cream Cheese Pie

* Avocado Soup
* Seafood Creole
* Cranberry-Nut Bread with Cream
  Cheese
* Vanilla Banana Pudding

* Low-Calorie Potato Soup
* Clam and Cottage Cheese Mold
  Boston Lettuce and Artichoke Heart
    Salad
  Ry-Krisp
* Fresh Fruit Compote

* Tangerine Seafood Cocktail
* Corn and Mushroom
    Casserole
* French-fried Brussels Sprouts
  Tomato Aspic Salad
* Vineyard Apple Crisp

  Tomato Madrilène
* Cabbage and Cracker Pie
* Orange-glazed Carrots
  Bran Muffins
* Hot Nectarine Sundae

Large Green Paris Artichoke
(⅕ natural size)

* Old-Fashioned Vegetable Soup
* Banana Omelet
* Blueberry-Nectarine Iceberg Salad
* Maple-glazed Coconut Buns

* Cream of Lettuce Soup
* Chicken-Vegetable Pie
  Romaine and Blue Cheese Salad
* Pineapple and Strawberry Cup

* Deviled Seafood
* Ratatouille
  Crusty French or Italian Bread
  Chilled Pears and Cheese

* Cucumber Soup
  Tuna Quadrattini
* Spiced Carrot Loaf Cake
* Vanilla Fruit Tart

  Tomato Bouillon
* Leek Soufflé
* Pineapple Slaw with Sour Cream
    Dressing
* Quick Gingerbread Upside-Down
    Apple Cake

* Cauliflowerets Vinaigrette
* Dill-stuffed Sea Bass with Parsley
    Sauce
* Glazed Mustard Parsnips
  Tossed Green Salad
* Chantilly Cream with Peaches

* Avocado-stuffed Celery
  All-in-One Barbecue
* Fruited Oatmeal Bread
* Minted Apricots

* Mushroom Canapés
* Tomato and Brussels Sprout
    Casserole

* Baked Rutabaga Cheese Chips
* Brown Betty Cranberry-Apple Pie

* Bisque of Brussels Sprouts
* Quick Chicken-Asparagus
    Hollandaise
* Celery Fritters
  Boiled Tomatoes
* Watermelon Bowl

Fresh Fruits and Vegetables for Your Health

Long-fruited Green Okra
(seed-vessels ⅓ natural size)

Health and Nutrition

Good nutrition, the most important contributing factor to good health, requires the adequate individual intake and interaction of the four basic food groups plus water. Fresh fruits and vegetables make up one of these four categories — the others are meat, fish, poultry, eggs and legumes; bread-cereals; and milk and dairy products. The nutritive value of fruits and vegetables, then, is obvious.

Although all four of the basic food groups provide vitamins, minerals, and other nutrients in varying amounts, only one food group can provide sufficient amounts of Vitamin C — that is fruits and vegetables. About 94% of the Vitamin C in the U.S. food supply comes from fruits and vegetables and no other food group can substitute in this contribution. *Note.* Since Vitamin C is not stored in the body to any great extent, fruits and vegetables should be consumed *regularly* (as part of a varied and balanced diet) by most healthy individuals.

It is significant, too, that fruits and vegetables supply half (51%) of the Vitamin A in our food supply, 20% of the iron, and almost half (43%) of the folic acid, an anti-anemia B vitamin. Of substantial importance, although less well known, is their contribution, in considerable amounts, of thiamine, niacin, and riboflavin plus the trace elements now believed necessary to the diet of humans — iodine, potassium, magnesium, manganese, zinc, and copper.

Fruits and vegetables again are the major contributors of the bulk or fiber necessary to good digestion and too often noticeably lacking in everyday diets in an era of super-refined foods. This indigestible material, often called roughage (this term can be misleading as its function belies its name — it is *not* rough on the intestinal tract), provides a medium for the growth of bacteria that help the body synthesize certain materials. It is the cellulose and hemi-cellulose (pectin) of fresh fruits and vegetables that create the intestinal bulk which then expedites the functions of the digestive tract, improves the retention of fluid in the upper intestine, lubricates the intestinal wall, and promotes normal peristalsis.

Another example of the importance of the fruit and vegetable food group is its tremendous contribution to oral health. In addition to the value of nutritive factors in fruits and vegetables combining to promote sound dental health in terms of tooth and gum structure, the physical character of many raw fruits and vegetables qualifies them as "detergent foods" by the American Dental Association. These foods perform an important mechanical function as tooth cleansers, clearing away to a great extent the residue of sticky high-carbohydrate foods such as candy, pastry, chewing gum, syrups, and jellies that tend to cling to the teeth, resist tooth brushing, and combine with mouth bacteria to produce decay sites. Detergent foods include celery, raw carrots, radishes, raw cabbage, cantaloupe, watermelon, honeydew melon, citrus fruits, pears, fresh pineapple, peaches, lettuce, strawberries, tomatoes, raw cauliflower, raw peppers, escarole, and raw turnips. These foods not only cleanse the teeth but provide relatively hard and crisp materials for chewing and promote firm healthy gums — again a supremely important factor in our oversweet, oversoft diets today.

With all the above virtues to recommend them, it hardly seems possible that fresh fruits and vegetables could also contribute heavily in the area of weight and cholesterol control — two factors considered essential in the prevention of heart disease today. Neverthless, it is true that almost all fruits and vegetables are virtually fat-free in their natural state, and because of their high water content (80–95%) they are very low in calories. Although fruits and vegetables (fresh and processed combined) constitute a third of the weight of all foods consumed, they provide less than a tenth of the calories. This applies especially to the fresh products that have no added sugar or starch — and in most cases more of the various nutrients than their processed counterparts.

Control of body weight and reduction in the consumption of foods with a high fat content has been proposed by the American Heart Association as a possible defense against common heart and circulatory disorders. Fruits and vegetables can be well used to help fulfill the desired quantity of food in the diet without supplying fat or adding excess calories. Fruits and vegetables, then, can be of real value to the weight-watcher. Yet it must be remembered that weight loss and weight maintenance depend wholly on the relationship between the total energy (calorie) intake and the total energy expenditure. According to the American Medical Association, there are no real health foods or reducing programs that are as satisfactory or as safe as maintaining a regular regime of suitable exercise and the good nutrition that results from the regular consumption of a *variety* of foods from the *basic four* categories of meat, cereals, milk, and fruits and vegetables.

It is the opinion of the American Medical Association that food, in variety and including fruits and vegetables, is a far more reliable source of vitamins and minerals than pills and, consequently, it advocates obtaining nutrients from foods, not drugs, except as a physician may prescribe supplements in specific cases. Indeed, even in the case of alkalizers, foods — apples, bananas, grapes, oranges, muskmelons, raisins, turnips, the legumes, tomatoes and white potatoes — have been found to produce a superior alkaline effect in the body. In fact, virtually all fresh fruits and vegetables have an alkaline reaction in the body, whether or not they have an acid taste. So unless directed to by your physician, avoid drugs; remember that fresh fruits and vegetables are among the body's best *natural* alkalizers, and with proper care the body generally takes care of its acid-alkaline balance very well.

In conclusion, despite all the seemingly obvious benefits to be derived from the fruit and vegetable food group, it is interesting to note the recent results of an extensive U.S. dietary survey conducted by two hundred professional nutrition investigators. The work extended over a period of ten years and the findings resulted in one major recommendation — the addition of more fruits and vegetables to the national diet.

Nutrient Highlights of Fresh Fruits and Vegetables

NUTRIENT COMPOSITION
(per 100 grams, 3½ ounces edible portion)

Apples

58 calories
84.4 g. water
0.2 g. protein
0.6 g. fat
14.5 g. carbohydrate
1 g. fiber
0.3 g. ash
7 mg. calcium
10 mg. phosphorus

0.3 mg. iron
1 mg. sodium
110 mg. potassium
8 mg. magnesium
90 Int. Units Vitamin A
0.03 mg. thiamine ⎫
0.02 mg. riboflavin ⎬ B Vitamins
0.1 mg. niacin ⎭
4 mg. Vitamin C

— Low in sodium.
— Low in calories: 1 medium apple (2½-inch diameter, 150 g.) contains 66 calories.
— Provide an alkaline reaction in the body.
— A dental detergent highly recommended by the American Dental Asociation.

Apricots

51 calories
85.3 g. water

1 g. protein
0.2 g. fat

12.8 g. carbohydrate
0.6 g. fiber
0.7 g. ash
17 mg. calcium
23 mg. phosphorus
0.5 mg. iron
1 mg. sodium

281 mg. potassium
12 mg. magnesium
2700 Int. Units Vitamin A
0.03 mg. thiamine
0.04 mg. riboflavin
0.6 mg. niacin
10 mg. Vitamin C

— Low in calories: three medium apricots (100 g.) contain 51 calories.
— Provide an alkaline reaction in the body.
— Rich in Vitamin A; six medium fruits supply more than the daily recommended dietary allowance.

Artichokes (boiled, drained)

8 to 44 calories (rising from time of
    harvest)
86.5 g. water
2.8 g. protein
0.2 g. fat
9.9 g. carbohydrate
2.4 g. fiber
0.6 g. ash
51 mg. calcium

69 mg. phosphorus
1.1 mg. iron
30 mg. sodium
301 mg. potassium
150 Int. Units Vitamin A
0.07 mg. thiamine
0.04 mg. riboflavin
0.7 mg. niacin
8 mg. Vitamin C

Asparagus (boiled and drained fresh spears)

20 calories
93.6 g. water
2.2 g. protein
0.2 g. fat
3.6 g. carbohydrate
0.7 g. fiber
0.4 g. ash
21 mg. calcium
50 mg. phosphorus

0.6 mg. iron
1 mg. sodium
183 mg. potassium
20 mg. magnesium
900 Int. Units Vitamin A
0.16 mg. thiamine
0.18 mg. riboflavin
1.4 mg. niacin
26 mg. Vitamin C

— Very low in sodium, only 1 mg. per 100 grams boiled spears. Ideal for a low sodium diet.
— Very low in calories: 1 cupful (175 g.) cooked cut spears contains 35 calories.
— Provides an alkaline reaction in the body.
— 1 cup (175 g.) provides three-quarters of the daily recommended allowance of Vitamin C; a third of the Vitamin A; a tenth of the iron for an adult.

Avocados

167 calories
74 g. water
2.1 g. protein
16.4 g. fat (incl. 3 g. unsaturated fatty
   acids & 9 g. unsaturated)
6.3 g. carbohydrate
1.6 g. fiber
1.2 g. ash
10 mg. calcium
42 mg. phosphorus

0.6 mg. iron
4 mg. sodium
604 mg. potassium
45 mg. magnesium
290 Int. Units Vitamin A
0.11 mg. thiamine
0.2 mg. riboflavin
1.6 mg. niacin
14 mg. Vitamin C

— Contain a substantial amount of the B vitamins.
— Contain food energy equal to lean meat.
— Highly digestible; provide an alkaline reaction in the body.
— Low in sodium; suitable for a low-sodium diet.
— Rich in fruit oil, which is relatively unsaturated.
— Partial substitution of avocados in the diet for hard animal fats has been shown experimentally to have a favorable effect in reducing the cholesterol level of the blood serum.

Bananas

85 calories
75.7 g. water
1.1 g. protein
0.2 g. fat
22.2 g. carbohydrate
0.5 g. fiber
0.8 g. ash
8 mg. calcium
26 mg. phosphorus

0.7 mg. iron
1 mg. sodium
370 mg. potassium
33 mg. magnesium
190 Int. Units Vitamin A
0.05 mg. thiamine
0.06 mg. riboflavin
0.7 mg. niacin
10 mg. Vitamin C

— Low in calories; high in bulk; filling and flavorful.
— Low in sodium: a medium-sized banana has only 0.41 mg. sodium.
— Banana sugars are 96% to 99.5% utilizable by the body.
— Have virtually *no* fat; equivalent weight-for-weight with the fat content of lettuce.
— Protective in preventing ulcer formation and permitting existing ulcers to heal.
— Provide an alkaline reaction in the body.
— Filled with a wide assortment of nutrients including Vitamin C; and since they are almost always eaten uncooked, full nutritive benefits are obtained.
— Thoroughly digestible, mildly laxative, they help to regulate body functions; their soft texture and blandness make them ideal for a therapeutic diet and

for infants and the elderly; a source of quick energy with readily assimilated sugars.

Beans, Lima (seeds only)

123 calories	2.8 mg. iron
67.5 g. water	2 mg. sodium
8.4 g. protein	650 mg. potassium
0.5 g. fat	67 mg. magnesium
22.1 g. carbohydrate	290 Int. Units Vitamin A
1.8 g. fiber	0.24 mg. thiamine
1.5 g. ash	0.12 mg. riboflavin
52 mg. calcium	1.4 mg. niacin
142 mg. phosphorus	29 mg. Vitamin C

— Suitable for use in a low-sodium diet; when boiled and drained, they have only 1 mg. per 100 grams (3½ oz.).
— Provide an alkaline reaction in the body.
— High in iron.
— A cup (160 g.), fresh, provides almost half recommended daily allowance of Vitamin C.

Beans, Snap

32 calories	0.8 mg. iron
90.1 g. water	7 mg. sodium
1.9 g. protein	243 mg. potassium
0.2 g. fat	32 mg. magnesium
7.1 g. carbohydrate	600 Int. Units Vitamin A
1 g. fiber	0.08 mg. thiamine
0.7 g. ash	0.11 mg. riboflavin
56 mg. calcium	0.5 mg. niacin
44 mg. phosphorus	19 mg. Vitamin C

— Low in calories: a cooked cupful (125 g.) contains 30 calories.
— Provide an alkaline reaction in the body.
— A cupful provides about a fourth of the daily recommended allowance of Vitamin C and useful amounts of Vitamin A, the B vitamins, and iron.

Beet Greens (boiled and drained)

18 calories	3.3 g. carbohydrate
93.6 g. water	1.1 g. fiber
1.7 g. protein	1.2 g. ash
0.2 g. fat	99 mg. calcium

25 mg. phosphorus

1.9 mg. iron

76 mg. sodium

332 mg. potassium

106 mg. magnesium (when raw)

5,100 Int. Units Vitamin A

0.07 mg. thiamine

0.15 mg. riboflavin

0.3 mg. niacin

15 mg. Vitamin C

— High in Vitamin A and iron: a cupful (180 g.) provides 80% more than the daily recommended allowance of Vitamin A and a third of the iron.

Beets (boiled and drained)

32 calories

90.9 g. water

1.1 g. protein

0.1 g. fat

7.2 g. carbohydrate

0.8 g. fiber

0.7 g. ash

14 mg. calcium

23 mg. phosphorus

0.5 mg. iron

43 mg. sodium

208 mg. potassium

15 mg. magnesium

20 Int. Units Vitamin A

0.03 mg. thiamine

0.04 mg. riboflavin

0.3 mg. niacin

6 mg. Vitamin C

— Low in calories: a cup (165 g.) contains only 50 calories.

— Provide an alkaline reaction in the body.

Blackberries

58 calories

84.5 g. water

1.2 g. protein

0.9 g. fat

12.9 g. carbohydrate

4.1 g. fiber

0.5 g. ash

32 mg. calcium

0.9 mg. phosphorus

0.9 mg. iron

1 mg. sodium

170 mg. potassium

30 mg. magnesium

200 Int. Units Vitamin A

0.03 mg. thiamine

0.04 mg. riboflavin

0.4 mg. niacin

21 mg. Vitamin C

— Low in calories: 100 grams (5/8 cup) contains 58 calories.

— Very suitable for a low-sodium diet: 1 mg. per 10 grams.

— Extremely valuable for producing bulk in the diet.

Blueberries

62 calories

83.2 g. water

0.7 g. protein

0.5 g. fat

15.3 g. carbohydrate

1.5 g. fiber

0.3 g. ash	6 mg. magnesium
15 mg. calcium	100 Int. Units Vitamin A
13 mg. phosphorus	0.03 mg. thiamine
1 mg. iron	0.06 mg. riboflavin
1 mg. sodium	0.5 mg. niacin
81 mg. potassium	14 mg. Vitamin C

— Relatively low in calories: a cupful (140 g.) contains about 85 calories.
— Provide a substantial amount of Vitamin C.
— Low in sodium: 1 mg. per 100 grams.
— Fresh, provide an alkaline reaction in the body.

Broccoli (spears boiled and drained)

26 calories	0.8 mg. iron
91.3 g. water	10 mg. sodium
3.1 g. protein	267 mg. potassium
0.3 g. fat	24 mg. magnesium
4.5 g. carbohydrate	2500 Int. Units Vitamin A
1.5 g. fiber	0.09 mg. thiamine
0.8 g. ash	0.2 mg. riboflavin
88 mg. calcium	0.8 mg. niacin
62 mg. phosphorus	90 mg. Vitamin C

— Low in calories — 1 cup (150 g.) contains 40 calories.
— High in Vitamins A and C with a substantial amount of iron and other minerals: 1 cup (150 g.) of cooked broccoli provides 75 percent of the recommended daily allowance of Vitamin A for an adult and twice the Vitamin C.
— Provides an alkaline reaction in the body.
— Like all green vegetables, it is valuable for bulk.

Brussels Sprouts (boiled and drained)

36 calories	1.1 mg. iron
88.2 g. water	10 mg. sodium
4.2 g. protein	273 mg. potassium
0.4 g. fat	29 mg. magnesium
6.4 g. carbohydrate	520 Int. Units Vitamin A
1.6 g. fiber	0.08 mg. thiamine
0.8 g. ash	0.14 mg. riboflavin
32 mg. calcium	0.8 mg. niacin
72 mg. phosphorus	87 mg. Vitamin C

— Low in calories: a half cup contains 23 calories.
— One cup (130 g.) provides almost double the recommended daily allowance

of Vitamin C, a tenth of thiamine (Vitamin B$_1$), and more than a tenth of the iron for an adult.

— Provide an alkaline reaction in the body.

— Valuable for bulk.

Cabbage

24 calories	0.4 mg. iron
92.4 g. water	20 mg. sodium
1.3 g. protein	233 mg. potassium
0.2 g. fat	14 mg. magnesium
5.4 g. carbohydrate	130 Int. Units Vitamin A
0.8 g. fiber	0.05 mg. thiamine
0.7 g. ash	0.05 mg. riboflavin
49 mg. calcium	0.3 mg. niacin
29 mg. phosphorus	47 mg. Vitamin C

— Low in calories.

— Provides an alkaline reaction in the body.

— Raw crisp cabbage is good for teeth and gums.

— A wedge (3½″–4½″) provides 82 percent of the recommended daily allowance of Vitamin C.

— Especially green cabbage — and the greener the better — is so high in Vitamin C that it ranks with orange juice.

— Ideal roughage; doctors agree that its addition (as in slaw) to a luncheon sandwich improves digestion in most cases as well as providing the nutritional value of the sandwich-and-drink lunch.

— Repeated experiments show that cabbage juice in many cases had a substantial effect in healing gastric ulcers or preventing their formation.

Cantaloupes

30 calories	0.4 mg. iron
91.2 g. water	12 mg. sodium
0.7 g. protein	251 mg. potassium
0.1 g. fat	16 mg. magnesium
7.5 g. carbohydrate	3400 Int. Units Vitamin A
0.3 g. fiber	0.04 mg. thiamine
0.5 g. ash	0.03 mg. riboflavin
14 mg. calcium	0.6 mg. niacin
16 mg. phosphorus	33 mg. Vitamin C

— Very low in calories: the edible part of half a melon 5 inches in diameter (185 g.) contains only 60 calories.

— Good source of Vitamins A and C; a half cantaloupe 5 inches in diameter provides more than the daily recommended allowance of Vitamin A for an adult and all of the recommended Vitamin C.

— Vitamin C increases as the melon ripens.
— Provides an alkaline reaction in the body.

Carrots

42 calories	0.7 mg. iron
88.2 g. water	47 mg. sodium
1.1 g. protein	341 mg. potassium
0.2 g. fat	23 mg. magnesium
9.7 g. carbohydrate	11,000 Int. Units Vitamin A
1 g. fiber	0.06 mg. thiamine
0.8 g. ash	0.05 mg. riboflavin
37 mg. calcium	0.6 mg. niacin
36 mg. phosphorus	8 mg. Vitamin C

— Low in calories.
— High in Vitamin A: a single carrot (1" x 5½") provides more than the daily recommended allowance.
— Provides an alkaline reaction in the body.

Casabas

27 calories	0.4 mg. iron
91.5 g. water	12 mg. sodium
1.2 g. protein	251 mg. potassium
Fat trace	30 Int. Units Vitamin A
6.5 g. carbohydrate	0.04 mg. thiamine
0.5 g. fiber	0.03 mg. riboflavin
0.8 g. ash	0.6 mg. niacin
14 mg. calcium	13 mg. Vitamin C
16 mg. phosphorus	

— Low in calories.

Cauliflower (boiled and drained)

22 calories	21 mg. calcium
92.8 g. water	42 mg. phosphorus
2.3 g. protein	0.7 mg. iron
0.2 g. fat	9 mg. sodium
4.1 g. carbohydrate	206 mg. potassium
1 g. fiber	24 mg. magnesium
0.6 g. ash	60 Int. Units Vitamin A

0.09 mg. thiamine
0.08 mg. riboflavin

0.6 mg. niacin
55 mg. Vitamin C

— Very low in calories: 3½ ounces contain 22 calories.
— Provides an alkaline reaction in the body.
— Raw or cooked, a good source of Vitamin C; one cup of raw cauliflower buds provides 115 percent of the recommended daily allowance of Vitamin C for an adult; one cup of boiled and drained cauliflower provides 110 percent of the recommended daily allowance of Vitamin C.

Celeriac (raw celeriac root)

40 calories
88.4 g. water
1.8 g. protein
0.3 g. fat
8.5 g. carbohydrate
1.3 g. fiber
1 g. ash
43 mg. calcium
115 mg. phosphorus

0.6 mg. iron
100 mg. sodium
300 mg. potassium
No Vitamin A
0.05 mg. thiamine
0.06 mg. riboflavin
0.7 mg. niacin
8 mg. Vitamin C

Celery

17 calories
94.1 g. water
0.9 g. protein
0.1 g. fat
3.9 g. carbohydrate
0.6 g. fiber
1 g. ash
39 mg. calcium
28 mg. phosphorus

0.3 mg. iron
126 mg. sodium
341 mg. potassium
240 Int. Units Vitamin A
0.03 mg. thiamine
0.03 mg. riboflavin
0.3 mg. niacin
9 mg. Vitamin C

— Very low in calories.
— Provides considerable amounts of Vitamins A and C.
— Ideal roughage.
— An excellent tooth cleanser.
— Useful in allaying hunger pangs during a weight-reduction period.

Cherries

70 calories
80.4 g. water

1.3 g. protein
0.3 g. fat

17.4 g. carbohydrate
0.4 g. fiber
0.6 g. ash
22 mg. calcium
19 mg. phosphorus
0.4 mg. iron
2 mg. sodium

191 mg. potassium
110 Int. Units Vitamin A
0.05 g. thiamine
0.06 g. riboflavin
0.4 g. niacin
10 mg. Vitamin C

— A half cup provides about a sixth of the recommended daily allowance of Vitamin C and useful amounts of other vitamins and minerals.

Chicory (See Endive, escarole, and chicory)

— One pound contains only 90 calories.

Chinese Cabbage

14 calories
95 g. water
1.2 g. protein
0.1 g. fat
3 g. carbohydrate
0.6 g. fiber
0.7 g. ash
43 mg. calcium
40 mg. phosphorus

0.6 mg. iron
23 mg. sodium
253 mg. potassium
14 mg. magnesium
150 Int. Units Vitamin A
0.05 mg. thiamine
0.04 mg. riboflavin
0.6 mg. niacin
25 mg. Vitamin C

— Very low in calories and high in Vitamin C; 1 cup (164 g.) cooked contains only 16 calories and provides 87% of the daily recommended allowance of Vitamin C.

Chives

28 calories
91.3 g. water
1.8 g. protein
0.3 g. fat
5.8 g. carbohydrate
1.1 g. fiber
0.8 g. ash
69 mg. calcium
44 mg. phosphorus

1.7 mg. iron
Sodium not stated
250 mg. potassium
5,800 Int. Units Vitamin A
0.08 mg. thiamine
0.13 mg. riboflavin
0.5 mg. niacin
56 mg. Vitamin C

— High in Vitamin C, Vitamin A and iron.

Coconuts (fresh coconut meat)

346 calories	1.7 mg. iron
50.9 g. water	23 mg. sodium
3.5 g. protein	256 mg. potassium
35.3 g. fat	46 mg. magnesium
9.4 g. carbohydrate	No Vitamin A
4 g. fiber	0.05 mg. thiamine
0.9 g. ash	0.02 mg. riboflavin
13 mg. calcium	0.5 mg. niacin
95 mg. phosphorus	3 mg. Vitamin C

Collards (cooked; leaves without stems)

33 calories	0.8 mg. iron
89.6 g. water	43 mg. sodium (in raw product)
3.6 g. protein	262 mg. potassium
0.7 g. fat	57 mg. magnesium
5.1 g. carbohydrate	7,800 Int. Units Vitamin A
1 g. fiber	0.11 mg. thiamine
1 g. ash	0.2 mg. riboflavin
188 mg. calcium	1.2 mg. niacin
52 mg. phosphorus	76 mg. Vitamin C

— Low in calories.

— High in Vitamins C and A and iron; one cup (190 g.) of cooked collards provides considerably more than the recommended daily allowance of Vitamin A and a tenth of the iron as well as other vitamins and minerals.

Corn, Sweet (boiled on the cob, drained)

91 calories	0.6 mg. iron
74.1 g. water	Sodium trace
3.3 g. protein	196 mg. potassium
1 g. fat	48 mg. magnesium
21 g. carbohydrate	400 Int. Units Vitamin A
0.7 g. fiber	0.12 mg. thiamine
0.6 g. ash	0.10 mg. riboflavin
3 mg. calcium	1.4 mg. niacin
89 mg. phosphorus	9 mg. Vitamin C

— Very low in sodium, with only a trace in 100 grams.

— Yellow sweet corn provides a fair amount of Vitamins A and C; one ear (5″ × 1¾″), cooked, provides about a tenth of the daily recommended allowance of thiamine (Vitamin B_1).

Cranberries (raw)

46 calories
87.9 g. water
0.4 g. protein
0.7 g. fat
10.8 g. carbohydrate
1.4 g. fiber
0.2 g. ash
14 mg. calcium
10 mg. phosphorus

0.5 mg. iron
2 mg. sodium
82 mg. potassium
40 Int. Units Vitamin A
0.03 mg. thiamine
0.02 mg. riboflavin
0.01 mg. niacin
11 mg. Vitamin C

— The quinic acid of cranberry juice is converted in the body to hippuric acid, a strong antibacterial agent under some circumstances.

Cucumbers

14 calories
95.7 g. water
0.6 g. protein
0.1 g. fat
3.2 g. carbohydrate
0.3 g. fiber
0.4 g. ash
17 mg. calcium
18 mg. phosphorus

0.3 mg. iron
6 mg. sodium
160 mg. potassium
11 mg. magnesium
Trace Vitamin A
0.03 mg. thiamine
0.04 mg. riboflavin
0.2 mg. niacin
11 mg. Vitamin C

— Very low in calories: 6 pared (⅛ inch thick) slices (50 g.) contain 5 calories.
— Provide an alkaline reaction in the body.
— One cucumber, pared (207 g.), provides about a third of the recommended daily allowance of Vitamin C.

Dandelion Greens (boiled and drained)

33 calories
89.8 g. water
2 g. protein
0.6 g. fat
6.4 g. carbohydrate
1.3 g. fiber
1.2 g. ash
140 mg. calcium
42 mg. phosphorus

1.8 g. iron
44 mg. sodium
232 mg. potassium
36 mg. magnesium
11,700 Int. Units Vitamin A
0.13 mg. thiamine
0.16 mg. riboflavin
18 mg. Vitamin C

— Low in calories: 3½ ounces (100 g.) contain 33 calories.
— High in Vitamin A and iron; a cup of boiled greens (180 g.) provides four

times the recommended daily allowance of Vitamin A for an adult, a third of the iron, and half the Vitamin C.

Dasheens, Corms, and Tubers (raw)

97 calories
73 g. water
1.9 g. protein
0.29 g. fat
23.7 g. carbohydrate
0.8 g. fiber
1.2 g. ash
28 mg. calcium
61 mg. phosphorus

1 mg. iron
7 mg. sodium
514 mg. potassium
20 Int. Units Vitamin A
0.13 mg. thiamine
0.04 mg. riboflavin
1.1 mg. niacin
4 mg. Vitamin C

— Eat only when cooked.

Dates (natural or dry)

274 calories
22.5 g. water
2.2 g. protein
0.5 g. fat
72.9 g. carbohydrate
2.3 g. fiber
1.9 g. ash
59 mg. calcium
63 mg. phosphorus

3 mg. iron
1 mg. sodium
648 mg. potassium
50 Int. Units Vitamin A
0.09 mg. thiamine
0.1 mg. riboflavin
2.2 mg. niacin
No Vitamin C

— Low in sodium.
— Provide an alkaline reaction in the body.
— Unusually high in iron; 3 to 4 pitted dates provide more than a third of the recommended daily allowance.

Eggplant (boiled and drained)

19 calories
94.3 g. water
1 g. protein
0.2 g. fat
4.1 g. carbohydrate
0.9 g. fiber
0.4 g. ash
11 mg. calcium
21 mg. phosphorus

0.6 mg. iron
1 mg. sodium
150 mg. potassium
16 mg. magnesium
10 Int. Units Vitamin A
0.05 mg. thiamine
0.04 mg. riboflavin
0.5 mg. niacin
3 mg. Vitamin C

— Low in calories: 3½ ounces contain 19 calories.
— Low in sodium.
— Provides an alkaline reaction in the body.

Endives, Escarole, and Chicory (raw)

20 calories	1.7 mg. iron
93.1 g. water	14 mg. sodium
1.7 g. protein	294 mg. potassium
0.1 g. fat	10 mg. magnesium
4.1 g. carbohydrate	3,300 Int. Units Vitamin A
0.9 g. fiber	0.07 mg. thiamine
1 g. ash	0.14 mg. riboflavin
81 mg. calcium	0.5 mg. niacin
54 mg. phosphorus	10 mg. Vitamin C

— Very low in calories — 3½ ounces of raw greens contain only 20 calories; a
  whole pound has only 90 calories.
— Provide an alkaline reaction in the body.
— 3½-ounce portion provides 60 percent of the daily recommended allowance
  of Vitamin A, a sixth of the iron, and a sixth of the Vitamin C.

Figs (fresh, not dried)

80 calories	0.6 mg. iron
77.5 g. water	2 mg. sodium
1.2 g. protein	194 mg. potassium
0.3 g. fat	80 Int. Units Vitamin A
20.3 g. carbohydrate	0.06 mg. thiamine
1.2 g. fiber	0.05 mg. riboflavin
0.7 g. ash	0.4 mg. niacin
35 mg. calcium	2 mg. Vitamin C
22 mg. phosphorus	

— Provide an alkaline reaction in the body.

Garlic (raw cloves)

137 calories	29 mg. calcium
61.3 g. water	202 mg. phosphorus
6.2 g. protein	1.5 mg. iron
0.2 g. fat	19 mg. sodium
30.8 g. carbohydrate	529 mg. potassium
1.5 g. fiber	Trace Vitamin A
1.5 g. ash	0.25 mg. thiamine

0.08 mg. riboflavin
0.5 mg. niacin

15 mg. Vitamin C

Grapefruit

41 calories
88.4 g. water
0.5 g. protein
0.1 g. fat
10.6 g. carbohydrate
0.2 g. fiber
0.4 g. ash
16 mg. calcium
16 mg. phosphorus
0.4 mg. iron

1 mg. sodium
135 mg. potassium
12 mg. magnesium
80 Int. Units Vitamin A (440 if pink
   or red)
0.04 mg. thiamine
0.02 mg. riboflavin
0.2 mg. niacin
38 mg. Vitamin C

— ½ medium-sized grapefruit (4¼ inches in diameter) provides 87 percent of
   the recommended daily allowance of Vitamin C and contains only 55 calories.
— Pink grapefruit has a substantial extra share of Vitamin A.
— Provides an alkaline reaction in the body.

Grapes (European type such as Thompson seedless, Emperor, Tokay, and
   Malaga)

67 calories
81.4 g. water
0.6 g. protein
0.3 g. fat
17.3 g. carbohydrate
0.5 g. fiber
0.4 g. ash
12 mg. calcium
20 mg. phosphorus

0.4 mg. iron
3 mg. sodium
173 mg. potassium
6 mg. magnesium
100 Int. Units Vitamin A
0.05 mg. thiamine
0.03 mg. riboflavin
0.3 mg. niacin
4 mg. Vitamin C

— Provide a good quota of vitamins and minerals of all kinds, although they are
   not outstanding for any one kind.
— Low in sodium.
— Grapes of all kinds have an alkaline reaction in the body.
— A half cup of Thompson seedless provides only 48 calories, good for low
   calorie sweetness and quick energy.

Honeydews

33 calories
90.6 g. water
0.8 g. protein

0.3 g. fat
7.7 g. carbohydrate
0.6 g. fiber

0.6 g. ash
14 mg. calcium
16 mg. phosphorus
0.4 mg. iron
12 mg. sodium
251 mg. potassium

40 Int. Units Vitamin A
0.04 mg. thiamine
0.03 mg. riboflavin
0.6 mg. niacin
23 mg. Vitamin C

— An excellent dessert for weight-watchers; low in calories, a 2″ x 7″ wedge (150 g.) contains 46 calories.
— Provide an alkaline reaction in the body.

Kale (boiled, drained leaves without stems and mid-ribs)

39 calories
87.8 g. water
4.5 g. protein
0.7 g. fat
6.1 g. carbohydrate
0.9 g. ash
187 mg. calcium
58 mg. phosphorus
1.6 mg. iron

43 mg. sodium
221 mg. potassium
37 mg. magnesium
8,300 Int. Units Vitamin A
0.10 mg. thiamine
0.18 mg. riboflavin
1.6 mg. niacin
93 mg. Vitamin C

— High in Vitamins A and C and iron: 1 cup (110 grams) cooked kale, leaves and stems, provides 150% of the daily recommended allowance of Vitamin A for an adult, 113% of the Vitamin C, and more than a tenth of the iron.
— Valuable for bulk as well as for vitamins and minerals, and a good regulator.
— Causes an alkaline reaction in the body.
— Low in calories: a cup contains only 45 calories.

Kohlrabi (thickened bulb-like stems of raw kohlrabi)

29 calories
90.3 g. water
2 g. protein
0.1 g. fat
6.6 g. carbohydrate
1 g. fiber
1 g. ash
41 mg. calcium
51 mg. phosphorus

0.5 mg. iron
8 mg. sodium
372 mg. potassium
37 mg. magnesium
20 Int. Units Vitamin A
0.06 mg. thiamine
0.04 mg. riboflavin
0.3 mg. niacin
66 mg. Vitamin C

— High in Vitamin C and provides useful quantities of other vitamins and minerals.

— 3½ ounces of boiled, drained kohlrabi provides 70 percent of the daily recommended allowance of Vitamin C.

Kumquats (raw)

65 calories	23 mg. phosphorus
81.3 g. water	0.4 mg. iron
0.9 g. protein	7 mg. sodium
0.1 g. fat	236 mg. potassium
17.1 g. carbohydrate	600 Int. Units Vitamin A
3.7 g. fiber	0.08 mg. thiamine
0.6 g. ash	0.1 mg. riboflavin
63 mg. calcium	36 mg. Vitamin C

Leeks (raw, bulb and lower leaf portion)

52 calories	1.1 mg. iron
85.4 g. water	5 mg. sodium
2.2 g. protein	347 mg. potassium
0.3 g. fat	23 mg. magnesium
11.2 g. carbohydrate	40 Int. Units Vitamin A
1.3 g. fiber	0.11 mg. thiamine
0.9 g. ash	0.06 mg. riboflavin
52 mg. calcium	0.5 mg. niacin
50 mg. phosphorus	17 mg. Vitamin C

— Low in calories.
— Contain useful amounts of iron and Vitamin C.

Lemons

27 calories	0.6 mg. iron
90.1 g. water	2 mg. sodium
1.1 g. protein	138 mg. potassium
0.3 g. fat	20 Int. Units Vitamin A
8.2 g. carbohydrate	0.04 mg. thiamine
0.4 g. fiber	0.02 mg. riboflavin
0.3 g. ash	0.1 mg. niacin
26 mg. calcium	53 mg. Vitamin C
16 mg. phosphorus	

— High in Vitamin C: 1 tablespoon (15 g.) of juice provides a ninth of the recommended daily allowance of Vitamin C; one medium-sized lemon (2⅖ inches in diameter) provides 63 percent of the recommended daily allowance of Vitamin C.

— A good fine substitute for flavoring in a salt-free diet.

Lettuce

13 calories
95.5 g. water
0.9 g. protein
0.1 g. fat
2.9 g. carbohydrate
0.5 g. fiber
0.6 g. ash
20 mg. calcium
22 mg. phosphorus

0.5 g. iron
9 mg. sodium
175 mg. potassium
11 mg. magnesium
330 Int. Units Vitamin A
0.06 mg. thiamine
0.06 mg. riboflavin
0.3 mg. niacin
6 mg. Vitamin C

— Very low in calories; a quarter of a 4¾-inch head (113 g.) contains only 15 calories.
— Provides an alkaline reaction in the body.
— Creates desirable roughage (cellulose) for good digestion; adding it to a sandwich improves both flavor and digestion.
— The greener types contain a useful amount of Vitamins A and C, iron, and other vitamins and minerals; Boston and Bibb lettuce are high in iron: 2 mg. in 3½ ounces.

Limes

28 calories
89.3 g. water
0.7 g. protein
0.2 g. fat
9.5 g. carbohydrate
0.5 g. fiber
0.3 g. ash
33 mg. calcium
18 mg. phosphorus

0.6 mg. iron
2 mg. sodium
102 mg. potassium
10 Int. Units Vitamin A
0.03 mg. thiamine
0.02 mg. riboflavin
0.2 mg. niacin
37 mg. Vitamin C

— Low in sodium.
— High in Vitamin C: 1 cup of juice (246 g.) provides 33 percent more than the recommended daily allowance of Vitamin C.
— Although limes have an acid taste, they provide an alkaline reaction in the body.

Mangoes

66 calories
81.7 g. water
0.7 g. protein

0.4 g. fat
16.8 g. carbohydrate
0.9 g. fiber

0.4 g. ash   18 mg. magnesium
10 mg. calcium   4,800 Int. Units Vitamin A
13 mg. phosphorus   0.05 mg. thiamine
0.4 mg. iron   0.05 mg. riboflavin
7 mg. sodium   1.1 mg. niacin
189 mg. potassium   35 mg. Vitamin C

— A good source of Vitamins A and C; one medium mango of 200 grams (providing 132 g. edible portion) provides more than the daily recommended allowance of Vitamin A for an adult and three-quarters of the Vitamin C.

Mushrooms (cooked, solids and liquids)

17 calories   0.5 mg. iron
93.1 g. water   400 mg. sodium
1.9 g. protein   197 mg. potassium
0.1 g. fat   8 mg. magnesium
2.4 g. carbohydrate   Trace Vitamin A
0.6 g. fiber   0.02 mg. thiamine
1.6 g. ash   0.25 mg. riboflavin
6 mg. calcium   2 mg. niacin
68 mg. phosphorus   2 mg. Vitamin C

— Low in calories: 1 cup (244 g.) contains 28 calories.
— A cup provides more than a tenth of the daily recommended allowance of iron.

Mustard Greens (boiled and drained)

23 calories   1.8 mg. iron
92.6 g. water   18 mg. sodium
2.2 g. protein   220 mg. potassium
0.4 g. fat   27 mg. magnesium
4 g. carbohydrate   5,800 Int. Units Vitamin A
0.9 g. fiber   0.08 mg. thiamine
0.8 g. ash   0.14 mg. riboflavin
138 mg. calcium   0.6 mg. niacin
32 mg. phosphorus   48 mg. Vitamin C

— Low in calories; 1 cup (140 g.) contains 35 calories.
— High in Vitamins A and C and iron; a cup provides 61 percent more than the recommended daily allowance of Vitamin A, more than the allowance of Vitamin C, a fourth of the iron, and a useful amount of other vitamins and minerals, including folic acid.

Nectarines

64 calories
81.8 g. water
0.6 g. protein
Trace fat
17.1 g. carbohydrate
0.4 g. fiber
0.5 g. ash
4 mg. calcium
24 mg. phosphorus

0.5 mg. iron
6 mg. sodium
294 mg. potassium
13 mg. magnesium
1,650 Int. Units Vitamin A
No thiamine
" riboflavin
" niacin
13 mg. Vitamin C

— Low in calories.
— Contain a valuable amount of Vitamin A: 1 nectarine (2½" x 2" in diameter) provides about a third of the daily recommended allowance of Vitamin A and a fourth of the Vitamin C.
— Provide an alkaline reaction in the body.

Okra (boiled and drained)

29 calories
91.1 g. water
2 g. protein
0.3 g. fat
6 g. carbohydrate
1 g. fiber
0.6 g. ash
92 mg. calcium
41 mg. phosphorus

0.5 mg. iron
2 mg. sodium
174 mg. potassium
490 Int. Units Vitamin A
0.13 mg. thiamine
0.18 mg. riboflavin
0.9 mg. niacin
20 mg. Vitamin C

— Eight pods of cooked okra (each pod 3" x ⅝") provide more than a fourth of the recommended daily allowance of Vitamin C, a tenth of the thiamine, and a twelfth of the Vitamin A.

Onions (raw)

38 calories
89.1 g. water
1.5 g. protein
0.1 g. fat
8.7 g. carbohydrate
0.6 g. fiber
0.6 g. ash
27 mg. calcium
36 mg. phosphorus
0.5 mg. iron

10 mg. sodium
157 mg. potassium
12 mg. magnesium
40 Int. Units Vitamin A (if yellow-fleshed)
0.03 mg. thiamine
0.04 mg. riboflavin
0.02 mg. niacin
10 mg. Vitamin C

— Low in calories; one raw onion (2½-inch diameter, 10 g.) contains 40 calories.
— 1 cup cooked onions provides a fourth of the daily recommended allowance of Vitamin C and a twelfth of the iron.
— Provide an alkaline reaction in the body.

Onions, Green (green portion only)

27 calories	2.2 mg. iron
91.8 g. water	5 mg. sodium
1.6 g. protein	231 mg. potassium
0.4 g. fat	4,000 Int. Units Vitamin A
5.5 g. carbohydrate	0.05 mg. thiamine
1.3 g. fiber	0.05 mg. riboflavin
0.7 g. ash	0.4 mg. niacin
56 mg. calcium	32 mg. Vitamin C
39 mg. phosphorus	

Onions, Green (raw, bulb and entire top)

36 calories	1 mg. iron
89.4 g. water	5 mg. sodium
1.5 g. protein	231 mg. potassium
0.2 g. fat	2,000 Int. Units Vitamin A
8.2 g. carbohydrate	0.05 mg. thiamine
1.2 g. fiber	0.05 mg. riboflavin
0.7 g. ash	0.4 mg. niacin
51 mg. calcium	32 mg. Vitamin C
39 mg. phosphorus	

— Green onions, including tops, are a good source of Vitamin C, Vitamin A and iron.

Oranges

49 calories	0.4 mg. iron
86 g. water	1 mg. sodium
1 g. protein	200 mg. potassium
0.2 g. fat	11 mg. magnesium
12.2 g. carbohydrate	200 Int. Units Vitamin A
0.5 g. fiber	0.1 mg. thiamine
0.6 g. ash	0.04 mg. riboflavin
41 mg. calcium	0.4 mg. niacin
20 mg. phosphorus	50 mg. Vitamin C

— One of the major and most economical sources of Vitamin C in food; one medium (3-inch) orange contains more than enough Vitamin C for the recommended dietary allowance for a day.

— Low in calories; a California navel orange (2⅘-inch diameter) contains 60 calories; a Florida orange (3-inch diameter) contains 75 calories.
— Low in sodium: 1 mg. in 3½ ounces of juice.
— Provide an alkaline reaction in the body.
— An excellent tooth cleanser, recommended by the American Dental Association; they also help prevent the softening and bleeding of the gums that occurs when Vitamin C is inadequate.
— The juice encourages the retention of calcium in the body.

Papayas (raw)

39 calories	0.3 mg. iron
88.7 g. water	3 mg. sodium
0.6 g. protein	234 mg. potassium
0.1 g. fat	1,750 mg. Vitamin A
10 g. carbohydrate	0.04 mg. thiamine
0.9 g. fiber	0.04 mg. riboflavin
0.6 g. ash	0.3 mg. niacin
20 mg. calcium	56 mg. Vitamin C
16 mg. phosphorus	

— Low in calories: 3½ ounces contain 39 calories.
— A cup of ½-inch cubes (182 g.) provides 170 percent of the recommended daily allowance of Vitamin C and more than half the allowance of Vitamin A.

Parsley (raw)

44 calories	6.2 mg. iron
85.1 g. water	45 mg. sodium
3.6 g. protein	727 mg. potassium
0.6 g. fat	8,500 Int. Units Vitamin A
8.5 g. carbohydrate	41 mg. magnesium
1.5 g. fiber	0.12 mg. thiamine
2.2 g. ash	0.26 mg. riboflavin
203 mg. calcium	1.2 mg. niacin
63 mg. phosphorus	172 mg. Vitamin C

— Very high in iron, Vitamins A and C; only 1.2 ounces provides the recommended daily allowance of Vitamin C.

Parsnips (boiled and drained)

66 calories	82.2 g. water

1.5 g. protein
0.5 g. fat
14.9 g. carbohydrate
2 g. fiber
0.9 g. ash
45 mg. calcium
62 mg. phosphorus
0.6 mg. iron

8 mg. sodium
379 mg. potassium
32 mg. magnesium (in the raw veg.)
30 Int. Units Vitamin A
0.07 mg. thiamine
0.8 mg. riboflavin
0.1 mg. niacin
10 mg. Vitamin C

— 1 cup (155 g.) provides a fourth of the recommended daily allowance of Vitamin C and a tenth each of the thiamine and iron.
— Provide an alkaline reaction in the body.

Peaches

38 calories
89.1 g. water
0.6 g. protein
0.1 g. fat
9.7 g. carbohydrate
0.6 g. fiber
0.5 g. ash
9 mg. calcium
19 mg. phosphorus
0.5 mg. iron

1 mg. sodium
202 mg. potassium
10 mg. magnesium
1,330 Int. Units Vitamin A (for
    yellow-fleshed varieties)
0.02 mg. thiamine
0.05 mg. riboflavin
1 mg. niacin
7 mg. Vitamin C

— Low in calories: a medium-sized peach (114 g.) contains only 38 calories.
— Low in sodium: 1 mg. per 100 grams.
— A good source of Vitamin A; 2 medium-sized yellow-fleshed peaches provide about half of the recommended allowance of Vitamin A.
— Provide an alkaline reaction in the body.

Pears

61 calories
83.2 g. water
0.7 g. protein
0.4 g. fat
15.3 g. carbohydrate
1.4 g. fiber
0.4 g. ash
8 mg. calcium
11 mg. phosphorus

0.3 mg. iron
2 mg. sodium
130 mg. potassium
20 Int. Units Vitamin A
0.02 mg. thiamine
0.04 mg. riboflavin
0.1 mg. niacin
4 mg. Vitamin C

— 1 good-sized pear (3″ x 2½″; 182 grams) contains only 100 calories.

— Contain a good spectrum of nutrients in useful amounts, including B vitamins and ascorbic acid.
— Provide an alkaline reaction in the body.

Peas (boiled and drained)

71 calories	1.8 mg. iron
81.5 g. water	1 mg. sodium
5.4 g. protein	196 mg. potassium
0.4 g. fat	20 mg. magnesium
12.1 g. carbohydrate	540 Int. Units Vitamin A
2 g. fiber	0.28 mg. thiamine
0.6 g. ash	0.11 mg. riboflavin
23 mg. calcium	2.3 mg. niacin
99 mg. phosphorus	20 mg. Vitamin C

— 1 cup (160 g.) provides more than half of the recommended daily allowance of Vitamin C, almost a third of the iron, half of the thiamine, and a sixth of the Vitamin A.

Peppers (raw, immature green sweet peppers)

22 calories	0.7 mg. iron
93.4 g. water	13 mg. sodium
1.2 g. protein	18 mg. magnesium
0.2 g. fat	420 Int. Units Vitamin A
4.8 g. carbohydrate	0.08 mg. thiamine
1.4 g. fiber	0.08 mg. riboflavin
0.4 g. ash	0.5 mg. niacin
9 mg. calcium	128 mg. Vitamin C
22 mg. phosphorus	

— Low in calories.
— Supplies much Vitamin C, some Vitamin A and other vitamins and minerals *plus* bulk; one medium-sized *cooked* pepper provides the entire daily recommended allowance of Vitamin C, and one medium-sized raw pepper (about six to the pound) provides a third more than the daily recommended allowance of Vitamin C.

Persimmons (oriental, cultivated)

77 calories	19.7 g. carbohydrate
78.6 g. water	1.6 g. fiber
0.7 g. protein	0.6 g. ash
0.4 g. fat	6 mg. calcium

26 mg. phosphorus

0.3 mg. iron

6 mg. sodium

174 mg. potassium

8 mg. magnesium

2,710 Int. Units Vitamin A

0.03 mg. thiamine

0.02 mg. riboflavin

0.1 mg. niacin

11 mg. Vitamin C

— 1 raw persimmon provides about half the daily recommended allowance of Vitamin A.

Pineapples (raw)

52 calories

85.3 g. water

0.4 g. protein

0.2 g. fat

13.7 g. carbohydrate

0.4 g. fiber

0.04 g. ash

17 mg. calcium

8 mg. phosphorus

0.5 mg. iron

1 mg. sodium

146 mg. potassium

13 mg. magnesium

70 Int. Units Vitamin A

0.09 mg. thiamine

0.03 mg. riboflavin

0.2 mg. niacin

17 mg. Vitamin C

— 1 cup raw diced pineapple contains 75 calories, which is moderate, and 24 mg. of Vitamin C, more than a third of the recommended daily allowance.

— Low in sodium.

— Provides an alkaline reaction in the body.

Plums and Fresh Prunes

PRUNE-TYPE PLUMS

75 calories

78.7 g. water

0.8 g. protein

0.2 g. fat

19.7 g. carbohydrate

0.4 g. fiber

0.6 g. ash

12 mg. calcium

18 mg. phosphorus

0.5 mg. iron

1 mg. sodium

170 mg. potassium

9 mg. magnesium

300 Int. Units Vitamin A

0.03 mg. thiamine

0.03 mg. riboflavin

0.5 mg. niacin

6 mg. Vitamin C

PLUMS OTHER THAN PRUNE-TYPE

48 calories

86.6 g. water

0.5 g. protein

0.2 g. fat

12.3 g. carbohydrate

0.6 g. fiber

0.4 g. ash

12 mg. calcium

18 mg. phosphorus
0.5 mg. iron
1 mg. sodium
170 mg. potassium
9 mg. magnesium

250 Int. Units Vitamin A
0.03 mg. thiamine
0.03 mg. riboflavin
0.5 mg. niacin
6 mg. Vitamin C

— Two plums (2 inches in diameter; 120 g.) supply only 60 calories; 1 cupful contains 94 calories.
— Low in sodium.
— Contribute useful amounts of Vitamins A and C, as well as other vitamins and minerals.

Pomegranates (raw pulp)

63 calories
82.3 g. water
0.5 g. protein
0.3 g. fat
16.4 g. carbohydrate
0.2 g. fiber
0.5 g. ash
3 mg. calcium
8 mg. phosphorus

0.3 mg. iron
3 mg. sodium
259 mg. potassium
Trace Vitamin A
0.03 mg. thiamine
0.03 mg. riboflavin
0.3 mg. niacin
4 mg. Vitamin C

Potatoes (partial composition of potatoes baked in the skin)

93 calories
75.1% water
2.6 g. protein
0.1 g. fat
21.1 g. carbohydrate
0.6 g. fiber
1.1 g. ash
9 mg. calcium
65 mg. phosphorus

0.7 mg. iron
0.4 mg. sodium
503 mg. potassium
Trace Vitamin A
0.10 mg. thiamine
0.04 mg. riboflavin
1.7 mg. niacin
20 mg. Vitamin C

— Very low in sodium.
— Provide 18% of Vitamin C; 1 medium baked potato (3 to the pound when raw) provides a third of the recommended daily allowance of Vitamin C, a tenth of the thiamine, and a variety of other nutrients.
— Highly digestible; the carbohydrate is 92% to 99% usable; the iron is 93% usable; and the Vitamin B_1 is more usable than even a like dose of the purified vitamin.
— Fresh mashed potatoes retain more Vitamin C than reconstituted dehydrated flakes or granules.

— Contain virtually no fat.
— Neither potatoes nor any other food increases the body's fat deposits until energy needs are met.
— $1 spent for potatoes provides more thiamine (Vitamin B_1) than the same amount spent for any other food. Potatoes are third (after citrus and cabbage) in yield of Vitamin C per dollar; second (after dry beans, peas and nuts) in yield of niacin and also of iron; and third (after fats and oils and flour, cereals and baked goods) in yield of calories, per $1.

Pumpkins (cooked)

33 calories	36 mg. phosphorus
90.2 g. water	0.7 mg. iron
1 g. protein	3,400 Int. Units Vitamin A
0.3 g. fat	0.02 mg. thiamine
7.0 g. carbohydrate	0.06 mg. riboflavin
1.2 g. fiber	0.5 mg. niacin
0.6 g. ash	Uncertain — Vitamin C
20 mg. calcium	

— 1 cup (228 g.) provides one and a half times the recommended daily allowance of Vitamin A.

Radishes

17 calories	1 mg. iron
94.5% water	18 mg. sodium
1 g. protein	322 mg. potassium
0.1 g. fat	15 mg. magnesium
3.6 g. carbohydrate	10 Int. Units Vitamin A
0.7 g. fiber	0.03 mg. thiamine
0.8 g. ash	0.03 mg. riboflavin
30 mg. calcium	0.3 mg. niacin
31 mg. phosphorous	26 mg. Vitamin C

— Low in calories.
— Have a substantial amount of Vitamin C (all available since it is not diminished by cooking): four small radishes (40 g.) provide a sixth of the daily recommended allowance of Vitamin C.
— Supply a tenth of the recommended daily allowance of iron.

Raspberries

57 calories	1.2 g. protein
84.2 g. water	0.5 g. fat

13.6 g. carbohydrate
3 g. fiber
0.5 g. ash
22 mg. calcium
22 mg. phosphorus
0.9 mg. iron
1 mg. sodium

168 mg. potassium
20 mg. magnesium
130 Int. Units Vitamin A
0.03 mg. thiamine
0.09 mg. riboflavin
0.9 mg. niacin
25 mg. Vitamin C

— Low in sodium.
— Provide an alkaline reaction in the body.
— 1 cup (123 g.) provides 50% of the recommended daily allowance of Vitamin C, 10% of the iron, other vitamins and minerals, and only 70 calories.

Rhubarb (cooked with added sugar)

141 calories (mostly the necessary added sugar)
62.8% water
0.5 g. protein
0.1 g. fat
36 g. carbohydrate
0.6 g. fiber
78 mg. calcium
15 mg. phosphorus

0.6 mg. iron
2 mg. sodium
203 mg. potassium
13 mg. magnesium
80 Int. Units Vitamin A
0.02 mg. thiamine
0.05 mg. riboflavin
0.03 mg. niacin
6 mg. Vitamin C

Salsify (Oyster Plant) (boiled and drained)

12 to 70 calories (depending on whether it is freshly harvested or has been stored, permitting some conversion to sugars)
81 g. water
2.6 g. protein
0.6 g. fat
15.1 g. carbohydrate
1.8 g. fiber
0.7 g. ash

42 mg. calcium
53 mg. phosphorous
1.3 mg. iron
266 mg. potassium
10 Int. Units Vitamin A
0.03 mg. thiamine
0.04 mg. riboflavin
0.2 mg. niacin
7 mg. Vitamin C

Scallions and Shallots

— Nutritional values are similar to green onions.

Spinach (boiled and drained)

23 calories

92 g. water

3 g. protein	50 mg. sodium
0.3 g. fat	324 mg. potassium
3.6 g. carbohydrate	88 mg. magnesium
0.6 g. fiber	8,100 Int. Units Vitamin A
1.1 g. ash	0.07 mg. thiamine
93 mg. calcium	0.14 mg. riboflavin
38 mg. phosphorus	0.5 mg. niacin
2.2 mg. iron	28 mg. Vitamin C

— 1 cup (180 g.) provides 3 times the daily recommended allowance of Vitamin A for an adult, 80% of the Vitamin C, 40% of the iron, and a substantial amount of B vitamins.

— Especially high in iron and is used in diets to increase iron intake.

— One cup contains 46 calories; it is highly nutritious but not weight-building, and good for digestion.

Squash

BAKED WINTER SQUASH

63 calories	0.8 mg. iron
81.4 g. water	1 mg. sodium
1.8 g. protein	461 mg. potassium
0.4 g. fat	17 mg. magnesium
15.4 g. carbohydrate	4,200 Int. Units Vitamin A
1.8 g. fiber	0.05 mg. thiamine
1 g. ash	0.13 mg. riboflavin
28 mg. calcium	0.7 mg. niacin
48 mg. phosphorus	13 mg. Vitamin C

BOILED AND DRAINED SUMMER SQUASH

14 calories	0.4 mg. iron
95.5 g. water	1 mg. sodium
0.9 g. protein	141 mg. potassium
0.1 g. fat	16 mg. magnesium (in one variety)
3.1 g. carbohydrate	390 Int. Units Vitamin A
0.6 g. fiber	0.05 mg. thiamine
0.4 g. ash	0.08 mg. riboflavin
25 mg. calcium	0.8 mg. niacin
25 mg. phosphorus	10 mg. Vitamin C

— Only 34 calories in a cupful of summer squash.

— Very low in sodium and suitable for drastically restricted low sodium diets.

— Provides an alkaline reaction in the body.

— A half cup of baked Hubbard squash provides almost the daily recommended allowance of Vitamin A, as well as a sixth of the Vitamin C, and other vitamins and minerals.

— A half cup of baked Butternut squash provides about 128% of the daily recommended allowance of Vitamin A, as well as useful amounts of other vitamins and minerals.

— Soft-skinned summer squashes, both green and yellow, contain a valuable amount of Vitamin C and useful amounts of Vitamin A and other vitamins and minerals.

— The Vitamin A of winter squashes, already high at harvest time, increases in storage.

Strawberries

37 calories	1 mg. iron
89.9 g. water	1 mg. sodium
0.7 g. protein	164 mg. potassium
0.5 g. fat	12 mg. magnesium
8.4 g. carbohydrate	60 Int. Units Vitamin A
1.3 g. fiber	0.03 mg. thiamine
0.5 g. ash	0.07 mg. riboflavin
21 mg. calcium	0.06 mg. niacin
21 mg. phosphorus	59 mg. Vitamin C

— Low in calories.

— High in Vitamin C: 10 large strawberries provide 100% of the recommended daily allowance of Vitamin C; 10% of the daily recommended allowance of iron for a man, or 6.7% of the allowance for a woman.

— A cup contains only 55 calories — they are a great dessert for weight-watchers.

— Low in sodium.

— Has an alkaline reaction in the body.

Sweet Potatoes (baked)

141 calories	0.9 g. iron
63.7 g. water	12 mg. sodium
2.1 g. protein	300 mg. potassium
0.5 g. fat	31 mg. magnesium
32.5 g. carbohydrate	8,100 Int. Units Vitamin A
0.9 g. fiber	0.09 mg. thiamine
1.2 g. ash	0.07 mg. riboflavin
40 mg. calcium	0.7 mg. niacin
58 mg. phosphorus	22 mg. Vitamin C

— One of the most all-around nutritious foods in the world — so nutritious that people have gotten along for considerable periods on a diet made up almost solely of this vegetable. They are even better, of course, with meat, milk, and other foods.

— 1 medium (2″ x 5″) boiled, then peeled, sweet potato (147 g.) provides more than twice the recommended daily allowance of Vitamin A for an adult, half of the Vitamin C, a tenth of the iron, a tenth of the thiamine, and other vitamins and minerals as well.

— Have an alkaline reaction in the body.

— Have a high content of carotene, which is converted to Vitamin A in the body, and the carotene increases during the usual period of storage before the sweet potatoes reach the retail market.

Swiss Chard (see Greens)

— High in iron, Vitamins C and A; 3½-ounce serving provides more than the recommended daily allowance of Vitamin A for an adult; 25% of the Vitamin C, a third of the iron, and other vitamins and minerals.

— One cup contains 30 calories.

Tangelos

41 calories
89.4 g. water
0.5 g. protein
0.1 g. fat

9.7 g. carbohydrate
0.3 g. ash
27 mg. Vitamin C

Tangerines

46 calories
87 g. water
0.8 g. protein
0.2 g. fat
11.6 g. carbohydrate
0.5 g. fiber
0.5 g. ash
40 mg. calcium
18 mg. phosphorus

0.4 mg. iron
2 mg. sodium
126 mg. potassium
420 Int. Units Vitamin A
0.06 mg. thiamine
0.02 mg. riboflavin
0.1 mg. niacin
31 mg. Vitamin C

— 1 medium-sized (114 g.) tangerine contains 35 calories.

— A good source of Vitamin C; one tangerine provides 43% of the daily recommended allowance of Vitamin C.

Tomatoes (ripe and raw)

22 calories
93.5 g. water

1.1 g. protein
0.2 g. fat

4.7 g. carbohydrate
0.5 g. fiber
0.5 g. ash
13 mg. calcium
27 mg. phosphorus
0.5 mg. iron
3 mg. sodium

244 mg. potassium
14 mg. magnesium
900 Int. Units Vitamin A
0.06 mg. thiamine
0.04 mg. riboflavin
0.7 mg. niacin
23 mg. Vitamin C

— Low in calories — a medium-sized (2" x 2½", 150 g.) tomato contains 35 calories.
— Valuable for Vitamins C and A and other vitamins and minerals: 1 medium-sized tomato (2" x 2½", 150 g.) provides 57% of the recommended daily allowance of Vitamin C for an adult and more than a fourth of the Vitamin A and a twelfth of the iron.
— Tomatoes retain Vitamin C very well and gain this vitamin as they color.
— Acid as eaten but base-forming or alkaline in the body.
— The U.S. Department of Agriculture recommends at least one serving of citrus fruit, tomatoes, or raw cabbage daily.

Turnip Greens (boiled, drained leaves, including stems, cooked a short time in a small amount of water)

20 calories
93.2 g. water
2.2 g. protein
0.2 g. fat
3.6 g. carbohydrate
0.7 g. fiber
0.8 g. ash
184 mg. calcium

37 mg. phosphorus
1.1 mg. iron
58 mg. magnesium (when raw)
6,300 Int. Units Vitamin A
0.15 mg. thiamine
0.24 mg. riboflavin
0.6 mg. niacin
69 mg. Vitamin C

— A cup (145 g.) provides 65% more than the daily recommended allowance of Vitamin C, 82% more than the allowance of Vitamin A, a sixth of the iron, a sixth of the thiamine, a fifth of the riboflavin, and other vitamins and minerals.

Turnips and Rutabagas (raw)

30 calories
91.5 g. water
1 g. protein
0.2 g. fat
6.6 g. carbohydrate
0.9 g. fiber
0.7 g. ash
39 mg. calcium
30 mg. phosphorus

0.5 mg. iron
49 mg. sodium
268 mg. potassium
20 mg. magnesium
Trace Vitamin A
0.04 mg. thiamine
0.07 mg. riboflavin
0.6 mg. niacin
36 mg. Vitamin C

— A good source of Vitamin C; they retain 61% of the vitamin when cooked. A cup of cooked, diced turnips (155 g.) provides more than half the recommended daily allowance of Vitamin C for an adult.
— Provide an alkaline reaction in the body.

Watercress (raw, leaves and stems)

19 calories	1.7 mg. iron
93.3 g. water	52 mg. sodium
2.2 g. protein	282 mg. potassium
0.3 g. fat	20 mg. magnesium
3 g. carbohydrate	4,900 Int. Units Vitamin A
0.7 g. fiber	0.08 mg. thiamine
1.2 g. ash	0.16 mg. riboflavin
151 mg. calcium	0.9 mg. niacin
54 mg. phosphorus	79 mg. Vitamin C

— High in iron and Vitamin A, with useful amounts of other minerals.
— Very low in calories.

Watermelons

26 calories	0.5 mg. iron
92.6 g. water	1 mg. sodium
0.5 g. protein	100 mg. potassium
0.2 g. fat	8 mg. magnesium
6.4 g. carbohydrate	590 Int. Units Vitamin A
0.3 g. fiber	0.03 mg. thiamine
0.3 g. ash	0.03 mg. riboflavin
7 mg. calcium	0.2 mg. niacin
10 mg. phosphorus	7 mg. Vitamin C

— Low in calories: contains 120 calories in a big wedge.
— Low in sodium: 1 mg. per 100 grams.
— Surprisingly nutritious — a 4″ x 8″ wedge provides half of the recommended dietary allowance of Vitamin C and half the allowance of Vitamin A, and other vitamins and minerals.

Helpful Hints

1. Apples are great as a midmorning or midafternoon snack which quickly leaves the stomach without affecting the appetite for the main meal.

2. For a quick summertime dessert, peel and pit apricots, cut them in quarters, sprinkle them with cinnamon sugar and top with softened vanilla ice cream. Substitute 1 cup of muscatel or white port for 1 cup of the water when cooking dried apricots.

3. Try introducing the artichoke to your children — they will usually like the delicate nutlike flavor of this educated thistle and enjoy the unusual process of tearing, dipping, and scraping the leaves against the teeth.

4. Asparagus makes a delicate and flavorful soup and a piquant salad garnish.

5. Avocados make a fine buttery spread for bread without the hard fats of butter.

6. Cooked bananas add a new and delightful flavor to meat loaf.

7. Try savory green beans with onions, bacon, and cloves.

8. Try lima beans in a casserole with bacon.

9. For a luncheon main dish, hollow out cooked whole beets and fill with ham, shrimp, or egg salad.

10. Serve beet greens creamed with bacon and hard-cooked eggs.

11. Blackberries are delicious in pancakes.

12. Use chilled blueberries to fill cantaloupe halves or sprinkle them liberally over peaches or mix with strawberries.

13. Broccoli is terrific in a cold salad with vinaigrette dressing. Have you ever made broccoli soup? It's creamy and delicious. Use a basic white sauce as the foundation, plus pureed cooked broccoli and a sprinkle of mace or nutmeg as you prefer.

14. Brussels sprouts blend beautifully with turkey and ham and make an unusually tasty soufflé.

15. For delicious extra flavor, cook cabbage with roasts.

16. A half cantaloupe filled with cottage cheese is a delightfully filling and tasty dish for the weight-watcher.

17. Babies several months old prefer the taste of carrots to many other foods.

18. Casabas are a perfect dessert for the weight-conscious.

19. Cauliflower is delicious raw and crisp as a dip and snack food.

20. Celery makes ideal nbbling for weight-watchers; add chopped celery leaves to the soup pot for a fragrant fresh herb quality in the soup.

21. Try dunking cherries in custard sauce or in vanilla or lemon fondue for your next backyard barbecue.

22. Chinese cabbage or celery cabbage is one of the most ancient vegetables — Chihli, Wong Bok, Michihli, Pak-Choi, Chi-hi-hi; it cooks almost without odor. For an exotic touch to a family dinner, prepare it with a thin cream sauce and a sprinkle of nutmeg; remember to shred the cabbage in pieces cut crosswise and to cook it quickly to retain its crispness; use a small amount of cooking water with a touch of soy sauce to enhance its flavor.

23. Chives are delicious in omelets.

24. A coconut is easily shelled in either of two ways. After draining out the milk, place the coconut in the freezer for about an hour *or* in a moderate oven (350°) for a short time. Then rap sharply with a hammer; the shell will shatter and the meat will come away easily.

25. Try collards and corn pone, a favorite in the South.

26. When choosing corn, remember that green husks indicate freshness.

27. Weigh-watchers, a good big cucumber has only 25 calories, 1 calorie per slice.

28. Try dandelion greens chopped with hard-cooked eggs.

29. Try dasheens, corms, and tubers as an interesting variation on your dinner table; bake, boil, or fry these vegetables of Chinese origin for a delicate nutty flavor. Eat *only* when cooked.

30. For quick energy, try dates — the "candy that grows on trees."

31. Eggplant is a versatile vegetable that may be sautéed, baked, fried, stewed, or used in casseroles; it is delicious in stuffing and a delightful surprise with a barbecue; try it also as a meat substitute main dish.

32. Eat endive, escarole, and chicory raw or cooked; there is no waste, and it is easy on the waistline.

33. Figs are a satisfying snack for those who mustn't eat candy.

34. Use a smidgen of garlic for flavoring meats, fish, soups, and stews. It has been said that "a tossed salad without garlic is like a wedding without flowers."

35. Try grapefruit sections with shrimp; or chilled halves with crushed strawberries; or broiled halves with honey. Eat plenty and stay slim. When making an herb butter sauce for fish, add a little grated grapefruit rind and about ½ teaspoon of fresh grapefruit juice for a tart and delicious new flavor.

36. Grapes are wonderful natural coolers and thirst quenchers and are better

than a cold drink on a hot day; try grapes and cheese for a quick and delicious dessert; and for a special treat serve chilled cantaloupe halves filled with a colorful variety of juicy grapes — amber green Thompsons, jet black Ribiers, juicy red Malagas and Emperors, greenish white Almerias and flaming mild-flavored Tokays.

37. Sprinkle honeydew wedges with lemon or lime juice or, for a special treat, fill with raspberry sherbet.

38. Kale is delicious with ham or pork, crisp bacon, or hard-cooked eggs.

39. Kohlrabi is something special in the cabbage family; its flavor is similar to, but more delicate than, that of a white turnip. For double nutritional value, eat both bulb and leaves — cook the leaves like spinach and the bulb like turnip. It's fine boiled and served hot or cold in salad; or steamed, peeled, and cut into julienne strips; ask your family to guess what it is!

40. Leeks have been enjoyed since ancient times; they are milder than green onions and are fine boiled and served with white sauce; use them to delicately flavor soups, salads, or vegetables.

41. Kumquats make unusual preserves. Use them for holiday fruit bowls; they are miniatures of the citrus kingdom.

42. Use lemon and water as a regulator.

43. Be sure to trim lettuce sparingly and discard as little of the darker green outer leaves as possible, as they contain considerably more Vitamin A and C and minerals than the inner leaves.

44. Limes are a delicious flavoring for fish, chicken, veal, and vegetables; use to spike a melon cup or to make a lime frappé. For a summer cooler, squeeze fresh lime juice into iced ginger ale and top with mint leaf and a maraschino cherry.

45. The mango is a luscious tropical fruit that has a flavor resembling apricot and pineapple; it tastes just as good as it smells.

46. Mushrooms are the gourmet's delight — once a rare delicacy, this elegant but inexpensive vegetable is now available all year to everyone; they are 100% edible — no waste — and contain only 28 calories per cupful.

47. Mustard greens are healthful and inexpensive. Their sharp nippy flavor makes them a delightful pot herb; boil them with a piece of fatty meat like corned beef, salt pork, ham, or bacon.

48. Baked nectarines are delicious — no peeling is necessary as the skin is very tender; they are perfect raw for the picnic basket.

49. Okra is indispensable in cooking authentic Creole gumbos; it also adds the French touch to stews and the stockpot. Boil and chill it for tangy combination salads.

50. Try onions stuffed with sausage, ham, or meat loaf; for a luncheon treat, add man-sized slices of onion to scrambled egg sandwiches on whole wheat toast.

51. Green-skinned and golden-skinned oranges are both fully ripe.

52. Papayas are good for digestion. Try this tropical "tree melon" à la mode. For weight-watchers it is also a delicious low-calorie treat when cut in sections with the seeds removed and served chilled with a wedge of lemon or lime.

53. Parsley is the star ingredient of fines herbes. For a quick broiled steak sauce, combine parsley, butter, and lemon juice.

54. Pep up stews with the nutty flavor of parsnips — it's great cold weather eating. Try parsnip chips for a special treat, and don't forget that to some people the soul of the soup is believed to be the parsnip.

55. Try peach Alaska for an elegant dessert or put up peaches at home just the way you like them — all you need are the peaches, jars and sugar. In Queen Victoria's England, peaches were worth about $5 each and were a treasured delight served in snowy white wool on special occasions.

56. For a luscious quick dessert, serve chilled pears and Brie. In the early eighteenth century, a Belgian priest who raised pears called them the "butter fruit" — it's still an excellent description.

57. Cold meat loaf and green pepper sandwiches are a special summer picnic treat. For economy, stuff peppers with minced ham or chicken.

58. A persimmon may look more like a colorful ornament than a fruit, but it is a real adventure in eating. The oriental persimmon is considered the national fruit of Japan, where it has been cultivated for over a thousand years. Chill it and eat it out of hand, and enjoy its delightful and unusual jellylike consistency. Have you tried fresh persimmon sherbet, baked persimmon pudding, or persimmon salad?

59. Pineapple cole slaw is a real summer treat.

60. Prune halves are delicious with cheese or on cereal; and plum pie and breakfast plum sauce mean really good eating.

Pomegranate (¼ natural size)

61. Pomegranate is as succulently delicious eaten out of hand as it is a colorful garnish for salads and desserts.

62. Although by no means a suggested diet, some people have existed solely on potatoes for as long as five months with only the addition of a small amount of fat (since potatoes are virtually fat free). They worked and stayed in good health. For speedy dinner preparation: boil and slice potatoes in the morning. Put them in a buttered casserole, pour melted butter over them with a sprinkling

of your favorite herbs, cover with aluminum foil, and refrigerate until evening. Then potatoes can be baked in a moderate oven for 30 minutes before dinner has to be on the table.

63. For something different and extra special, bake pumpkin bread and pumpkin cookies; for the kids, make frozen pumpkin custard.

64. Radishes are cultivated around the world for a variety of uses. In Egypt, only the leaves are eaten. In India, a variety of radish is grown for its fleshy, edible seed pods which reach lengths of 8 to 12 inches. In the Orient, radishes are grown as stock feed and for a winter vegetable that can be stored. In China, one kind of radish without an enlarged root is grown for the oil in its seeds. Why not try something different in your own kitchen — stir-fry radishes? Slice and cook the radishes for one minute in butter or oil in a skillet over high heat, sprinkle with salt and pepper, and serve!

65. Two super-cooling desserts are delectable rhubarb whip and rhubarb sherbet; for a hot weather thirst quencher, try a rhubarb highball; and for a delightful breakfast surprise, serve rhubarb marmalade.

66. Salsify, the "vegetable oyster" that is only occasionally available, contains nutrients similar to carrots and has a mild, sweet and oysterlike flavor a little bit like parsnips; prepare like carrots or parsnips.

67. Try a spinach ring with mushrooms or serve it Dutch-style with bacon; don't forget to use raw spinach leaves for an attractive and nutritious addition to tossed salad.

68. Cook summer squash often, it is 100% edible with no waste; and for good hearty eating, bake a squash pie.

69. When cooking prunes, substitute 1 cup claret or Burgundy for 1 cup of the water and add 2 or 3 whole cloves, a stick of cinnamon, and a slice of lemon.

70. For an exotic climax to a "Renoir picnic" or a candelight dinner à deux, try fresh strawberries and chilled champagne.

71. French fry sweet potatoes with sausage; a cold weather treat means roast pork and yams; or mash with cream, butter and a little nutmeg and brown in the oven. Don't forget sweet potatoe pie and pudding.

72. Swiss chard is a two-in-one vegetable; cook the leaves like greens and the white stems like celery. It is best steamed to preserve its delicate, asparaguslike flavor.

73. Tangelos, a cross between the tangerine and grapefruit, have a unique flavor blend of both fruits. They're as good for juice, fruit cups, salads and marmalade as for eating out of hand.

74. Tangerines are a natural for Christmas stockings and school lunchboxes — children love to zip the skins off and enjoy the sweet fruit flavor.

75. For a satisfying bedtime snack, try an ice-cold tomato with salt and pepper and a slice of whole wheat bread and butter.

76. Turnips are good raw or cooked: use nippy and crunchy raw turnip curls or very thin slices in salads, or shred and toss them with sliced green onions. For a delicious dinner side dish, sprinkle cooked and mashed turnips with grated cheese and broil a few minutes.

77. Turnip greens and "pot likker" — fine with beef and pork.

78. Be sure to eat the tender stems as well as the leaves of watercress.

79. For a cool drink, eat a wedge of watermelon.

80. For vegetable salads, remember to clean the vegetables thoroughly, paring if necessary. Vegetables such as potatoes and asparagus may be cooked ahead of time and chilled before adding to a salad or serving with dressing.

Acknowledgments
Index

Chinese Cabbage
(1/10 natural size)

Acknowledgments

The author gratefully acknowledges the information and materials supplied by the following organizations:

Accent International
American Mushroom Institute
American Spice Trade Association
Armour and Company
Campbell Soup Company
Corn Products International
Durkee Famous Foods,
    SCM Corporation
General Foods Kitchens
H. J. Heinz Company
Kellogg Company
Knox Gelatine Company

The McIlhenny Company (Tabasco)
Pepperidge Farm Inc.
Oscar Mayer and Company
Sunkist Growers, Inc.
Tuna Research Foundation
United Fresh Fruit and Vegetable
    Association
U.S. Department of Agriculture
    Consumer and Marketing Service
Vanilla Information Bureau
Wine Institute of California

Index